What Others Are Saying

"The diagnosis of a life-threatening autoimmune disease sets in motion reactions, consequences, and decisions for not only individuals but also all who love and care about them. However, the major responsibility is on individuals, their attitude, determination, and faith. This memoir sets out, in uplifting detail, the part faith and attitude play in facing one of life's greatest trials, and emerging whole, positive, and seeking to help others in their journey."
Dinah L. O'Brien, Director, Plymouth Public Library

"This book will compel you to stop, think about your life, thank your guardian angels, and realize the blessing all around you! Andrew's story will have you focus...on what matters most!"
Ernest F. Oriente, President of PowerHour®

"This book is a Blessing! ...full of valuable insights and inspirations. I recommend it to anyone who wants to dramatically improve their life perspective!"
Patty Morgan-Seager, Inspirational Speaker and Trainer, Certified Laugh Leader

"If anyone should know how to celebrate life, it is Andrew. This very touching story is perfect for anyone who has, or is overcoming an adversity of huge proportion. Most of us will never go through an event like this brave young man went through, but all of us have or will experience great challenges; this book will help you through."
Anne Sadovsky, CSP, Host of Fair Housing Focus on MultifamilyProTV.com

"Anyone who is facing a challenge with health issues or really any major issue in life will find hope, support and inspiration in Andrew Botieri's book. *A Celebration of Life: A Story of Hope, a Miracle, and the Power of Attitude* is an enjoyable read that expresses how faith, attitude and support can help us all through all that life hands us. Andrew Botieri has opened a window to his personal life and that light shines for all of us who are looking for answers to what appear to be unanswerable questions. He has done a great service for all of us."
Dr. John F. McEwan, Ed. D., President, Cardinal Spellman High School

A Celebration of Life

A Story of Hope, a Miracle, And the Power of Attitude

Andrew Louis Botieri

Find your *FREE* ebook offer in the Bibliography and Resource section at the end of this book.

© 2012, 2013, 2014 Andrew Louis Botieri

Second Edition, 2014

Digital Edition, 2013

Nino-Ida Publishing

Plymouth, Massachusetts

ISBN 978-0-9853996-2-7

No part of this publication may be reproduced, stored in a retrieval system, or transmitted, in any form or by any means, electronic, mechanical, photocopying, recording, or otherwise, without the written prior permission of the author.

Cover design by Greg Caulton, www.stayintouch.org

Printed in the United States of America

Contents

What Others Are Saying i
Dedication vii
Disclaimer viii
Foreword ix
Foreword Deux xi
Preface xxvii
1 The Emergency Room 1
2 Thursday, June 29, 7 A.M. 3
3 The Call Every Parent Dreads 13
4 You Have Sclero What? 23
5 The Power of Miracles, Part 1 32
6 Growing Up in Mayberry 59
7 My First Guardian Angel 82
8 The End and Beginning of a Journey 87
9 A Cat Has Nine Lives 103
10 The Learning Years 119
11 Fate Comes a Knockin' Again 165
12 The Beginning of the End 167
13 The Powerful of Attitude 200
14 Coming Back Home to My Roots 209
15 The Power of Miracles, Part 2 213
16 Why This Book? 223
Afterword: So, What Have I Learned? 229
Bibliography and Resources 233
Who the Heck Is Andrew Botieri? 234

Dedication

This book is dedicated to the victims of scleroderma and to those who suffer from the pain, the discomfort, and humiliation of this autoimmune disease that has no cause or cure. My dream is they do find a cure, but in the meantime, have faith, pray for strength, and give yourself a daily dose of positive attitude.

A big thanks to my editing and book production guru, Claudia Gere, who helped me through my first book. I also dedicate this book to my family and friends, to all the others who prayed for me, who helped me through this ordeal and to those in my family who have gone before me. See you on the other side, someday.

A portion of each book sale will go to the Scleroderma Foundation of New England. (scleroderma.org/chapter/newengland)

Disclaimer

The information in this memoir is to the best of my recollection as are the comments and descriptions from those who have contributed their stories and remembrances.

Foreword

Since 1988 I have worked in the publishing and multi-housing industry and have had the pleasure of meeting some very dynamic leaders over the last several decades. In 1990 I was fortunate enough to meet Andrew Botieri and have enjoyed his infectious and bigger-than-life personality. Andrew has a can-do attitude and knows how to bring out the very best of those around him. I can remember some of his powerful weekly sales meetings with his team in the Inland Empire and Los Angeles that began with the words, "If it's to be, it's up to me!" And in a snap, Andrew and his team would be rocking into their sales days.

You see, Andrew has never had to worry about sales quotas or reaching his financial budgets. From Phoenix to Southern California to Philadelphia and in other key markets around the country, Andrew has coached, trained, and mentored his sales teams to success, navigated some very challenging turnaround situations, stepped into markets where others had failed. The hotter the kitchen; the more you want Andrew in your corner. Andrew knows how to turn coal into bright sparkling diamonds.

But this book is not about sales or leadership success. Andrew has written *A Celebration of Life* because he nearly died on June 29, 2000. He tells the story of his near-death and the long, long road of his medical recovery. Reading it will cause you to pause and look at your own life in a new and different way. This book will have you stop to find the roses of joy in your life, will challenge you to plant your life roses deep and strong, and will ask you to savor the blessings of the roses in your life, each and every day.

In these chapters, Andrew describes the guardian angels in his life, the power of prayer, the love of his family, and the importance of focusing on doing the things in life that you most love. And you will hear from Andrew's parents and siblings as they describe their love for Andrew and the support and prayers they gave him over the years and throughout his journey with scleroderma.

In closing, this book is also a celebration of Andrew's love for his Father who is dancing with the angels and smiling proudly on his son.

—Ernest Oriente, President and Founder of PowerHour®

Foreword Deux

Typically a foreword is written by someone other than the author. Some rules are meant to be bent. This foreword is a collaboration of myself and Dr. Robert Simms, MD Section Head, Rheumatology Boston Medical Center.

This June 29*th* will mark just over a decade since a medical crisis, brought on by a rare autoimmune disease called scleroderma, almost took my life. Since my crisis, I have met and read about so many wonderful people with scleroderma and their families. After attending and speaking at last year's National Scleroderma Patient Education Conference in Atlanta, I was blown away by the hundreds of people who were there with all varying forms and stages of the disease. I was humbled by the many people I met who've been afflicted by scleroderma and suffer so much more than I do. I almost felt unworthy to be there. In fact, it's something I still struggle with.

I was honored to present a session that included a discussion about my book, *A Celebration of Life,* and the fact that I was a male survivor of scleroderma, which is rare. After my talk, I autographed several of my books and enjoyed writing inscriptions of hope and faith. Many of the people I met there I still keep in touch with, and it is a blessing to know them and be a part of their lives.

What I have found amazing and still do today, is the strength I have witnessed in those afflicted with scleroderma who I've met at events around the country. I am hoping by relaunching my book with this updated foreword, I can bring a new level of awareness to the public and to those who are wondering if they may have contracted scleroderma. Today, with insights into new therapies, drugs, and techniques, I wanted to update the state of help available to sufferers of scleroderma and their families—because that help is far more available today, than it ever was before.

Though this disease seems to have been around for millenniums, with the first possible reference to scleroderma by Hippocrates who lived from 460 to 370 BC, the National Scleroderma Foundation was only established in 1998. The Foundation's mission has been and continues to be to educate patients, their families, the medical profession as well as the general public through its various awareness programs. It also spearheads and coordinates fundraising events around the country for much needed research and advocates on Capitol Hill in Washington, DC to get the attention of our national politicians who can help direct additional dollars to research and funding.

One of the other initiatives that are new, or at least weren't around when I was first diagnosed, is a new innovative online resource called "Interactive Body Tool" for people recently diagnosed or those who think they may have scleroderma. You find the tool by visiting the National Scleroderma Foundation website at www.scleroderma.org/body (accessed May, 2014). This new interactive tool demonstrates the affects scleroderma has on a person's body from the skin, kidneys, lungs, gastrointestinal system, and other areas. It is an amazing tool I wish I had when I was first diagnosed.

According to *Scleroderma Voice* magazine (Winter 2013), in the summer of 2013, US Representative Lois Capp (D-CA) read a statement in the US House of Representatives to recognize June as National Scleroderma Awareness Month. "Given the unpredictable progression of the disease, scleroderma, like many other autoimmune diseases, is difficult for medical practitioners to accurately diagnose and even more difficult to treat as there are currently no disease-specific treatments.

As we recognize the need for awareness of the troublesome disease, we can and must do more for the thousands of Americans who are diagnosed with this condition every year." Capps, along with Representative Peter King (R-NY), is an original sponsor of H.R. 1429, the Scleroderma Research and Awareness Act. This bipartisan legislation works to intensify research into scleroderma by the National Institutes of Health (NIH). Also in June, Representative Kirsten Gillibrand (D-NY) reintroduced the Senate version of the legislation S.1239. It is wonderful to see our national leaders beginning to take an interest in creating awareness for and fighting scleroderma. In my opinion, it is still the most devastating "unknown" disease we deal with that affects so many people.

What I find so interesting is that ALS or Lou Gehrig's disease, which is also a devastating illness, only affects about 25,000 to 30,000 people at any given time versus 250,000 to 300,000 for those afflicted with scleroderma. But, ALS is more well-known. So, receiving this national attention and spotlight is welcome for those who suffer with the disease and want to create awareness to find a cure.

What People Should Know About Scleroderma

With very little being discussed in the public mainstream, there a many misconceptions as well as a lack of information readily available. Here are brief answers to some of the most common questions. Much of this information comes from the Scleroderma Foundation website (www.scleroderma.org).

How do we talk about scleroderma?

There is a big initiative to use the term "person with scleroderma" instead of "scleroderma patient." The person with scleroderma may be a "patient" in the physician's office, hospital or clinic, but he or she is much more than that. Thinking of oneself as a total person with a full life to lead may help to keep scleroderma in perspective and enable one to maintain a positive but realistic attitude.

What is scleroderma and how is it defined?

Scleroderma, also known as systemic sclerosis, is a chronic connective tissue disease generally classified as one of the autoimmune rheumatic diseases. The word "scleroderma" comes from two Greek words: "sclero" meaning hard, and "derma" meaning skin. Hardening of the skin is one of the most visible manifestations of this disease, and symptoms change from patient to patient. Scleroderma is not contagious, infectious, or cancerous; however, the cause is still unknown.

How serious is scleroderma?

The symptoms of scleroderma vary greatly for each person, and the effects of scleroderma can range from very mild to life threatening. The seriousness will depend on which parts of the body are affected. So prompt and proper diagnosis and treatment by qualified physicians may minimize the symptoms of scleroderma and lessen the chance for irreversible damage.

How is scleroderma diagnosed?

The discovery process may require consultation with rheumatologists (arthritis specialists) and dermatologists (skin specialists) and call for blood studies and numerous other specialized tests depending upon which organs are affected. Of the estimated 300,000 Americans that have scleroderma, about one third of these people have the systemic form of scleroderma (which I was afflicted with). Since scleroderma presents itself with symptoms similar to other autoimmune diseases, diagnosis is difficult. There may be many misdiagnosed or undiagnosed cases; (I was misdiagnosed for nine months with rheumatoid arthritis). Localized scleroderma is more common in children, whereas systemic scleroderma is more common in adults.

Overall, female patients outnumber male patients about 4-to-1. Factors other than a person's gender, such as race and ethnic background, may influence the risk of getting scleroderma as well as the age of onset and the pattern or severity of internal organ involvement. The reasons for this are not clear. The onset of scleroderma is most frequently between the ages of 25 to 55, though lately there has been research on the increase of juvenile scleroderma which is affecting young children. In the *Scleroderma Voice* magazine, Summer 2014 issue, there are multiple articles giving insight into juvenile scleroderma. Although scleroderma is not directly inherited, some scientists feel there is a slight predisposition to it in families with a history of rheumatic diseases. Some studies possibly relate the onset to increased stress levels in individuals.

What are the common emotional reactions?

A common reaction to being told one has a disease such as scleroderma is, "Why me?" It's unknown why some people develop the disease and others do not. A person newly diagnosed with scleroderma may feel alone and uncertain about where to turn for help. He or she may experience a number of other feelings and emotional reactions from time to time, including initial shock or disbelief, fear, anger, denial, self-blame, guilt, grief, sadness, or depression. Family members may have similar feelings. Sharing them with family and friends or with others who have had similar experiences can be helpful. Since one does not bring scleroderma upon himself or herself, one shouldn't feel guilty or responsible for the illness. When I was diagnosed, I was living on the West Coast 2300 miles away from my family. I can assure you, I felt very alone.

What is the treatment for scleroderma?

Currently, there is no cure for scleroderma, but there are many treatments available to help particular symptoms. To help reduce the onset of heartburn and other gastronomical issues, a person with scleroderma may have to change their diet. Acid reflex is frequent in those who experience deterioration in their esophagus area, so learning to eat smaller quantities throughout the day (as I did) versus overeating once or twice a day can be a big help.

It's also helpful to not drink large amounts of water or liquids before going to bed as you increase the likelihood of acid reflex. People with scleroderma who experience severe cases of acid reflex may have to take OTC drugs like Prilosec (as I do) and are instructed to elevate the head of their beds by placing a couple 2x4 boards under the legs so the bed pitches downward.

Other breakthroughs involve a person's clothing. Many don't realize it, but the skin of a person with scleroderma can be sensitive and painful to the touch of regular clothing. New lines of apparel are now available that allow easy on and off pants, shirts and dresses. Snaps have also replaced buttons, as the fingers of a person with scleroderma have trouble buttoning or unbuttoning clothing. I still struggle with this on occasion, but am grateful to feel so much better.

Some treatments of scleroderma are directed at decreasing the activity of the immune system. Some people with a mild case may not need medication at all and occasionally people can go off, when their scleroderma is no longer active. Because there is so much variation from one person to another, there are variables as well in the treatments prescribed. Basically, there are four types of scleroderma: localized, morphea, linear, and systemic scleroderma. These four types are described in depth in Chapter 4.

Unlike when I was diagnosed with systemic scleroderma, there have been many breakthroughs and continued research and study on ways to alleviate some of the pain, discomfort, and disabilities associated with scleroderma. One area that affects many is Raynaud's phenomenon which occurs when the excess collagen settles into a person's hands and fingers and begins to cut off circulation. Many people who are diagnosed with Raynaud's will experience purplish-blue discoloration and slight numbness in their fingertips during cold weather. In extreme cases, others will encounter painful ulcers around their fingertips and wearing gloves on cold days can be a big help in reducing those effects. It is quite serious, and I have several friends with scleroderma who have had portions of their fingertips surgically removed as the areas became gangrene. Today, doctors have been performing surgeries on the wrist and hand areas to try and open up the blockage of collagen to improve the circulation, thereby reducing the effect or severity of Raynaud's phenomenon.

How will building a health and support network help?

Participating actively in one's own health care is of prime importance to the person with scleroderma. It is equally important to cooperate and communicate effectively with the physician who is managing the disease. Family and friends can provide emotional support for the person with scleroderma, encouraging them to follow the recommended treatment program and assisting them in carrying out activities they find difficult.

Joining a support group, such as one affiliated with the Scleroderma Foundation, enables the person with scleroderma to meet and exchange information with others who have similar problems, as well as learn more about the illness. The Scleroderma Foundation (www.scleroderma.org, accessed May 2014) also manages an online support group community at www.inspire.com/groups/sclerodermafoundation.

Although living with scleroderma may be a challenge, it is fortunate that support groups can be found around the country. These groups help the person with the disease as well as their families who cope with its progressive nature since there is no known cure. When I was finally diagnosed, I suffered in silence; there were no support groups when I was sick. After my crisis, I felt alone, like I was the only one who had scleroderma—especially because my doctors told me that not many men were known to contract the disease and survive. What I did find out in the years that followed was that I was not alone.

With June being National Scleroderma month, the leading North American scleroderma advocacy and research organizations—the Scleroderma Foundation, Scleroderma Research Foundation, and Scleroderma Society of Canada joined forces and launched a social media campaign for people to learn more about this unknown and often misunderstood disease. The campaign is named Hard Word. Harder Disease. It has run on social media platforms, Facebook, and Twitter using the hashtag #hardword throughout the month of June. A microsite, hardskin.org, serves as the landing page for pledge and general information about scleroderma with links to additional resources.

On another note, I am so honored to have my physician, who specializes in the treatment of scleroderma, Robert W. Simms, MD of Boston University Medical Center in Boston, Massachusetts add some of his thoughts and promise in the arena of treating scleroderma.

"Overall therapy for scleroderma remains a significant challenge; however, emerging evidence from studies of immune suppression or immune system ablation followed by stem cell transplantation for patients at risk of serious complications has shown significant promise. These studies have built on evidence of the benefit of immunosuppressive agents in interstitial lung disease associated with scleroderma.

"New effective therapies for pulmonary hypertension associated with scleroderma have also provided clinicians and patients many more options for this serious complication of the condition. Some of these medications, especially the phosphodiesterase inhibitors (sildenafil and similar medications) are also effective in clinical studies of digital ulcers. Advances in lung transplantation have also improved outcomes in patients with scleroderma. Finally, there is very active research in mapping the molecular pathways of disease in scleroderma. These studies have enabled identification of new therapeutic targets which will lead to the development of immunologic 'smart bombs', some of which will be ready for human trials in the very near future."

So, as you can see, scleroderma can affect so many people, in so many ways. And, with the continued financial support of the general public, I feel that over the next few years major breakthroughs will occur enabling people with scleroderma to live a more fulfilled and rewarding life.

Let me add that I am so blessed on many levels; first, my systemic scleroderma has been at bay or inactive for over ten years, and thankfully I'm on minimal medication. This has allowed me, through my book and speaking opportunities, to meet many incredible people with scleroderma who have amazing strength and perseverance. They are truly wonderful people as are the volunteers and family members who give up their time to help and support their loved ones.

As a scleroderma survivor, I am also passionate to reach out to people who have given up hope for a cure and to those who feel they are all alone. You are not! I've also connected with others outside the scleroderma family who've found my book helpful in delivering a message of hope and perseverance to help put their lives back into perspective with whatever adversity they may be facing. You can also visit www.scleroderma.org to find more about this disease and how others are coping with it.

Five Lessons I Learned From Almost Losing My Life

Since I almost lost my life over a decade ago, my gifts are many, but most important is that I have been able to create a balance in my life and make a difference in the lives of other people. My near death experience and lessons that I learned caused me to rethink every day and my intentions for living.

1. Stop and smell the roses—reduce your stress

In our out-of-control lives, it is so easy to get caught up in chasing one's own tail. We are the only country in the world where people continue to work more and more hours than any other country. For what? More money? More prestige or power? More stress? I was on this merry-go-round until I almost died from scleroderma. I know my disease was brought on, in part, due to the stress I was experiencing in my executive position with AllApartments. When I look back on it all—the money, the position, the prestige—if I had died at 40, what good would all of that have accomplished? Nothing! How many people do you know who didn't make those all important changes in their lives and either got seriously ill or lost their life through an illness?

Since the publishing of my book in 2012, I've been overwhelmed by the people who have called, emailed, and spoken to me at my book signing events, who have taken solace and found inspiration in my book and words. I was originally inspired to write my book to get people's attention, and I am so grateful many have paid attention. So what can we do to help deal with the stress we have in our lives? Well, we can't remove stress; it doesn't work that way. But a lot of the stress we carry around with us is self-induced. So, if we can self-induce stress, then we can self-un-induce stress, but it has to be a conscious effort on your part, like anything in your life that helps create positive reinforcements. Stress is everywhere we turn. We can't run from it; we can only control it.

So what is stress and what causes it? Here's a great analogy. Take a balloon and start blowing it up. As you watch the balloon expand, keep blowing into it until finally the balloon pops! This is what happened to me. I became a workaholic working 75 to 80 hours a week, seven days a week, and I wasn't taking care of myself. Stress is sneaky and comes in many shapes and forms. Some of the biggest stress factors are overworking and never finding the time to relax. Unfortunately, I wasn't even exercising to release stress from my body (remember the balloon analogy?) Even the smallest little break from your day-to-day grind can be rewarding. But you must make an effort to schedule that break into your day. Just like you'd schedule your doctor or dentist appointment or your child's ballgame, you must also do this to start disciplining yourself to carve out these precious moments. Do it now, before it's too late!

Quick tip. Before you move on to lesson two, take out your calendar and schedule your "roses" moments, even if it's to sit outside in the morning before work for five minutes to just reflect on your day, your week, your life, and where it's going. After about a week or two of this five-minute reflection, move on to ten minutes. If you can't carve out ten minutes in the morning or ten minutes at the end of the day, then you have some serious issues. Find out when your children's school or sporting events are coming up so you can make sure to schedule them into your calendar, thereby scheduling them into your life. You should never be in a position where you someday say, "I should have..." So what are you waiting for?

2. Creating balance in one's life

Balance, what's balance? It's something everybody strives for but few find. It's the ability to have a grasp on all the major aspects of your life and for the most part, for them to be in harmony. The harmony comes from internal forces and outside forces. The internal forces are your compassion and mind, both in challenging yourself and learning to relax the mind. And then there's your health, making sure you are eating and exercising properly. The outside forces that can affect your balance are work, friends, family and your passions. You should strive to love what you do for work—life is too short not to. If you don't enjoy what you're doing for work or a career, only you have the ability to make a change, and remember, change is good!

One of the most important things that can help you keep a balance is the connections you have and maintaining those connections with your family and friends. Our lives can get so hectic we sometimes pull further and further away from this center of strength. I was guilty of this when I lived on the West Coast and lost contact with many friends I grew up with. I can also say I didn't keep in touch with my family as much as I should have. I can remember coming home from work and on my answering machine was my mother saying, "I was just checking to see if you were still alive?" Back then I used to chuckle; today it isn't funny at all.

The last area that needs your focus is to follow your passions. The spark of life, the essence of existence is experiencing and enjoying the things in life you are passionate about. Your ability to harness all of these areas and keep them in some kind of harmony is critical to maintaining balance. But it isn't easy; if it was, everyone would be doing it. Finding balance may always be a constant battle, if you choose to fight.

Finding balance in even the smallest of accomplishments must be applauded. Why? Like a baby's first step, each step creates a forward motion, a good habit, and little by little you begin to reinforce those positive life choices that will enable you to begin creating that all-elusive balance. Even though I feel I've found a better balance in my life; I still find myself falling back to my old work habits more than I should. Part of it is the competitive spirit most of us enjoy, and then there is the fear of failure. Perhaps it's a work ethic thing. When that happens, I take stock in how I got there in the first place (stress), and I am able to pull back and regain some of the balance I lost. But, it takes both a conscious and subconscious effort.

Before you see a goal in front of you, first see it in your minds' eye. Identify those obstacles in your life that are keeping you from "being." Everyone has a bad habit or two. Nothing is more rewarding than when you've turned a bad habit into a positive life motivator. "If it's to be…It's up to me!" Or the opposite would be, letting your personal road blocks keep you from fully realizing your life dreams. If you don't begin to bring balance into your life starting now, you may never find it or if you do, it may be too late.

Quick tip. To begin claiming back some balance, start by giving yourself five minutes in the morning and five minutes at night to "being." What is being? It's the state of living in the moment, the state of knowing who you are and where you are going. It's carving the time out of your day to dream and ponder where you want to be. It's figuring out what you really want in life and what it is going to take to get there. Some will call it meditation. Give yourself an internal check with your compassion, your mind, and your health. Do you feel you have a grasp on these areas? Where can you improve?

As for your external forces of work, friends, family, and your passions, take an assessment and ask yourself if you are satisfied with how these are unfolding in your life. From a professional standpoint, ask yourself, what will I accomplish today? What are my top three priorities? What are my "fires" for tomorrow? Now, begin to dream out further than just today. Begin by thinking about one year, five years, and ten years. What does that look like to you? Before you can realize these dreams, you must first find and maintain a balance in your life. Once you get a better handle on your life, then you can start carving out the moments that will always be precious to you.

3. The act of giving back

Whether you've had a brush with death, like I had, or not we must all make a stronger effort to give back to others who are less fortunate than we are. That's what has made our country and its people the best in the world. If we lend a helping hand now, when it's time for someone to help us, it becomes reciprocal. It's the pay it forward mentality. But, many of us stop short because we say we don't have time. If you live till 70 years of age, you'll have lived for over 610,000 hours. So let me ask you…you mean you can't carve out one to two hours a month to volunteer for something? I mean, really? It's easy giving money to a cause that you're passionate about, and that's wonderful. But, there is nothing more rewarding than rolling up your sleeves and getting your hands a little dirty. Get involved! You may actually feel like you've helped move the football across the goal line. Many times you might feel you accomplished this as a team. You may also walk away with a smile on your face and pride in your spirit.

Over the years, I've been blessed to volunteer for several great nonprofit organizations, Big Brothers, Meals on Wheels, and Mayflower RSVP where I was a reading tutor for second graders, as well as to sit on the boards of nonprofits, The Plymouth Library Corporation and Project Arts of Plymouth. There are so many organizations out there, mostly nonprofit, which always fall short of their goals because not enough people reach out to help, either with action or donations. Though I volunteer now, when I was a workaholic and engrossed in my work and my life, I didn't. And that is a regret I still carry today.

Quick tip. As I mentioned when you turn 70, you've lived for over 610,000 hours. Start today and "allow" yourself to set aside a few hours a month and give back, volunteer. I think today we can look at our youth who seem to volunteer more frequently than I did when I was growing up. If you are passionate about animals, volunteer at a shelter or donate old towels to their cause so they can have new bedding. See, you've just helped out a great cause! What are you passionate about? Where can you put that passion into action? If you love nature, volunteer for a conservation group. If you love children volunteer as a reading tutor or help out at your local school. If you like sports, many youth organizations need volunteers to help with the kids. So what will you do? The key is to be unselfish with your free time rather than selfish. We know we have the time to give! Please email me on how you've decided to give back! (Andrew@AndrewBotieri.com)

4. Importance of family traditions

Maybe it was the generation I grew up in, or maybe it was the stories of my parents and grandparents who helped us relive an era that we never experienced. Nothing made me want to sit still more as a young child than listening to my Gramp or Noni tell stories of their days growing up and their decision to come to America from Italy. The hardships, the joys, and the family traditions. I especially loved the stories Gramp told me about his days playing baseball, and I'm sure he was the one who instilled in me my love of baseball. Growing up we learned to prepare many wonderful Northern Italian dishes, but the most memorable for me and my siblings—that we still celebrate today—was watching and helping my grandfather make homemade Italian sausage, which he learned from his family in Cento, Italy.

After Gramp passed, my father and his kids picked up the tradition. Then, after Dad passed away in 2009, my sister Karen, brother Michael, and I got together to carry on the family tradition. So, two to three times a year, we get together at my Mom's, and we knock out about 100 pounds of Italian sausage. We do it for many reasons aside from the fact we *love* the sausage. When we make it, it's just like Gramp and Dad are there with us, guiding us to make sure we do it right. We even talk to them during the process. But mainly we do it because it's a family tradition. It's that intangible tradition that binds us together aside from the blood that flows through our veins.

All through history people come and people go, but it's a family's traditions that keep generation after generation connected. Let me ask you, what family traditions do you remember as a child? Are you still engaged in those traditions? What will you pass on to your children so that 50 or 100 years from now, you and other family members are remembered and celebrated?

Quick tip. If you've let those family traditions fade away, like a flame extinguished by the wind, it's time to make a stand to bring back what connects you to your past. Find one tradition that you used to do when you were younger and bring it back alive. Leave this legacy and tradition to your children. Get them involved and watch with pride as they embrace their history. They will thank you, and your family who went before you will smile down from Heaven.

5. Making a difference in the lives of others

Part of what defines a person's character isn't so much how much they make, but how they've made a difference in the lives of others. Let's face it; the people who have the biggest impact on our society over the centuries have been parents. It is an awesome responsibility, and it should never be shirked. The proper raising and education of our youth is critical to the well-being of our nation and its longevity.

When you look back on how you got where you are today, who was the person or persons who made a difference in your life? A parent, a grandparent, a teacher, a coach, or a mentor? I know I am where I am today because of the mentors who came into my life: Mr. Antal, Gary Austin, Tony Ashe, and Ernest Oriente. Was it coincidence or fate that they came into my life at different intervals and in different parts of the country? I know it was fate. Part of why I give back is because of what one of my mentors, Tony Ashe told me, "Now that I have given guidance and knowledge to you, you must give it to help others; pass it on."

It's so easy to get caught up in our lives and selfish with our time in today's fast-paced, out-of-control world. Some people focus on the bigger house, the newer car, the extravagant vacation home. Now, don't get me wrong, I like nice things and have worked very hard to achieve my success so I can enjoy the better things in life. However, I almost died never being able to enjoy the fruits of my labor. I think the greatest thing about people I see making a difference in the lives of others is that they do it from their heart and from their compassion. And, what's best is that they don't ask for or want any recognition for what they do. That is the definition of selfless!

Quick tip. Where can you make a difference in the life of someone else? I challenge you! Be a Big Brother or Big Sister if you have no children of your own. Be a mentor to someone and the reward will come back to you tenfold! Please email me about how you've made a difference in the life of someone. I'd love to hear from you! (Andrew@AndrewBotieri.com)

As for me, the last 14 years have been quite a journey. I lost my Dad in November of 2009. He was an incredible man, the town barber for 58 years. There is also a Little League field in Hanson, Massachusetts named after him. Quite an honor! As I finished writing this foreword, my Mom passed away from lung cancer. She was an incredible woman and mother. Even with these losses, I continue to be on my life's journey to seek out ways I can make a difference in the lives of others. My parents made a huge difference in the lives of their kids as well as all those who came into contact with them.

On occasion, I still get flare ups with scleroderma, but mostly in my hands, and sometimes I'm quick to fatigue. But of my many blessings, I got back something I thought I might lose forever, my ability to play guitar. I know many of you can relate to losing the ability to do something you loved to do, to have it taken away. Several years back, as the symptoms of scleroderma began to regress, I was able to slowly begin picking up the guitar again. I now perform at local establishments around the Plymouth area, though after about three hours of playing, my fingers and hands get stiff and sore for a few days. But, the enjoyment I receive from performing and bringing together childhood friends, new friends, family, and cousins is certainly worth the couple days of discomfort.

I hope that those who read on will find ways throughout my book to listen to the many life lessons, not just from me but from others who have made a difference in my life. God Bless!

—Andrew Botieri- Author & Inspirational Speaker

—Dr. Robert Simms, MD Section Head, Rheumatology, Boston University Medical Center, Professor of Medicine, Boston University School of Medicine

Preface

They say there is a book in all of us. Everyone has a story. Though, like me, you probably wonder who would read your book. Why would they want to? Is your message powerful enough to not only get people to read your book, but compel them to take action? To ponder and think about your message?

It took a brush with death to finally motivate me to write this book. At first I felt awkward writing about myself and my medical crisis. But the more I shared my story, and after publishing an article in a national magazine, people close to me said, "You have a strong message to tell others." The story was so compelling that my article was read in churches of many denominations all across our country.

There are several messages throughout this book; messages of family and tradition, of hope and faith, of perseverance, and the power of prayer and attitude. My wish is for everyone who reads this book that it has an impact on you, that it gets your attention. I hope it helps you reevaluate your life and enables you to strive for balance. Don't wait for a near death event like I had, to wake you up and smell the roses.

God Bless. —Andrew

CHAPTER 1

The Emergency Room

It was a quiet morning at the Arizona Heart Hospital in Phoenix except for the sounds of intercom pages and the bleeps and bloops of the ER machinery. The following is a dramatization of what happened there around 9:15 a.m. on the morning of Thursday, June 29, 2000.

"We've got a 911 call from the Phoenix Nephrologist's office down the street, Dr. Pietre's office. The ambulance is on its way," a nurse shouted with urgency.

"Who's the patient?" asked a doctor just finishing up his morning coffee.

The nurse responded, "Male, 40 years old, 185 pounds, appears to be in acute renal failure; he's unconscious, with severe convulsions, and unresponsive. Dr. Moorshedian is with him."

The head doctor instructed his team, "Okay, let's get ready; they'll be here any minute."

Then a voice broke over the intercom, "911 patient arriving."

Two EMTs accompanied by a young physician in his white coat, emerged, rushing from the back of the ambulance, gurney and patient in tow as they broke through the emergency entrance doors. The physician looked no older than his late twenties. Dr. Kris, as his colleagues and patients call him, was focused on what needed to be done to save this patient's life. He began shouting out orders like a drill sergeant but in a much softer and effective manner to the emergency room staff. They rushed the patient into the ER where a group of doctors begin to work feverously on the sick man.

One physician from the ER tried to take charge, but Dr. Kris wouldn't have any of it. He instructed the assembled group of doctors and nurses, "The man has suffered acute renal kidney failure and is in hypertensive crisis brought on by scleroderma."

To combat most cases of hypertensive crisis, doctors will prescribe a beta-blocker to help bring down the blood pressure. Normal blood pressure is 120 over 80. Dr. Kris saw this patient's blood pressure hover around 270 over 170 and he knew that beta-blockers wouldn't bring the blood pressure down quickly enough, so he asked for ACE inhibitors. The patient's blood pressure was twice the normal pressure. Pressure this high, for even short periods of time can cause a fatal heart attack or stroke.

"What's the patient's name?" A nurse asked.

Dr. Kris responded, "Andrew Botieri, he's had two convulsions and is unresponsive. He may lapse into a coma."

A second doctor, in an alarmed voice barked, "The patient stopped breathing! We need to intubate immediately!"

They inserted a breathing tube down the patient's throat allowing a respirator to breath for him.

A second nurse responded, "Okay, tube inserted, got him!"

A doctor shouted, "We need x-rays and scans! Stat!"

The doctors continued to work at a fast pace on their critically ill patient. At one point, the patient began to stir from his coma, as he did, he became agitated, pulling out IVs and the cardiac monitor lines off of his chest. The doctors rushed in holding him still while one injected him, placing him into a drug induced coma and out of harm. Keeping him still and reducing his extremely elevated blood pressure was critical. Without these events happening, the patient could die.

The doctors had been working on the patient for a few hours and had made little progress. The patient was lying in the ER, clinging onto life. One doctor mentioned under his breath, "The patient may not survive the morning."

CHAPTER 2

Thursday, June 29, 7 A.M.

You've all heard or read accounts where people recall a specific event in their life and how that event created a significant moment that would change their life forever. My significant event occurred on June 29, 2000.

It was a little before 7:00 a.m. I awoke just before the alarm went off, as I always seem to do. I guess it's all those years in corporate America getting up early to get a jump on each business day. Isn't it funny how our inner alarm clock seems to go off seconds before the actual alarm does? Sometimes it drives me crazy, especially on weekends when I'd like to sleep in and my inner clock goes off at 5:30 a.m. Boy, I hate that. You know what I mean?

But this brings up an interesting point. If we can condition or discipline our minds and bodies to wake up before an alarm clock goes off, why can't we use the same discipline to accomplish other tasks or overcome other challenges? What else could we achieve? How far can we push ourselves? As the morning unfolded, I was about to find out.

I was a little anxious this particular morning as I had an important, I guess maybe a slightly urgent, appointment with a kidney specialist, known as a nephrologist. The reason for the appointment? In October 1999, after eight months of being misdiagnosed with Rheumatoid Arthritis, I was correctly diagnosed with a rare autoimmune disease called scleroderma, a deadly disease that at this time has no known cause or cure. (You'll read more information about scleroderma in Chapter 4.)

I had returned from a four-day apartment industry conference in New Orleans on June 25, 2000, with my former company, Spring-

Street/Homestore. (HomeStore, is now called Move.com, a publicly traded Internet based apartment listing search service). The event was the National Apartment Association's Annual Trade show and Conference.

I'd been feeling extremely fatigued over the weeks leading up to the conference, but as always, I shook it off as the been-working-too-hard routine. But nothing would compare to the fatigue I felt during and after my return from New Orleans. Between the long working hours, the round trip flight from Phoenix, and a few nights of partying on Bourbon Street, which I'm sure didn't help my situation, I was feeling pretty exhausted on a daily basis. Had I known I was this sick, I would've not only behaved myself but probably would've stayed home.

The trade show was a success, mainly because our sales team was highly motivated to begin with and we set forth a unique sales strategy to capitalize on our face-to-face selling opportunities with our clients and prospects at the trade show. As the VP of sales for All-Apartments/SpringStreet in '98 and '99, I'd make this event and other trade shows a game with my team by placing money incentives on new sales and renewals during the show. We worked hard and played hard as well. There was so much positive energy and the team hustled and had fun doing it. Why shouldn't work be fun? If you can't have fun at work, why do you even bother to show up?

> *When you love what you do for work, it ceases to be work.*
>
> —Andrew Botieri

The National Apartment Association (NAA) always does an outstanding job putting together powerful educational programs and networking opportunities for both members and industry vendors. Over the years, they've secured notable speakers like, former secretary of state Colin Powell, Pro Football Hall of Fame quarterback and TV analyst Terry Bradshaw, New York City's former mayor Rudy Giuliani and former president Bill Clinton. I was tired and exhausted from the long hard week and couldn't wait to get home. If only I knew, a fuse caused by stress had been lit inside of me and my body was headed for a collision course, and I was just along for the ride.

The day after returning from New Orleans, on Monday, June 26, I woke to get ready for work. I had slept about ten hours, but still had no strength or motivation. I lay in bed willing myself to get up, but did not have the energy. For someone as highly motivated as myself, this was a very strange feeling. I knew something wasn't right. Eventually I got up and made my way into the office.

When I arrived at the office, a co-worker and close friend, Stacy, told me I didn't look good. "Thanks and how are you?" I said sarcastically. I was tired and didn't feel good, so she asked me to see my doctor. Back in the Spring of 1999 when my hands and feet were bothering me, Stacy urged me to see a doctor then. At first I was going to argue with her, but I knew something was wrong and knew she was right. This was one of the first times I didn't put up a fight. I called my doctor and was told to come in to have some blood drawn; hoping the results could shed light on my extreme fatigue.

> Creatinine measures the amount of toxins in your kidneys. The average person has a level of around .5–1.5, and mine was about 2.1 at the time. Unknown to me, the toxins were beginning to elevate because my kidneys were being slowly attacked by scleroderma. As your kidneys slowly shut down, you begin to lose your ability to urinate and as that happens, your kidneys begin to retain more and more toxins. Eventually those toxins begin to seep back into your major organs creating all kinds of health and medical issues. This waste and toxic liquids can do irreversible damage to your kidneys.

Dr. Blau took my vitals and noted my blood pressure was a bit elevated. I'd been on low dosage blood pressure pills since they diagnosed me with scleroderma in 1999, so he suggested an increase in dosage. He wrote a prescription and said if my blood work showed anything he'd call me immediately. I felt only slightly relieved. He was the same doctor who, after my first appointment complaining about the pain and tingling in my hands and feet in the spring of 1999, said it was probably arthritis, when in fact, it was the beginnings of scleroderma. So I didn't have the best of confidence in him, but he was local and all I was doing was getting some blood work done. I was so tired I couldn't even concentrate. I decided to take the rest of the afternoon off, go home and get some rest.

Later that afternoon, Dr. Blau called to say he was concerned with some of my blood results. His biggest concern was the elevated levels of my creatinine and elevated blood pressure (see sidebar).

> **What Your Kidneys Do**
>
> As blood flows through our kidneys it filters out our waste and drains off excess water, which is then expelled from the body as urine via our bladder. In this way the urinary system clears the blood of toxins and regulates its water content. The kidneys clean about 2.7 pints of blood a minute and urine is 95 percent water; the rest is toxic waste.
> *National Kidney Foundation (http://www.kidney.org)*

He told me in layman terms something was going on with my kidneys and it was imperative to get an appointment as soon as possible with a kidney doctor. The kidney doctor, or nephrologist, could make a proper diagnosis based on the reports we got back. Why he didn't send me to a hospital that day, I'm not sure. As I later learned, these toxins were acting like a poison, slowly making me deathly ill, literally. His office called and made me an appointment for Thursday, June 29 at 9:00 a.m.

Wow, of all the phone calls I've received in my lifetime, this call rattled my world. I felt nauseous and my knees got weak, so I had to lean up against the wall. I felt as if I was hit by a stun gun. My mind and body went numb. I was in total shock! I knew I had this disease, scleroderma, and in some cases it can be fatal. It can't affect me like *those other* people who I'd read about in the various scleroderma books after being diagnosed. But wait, I'm Andrew. It's not supposed to happen to me. Why is it we believe bad things only happen to others and not ourselves? If someone else is thinking the same way, then couldn't you be that *other person*? Just a thought.

I hung up the phone and stood staring out the sliding glass door overlooking the desert landscape of the McDowell Mountains in North Scottsdale. Everywhere you looked were Saguaro, Prickly Pear and dozens of other types of cactus in the shadows of the beautiful mountains. It was such a surreal moment, all this beauty in front of me and something was going on with this disease. This was the first time I really felt threatened since being properly diagnosed in October of 1999. Up until this point I kept telling myself, "I can beat this." After this call I now asked myself could this really be happening to me? Now what?

As I continued staring into space, I tried to take it all in. Did I really have that phone conversation with my doctor or was it a dream? Looking up into the sky towards the heavens, I dropped to my knees and began to pray to Jesus. I asked Him to watch over me and protect me, and then I prayed to my guardian angel to keep an extra eye on me. I kept repeating over in my head a little prayer "May God's bright light be my protective shield." I kept repeating this throughout the rest of the evening. Still today, I say this prayer every time I take off and land when flying.

> **Scleroderma**
>
> Here's a quote from the book *The Proven Therapy That Can Save Your Life* by Henry Scammell.
>
> *Scleroderma, which afflicts 400,000 Americans, starts off like skin cancer but is far more deadly. Long considered incurable, for many of its victims it is a slow, painful killer.*

I began pacing around the house, not knowing what to do or what to think. After some pondering, I knew I had to call my parents and let them know what was going on without going into too much detail so as not to alarm them since they were back in Massachusetts, 2300 miles away. I've always been private about things in my life, even with my family. I could feel their angst on the other end of the phone. It was killing them because they couldn't be with me to provide comfort and support. I told them everything was going to be fine. At least now we knew what was causing the fatigue, so the specialists could take over. If only it would be that simple.

Throughout the night, my mind would wonder off saying, "Kidney failure? What, me? This couldn't be!" My life was moving along just as planned. A great job, making great money, living in Scottsdale. I bought a four-bedroom home in a beautiful community, a two-car garage with a swimming pool overlooking the beautiful McDowell Mountains. Now everything I've worked so hard for was being threat-

> The best laid plans of mice and men often go astray.

ened by a disease called scleroderma. An old saying made popular by John Steinbeck in *Of Mice and Men* came to mind.

Over the past few weeks, I kept putting off possible reasons for my fatigue. With juggling so many business issues, I didn't spend much thinking time on why I wasn't feeling well. I plowed through my days like I'd always done, like my dad did, and his dad before him. It was the work ethic instilled in me from an early age. In my opinion work ethic is a learned behavior.

I knew I hadn't been taking enough time to recharge my batteries. Was it my passion for work? Maybe I was a bit obsessed about my career. Was it the challenge of leading and contributing to the success of a company? Was it the enticement of cashing my stock options and making substantial money? Regardless of the driver, I felt out of balance, but I didn't realize at the time how out of balance I was. When was I finally going to admit to myself maybe I'd become a workaholic?

Wednesday night before my appointment with the kidney doctor, I started getting a headache, which was unusual, as I hardly ever got headaches. Even with all the controlled chaos I thrived operating in over the years, I never got headaches. Before I went to sleep, I took some Motrin, grabbed a cold wet face cloth, and placed it across my forehead to relieve the throbbing. It seemed to work and shortly I fell asleep. But this was going to be the beginning of an anguishing and almost fatal journey.

When I woke the next morning, my head was now pounding to the rhythm of a bass drum; the pressure was intense. I felt weak and had no energy to get out of bed. As I struggled to motivate myself, I glanced up at the ceiling fan, slowly turning in a hypnotic rhythmic drone. The blades of the fan seemed out of focus. I rubbed my eyes to focus, but as they cleared, I still couldn't focus my eyes on the blades. Wow, I must really be tired! After a few minutes, I lethargically rose from the bed feeling like a plain ole' tired dog and slowly shuffled into the bathroom.

I made my way to the sink, turned on the faucet and splashed cold water on my face. The coolness felt great for a brief while, though within seconds the throbbing came back. Now what?! As I towel dried my face and hands, I noticed my hands going in and out of focus, like the ceiling fan. I couldn't clearly recognize my individual fingers. I put my hands up in front of my face and they continued to fade in and out. What could be happening to me?

You always wonder how you'll react in a crisis, especially a crisis that appears to be serious. What will you do? Will you panic? Will you remain calm? Will you attack the problem or situation with clarity, assessing the best course of action or will you succumb to the inevitable and create an opportunity for failure? Have you ever faced something unexpected? How did you react? What was the outcome of your actions?

I could feel myself getting weaker. I recalled a baseball scenario. It's bottom of the ninth, two outs, bases loaded, you're down by two runs, and you're up at the plate. Having played a lot of competitive baseball, this scenario was the perfect butterflies-in-the-stomach feeling. I knew if I didn't do something and do it quickly, I'd be in big trouble. I recalled the story of a mother lifting up the side of a car to free her child from underneath. Adrenaline! I needed to find mine and find it quick. As I like to say, "Each and every day we make choices that shape and mold our destiny." All of this stuff was racing through my mind. I knew something was wrong but didn't realize how wrong.

As each minute passed, my eyesight became weaker and my head pounded even more; it was now constant. But I still didn't seem to have a high sense of urgency. I had to call someone for a ride. I couldn't drive myself; hell, I couldn't even see. The fact I didn't call 911 goes to show I didn't think this was life threatening.

The first person I attempted to call was Stacy, who lived down the street. I knew her phone number by heart. As I picked up the phone, something disturbing happened. Not only couldn't I remember her number, I couldn't remember her name. I could see her in my mind's eye, but couldn't put a name to her face. That freaked me out, but I had to stay focused on getting through this. I thought "What the hell is going on?" "What's happening to me?" I then tried another friend and co-worker, Craig, who also lived down the street, but the same thing occurred. I couldn't remember his name or phone number.

For a moment, I felt all alone, almost secluded. I felt like the walls were closing in. I was 2300 miles away from my family, standing alone in my kitchen, holding a telephone, not sure what my next move was. I said the "Hail Mary" prayer and asked God for strength and guidance. The burst of fear and panic I'd been feeling was now replaced with calmness and clarity.

I had to keep my composure. I knew I needed a plan, a plan of action, and I had to put it into motion quickly. I got focused and remembered another good friend and co-worker Rob McCarthy. I tried to think of his first name, but couldn't. But, by the Grace of God, I remembered his last name.

My vision continued to deteriorate. Objects were beginning to blur and some, like my bedroom set and other furniture were just dark shadows. Fear now crept up from the gallows of my soul and another jolt of panic went through me like a lightning bolt. Again, I knew I had to be pro-active with a purpose, for if I didn't, it might not fare well. One thing I had to fall back on was my faith. I prayed to Jesus and hoped my guardian angel was in the room with me.

As I looked at the telephone, I realized I couldn't make out the numbers on the key pad, "Oh shit!" How scary! I ran my fingers down the number pad and located the "0" for operator. I pushed the button. The two to three rings seemed like an eternity. An operator came on the line and asked how she could help. I told her of my medical situation and that I couldn't see the numbers on the phone dial. I urgently asked her for help. "Should I dial 911?" she asked. For some reason I resisted and asked her to look up a number of a friend who would pick me up and drive me to my scheduled appointment. I obviously still didn't realize how serious of a predicament I was in. If I had, I might've urged her to call 911.

I told her I couldn't remember his first name, but knew his last name and there were two zeroes side-by-side in the last four digits of his phone number. How I remembered that at that moment, still baffles me today. Now, you may be wondering. How many McCarthy's are there in the Phoenix area phone book? A very good question. At the writing of this chapter, there were over 80.

The operator went right to work. As she continued searching the long list of names, she sensed my anxiety and confusion and tried to keep me engaged, talking with me, trying to keep me calm and relaxed. She kept asking how I was doing and how I was feeling. I don't recall much more of our conversation, though I do remember she connected me to Rob.

His phone rang. The operator stayed with me until Rob picked up. She wished me good luck and told me to hang in there. I wish I remembered her name; she was so patient, compassionate, and had a big part in saving my life.

I quickly told Rob what was going on. Rob had been one of my team leaders in the early days of AllApartments. We had a good working relationship and spent time outside the office. Let's face it, when you work 12 to 14 hours a day with a group of people, you get to know them very well. You either bond with them or you don't. Rob and I bonded well. Isn't it interesting in many cases we spend more time with people at work than we do our own families? Every market across the country I've worked in, those sales teams eventually became my surrogate family.

Rob asked if I was okay. I said, "Yes," but I wasn't feeling well and needed a ride to my nephrologists' office. I told him my vision was fading. I'm not sure if Rob asked me if he should dial 911. If he did, I probably said, "No." I still wasn't fully aware of how critical my condition was. Rob said he'd be over as fast as he could.

As soon as I hung up, the phone rang. It was Stacy. I asked Rob before hanging up to call her and let her know what was going on. She stayed on the phone with me till Rob arrived.

After putting the phone down, I walked to the front door waiting for Rob. What seemed like an hour was only about 10 to 15 minutes. By the time he got to my house, I probably wasn't looking so good, and I know I wasn't feeling well either. By this time I could barely make out any object in front of me. Rob came in, we had some small talk, and then he led me to his car and placed me in the passenger seat. As we drove to the appointment, Rob was trying to create small talk, but I wasn't much for talking. I do remember his voice was full of concern. With my head against the side window, I thought, "How did I get here? What was going to be the outcome of this?" I knew one thing: I needed to stay calm and keep my wits about me if I was to get through this. I reached down and tapped into some positive energy and felt a surge run through my body.

We raced towards downtown Phoenix, through the side streets of Scottsdale as the 202 Freeway was backed up with morning traffic. As I looked out the passenger window I only saw a gray blur surrounding me. A nauseous feeling started to overtake me. I quickly put the window down and vomited out the window, much to Rob's horror. I'd have been more than happy to pay for his car wash! Later I found out the vomiting was the beginning signs of kidney shutdown. At this point, I started to feel myself fall in and out of consciousness. How was this going to end? I thought of Mom, Dad, my sisters, my brother and Noni. They were so far away, who was going to help me?

The next thing I heard was Rob saying we were at the doctor's office. The last thing I remember was being placed in a wheelchair and wheeled into their office and without warning I slumped over to my right side and blacked out.

It was a little after 9:00 a.m. Phoenix time on the morning of June 29, and for the next 28 hours, I lay in a coma, on a respirator, teetering on the brink of death in a Phoenix emergency room. I had absolutely no idea what was happening. Not even my family knew what was going on at this moment.

CHAPTER 3

The Call Every Parent Dreads

A telephone rings on a beautiful summer afternoon at the quiet home of Don and Betty Botieri in Hanson, Massachusetts. Mrs. Botieri is surprised to hear Andrew's close friend and co-worker Stacy on the other end of the phone. Betty recalls how frantic Stacy's voice was. Here what she remembers:

> It was about two o'clock in the afternoon, Thursday, June 29. I received a call from Andrew's assistant, Stacy. She frantically began telling me how that morning Andrew was on his way to a kidney specialist driven by his co-worker Rob. With urgency in her voice, Stacy told me that something was wrong and Andrew went into convulsions and was rushed to a local hospital. I later found it was the Arizona Heart Hospital. I immediately called my other children who rushed to our home.
>
> My daughter began calling various airlines to get my husband and me out on the earliest plane to Phoenix. Even my husband's cousin's wife, Mal, who owned a travel agency, jumped on the Internet to help us find a flight out to see my sick son. To our dismay, we couldn't get a flight out until 7:00 a.m. Friday, the next morning. My daughters (Carol and Karen) began calling family and friends from all over to let them know what was going on. None of us could believe it, not our Andrew. Not my Andrew! He was always so healthy and took care of himself. I knew he worked very hard, sometimes maybe too hard. But not this, please help us God! I didn't know what to do. My first born son was lying in a hospital two thousand miles away, and I couldn't help him. All my life I'd been there for my children, and now I couldn't do a thing. I felt helpless. I felt numb. I was frantic and couldn't believe this was happening. I began to pray.

For the rest of the day, I paced around the house, not knowing how to keep busy. My daughters, husband and I just sort of walked around in a fog Thursday night. My mind kept going back to my son lying there, alone in the emergency room of that hospital. None of us knew what to say so we kept busy with lots of small talk. The one saving grace was knowing that Andrew's cousin's husband, Jim, was with Andrew at the hospital. That night I tried to get a little sleep but I couldn't. My nerves were too much. I kept saying prayer after prayer. It was all I could do. I kept asking God to please let him be alive.

We left for the airport at 5:00 a.m. on Friday morning, June 30. My nerves felt as though they were trying to push through my skin. We arrived at Logan Airport in Boston and checked in. We rushed through security and headed to the gate only to find out our flight would be delayed until 9:30 a.m. I couldn't believe it; I wanted to see my son. All I could do was pace and pray. I was so nervous at times I wanted to scream at someone to get me to Phoenix. At 9:30 a.m. they announced that our flight was now being pushed to noon. 'You've got to be kidding me,' I said out loud. I was fit to be tied! I went up to the gate counter, looked at the lady behind the counter and starting crying. My emotions and frustrations seemed to flow out of me, and I begged them to get me on another airline, but to no avail. All we could do was wait, so we got a bite to eat in the airport concourse to wait for our noontime departure.

When we finished eating, we came back to the gate. Then to my horror they announced, that our flight was now being delayed until 2:00 p.m. I went up to the young lady at the counter, crying, telling them I needed to fly out to see my sick son. They were trying to be helpful but they couldn't find another flight out for us. I sat in a chair totally distraught. I was a basket case. This can't be happening to me and my family.

A few hours later, we finally made it off the ground. In the past, I've flown to Phoenix, California, and even Italy. Flights that were longer than this and all I could think of was how long this flight took. It was like each minute slowly ticked off of my watch. It seemed to take an eternity to land in Phoenix. My husband and I did very little talking on the plane, but we held hands in silent support along with our thoughts and fears for the duration of the trip.

Prior to my parents' flight out to Phoenix, my sister Karen, had placed an urgent call to our cousin Paula, who lives in Phoenix, with the distraught news about my medical condition. Paula was at her summer beach house in Plymouth, Massachusetts so she asked what hospital I was transported to and was told the Arizona Heart Hospital.

Paula couldn't believe it, not only the news about me, but the hospital I was taken to. The Arizona Heart Hospital and Institute (AHI) was not just a hospital, it was a state-of-the-art heart hospital that specializes in the prevention, detection, and treatment of cardiovascular disorders and heart disease through patient assessments and custom designed life plan strategies. Pro-active versus reactive measures before a heart attack or heart disease sets in. AHI is distinct for being the nation's first free standing clinic built solely to combat heart and blood vessel disease. What made this even more ironic was my cousin Paula retired as the right-hand person for the Arizona Heart Institute's founder, Dr. Ted Diethrich.

Paula immediately called her husband Jim who was in Phoenix to tell him the news. Ironically, Jim was on his way to the hospital. As I mentioned, not only did my cousin Paula work and collaborate with the founder of AHI, but her husband's communications company, Banahan Communications, was the hospitals PR agency, so Jim pretty much knew everyone at the hospital.

Jim pulled into the hospital lot, parked his car and dashed into the hospital's ER entrance where he asked for Dr. Ted. Jim was told he was in surgery and wouldn't be out for a while. Jim looked at his watch and then looked around the ER and recognized Stacy, standing next to Rob, from an Easter dinner I'd taken her to at my Aunt's house in Phoenix a few months earlier. Jim went over and asked her to fill him in on what had happened.

With much emotion, Rob explained to Jim about picking me up at my house and how I collapsed at the doctor's office. Rob said the nephrologist's office dialed 911 and rushed me here to the hospital. They still weren't sure what had happened to me. Jim recalled when he looked in the eyes of Rob and Stacy, all he could see was fear.

It was at this point Jim knew my situation was a lot more serious than he or anyone in my family was aware of. Since Jim couldn't get a hold of Dr. Diethrich, he walked directly into the ER where I was laying while the doctors worked diligently on me. Jim couldn't believe what he saw. I was lying there, unconscious, and I "Looked like death," he said. My face was grey. He almost didn't recognize me.

Jim was able to get a little more information from the attending doctors, but he desperately needed to speak with Dr. Diethrich personally. Jim placed a call to Paula to let her know he was at the hospital, and when he had a chance to speak with Dr. Ted, he'd call her back. Jim confided to Paula, "Andrew doesn't look good at all."

A short while later Jim got to speak with Dr. Ted after he emerged from surgery. Jim said Paula's cousin, Andrew, was in the ER and needed to find out what was wrong with him. Jim mentioned to Dr. Ted he had met me at his son Tad's wedding back in the late eighties when I first lived in Phoenix.

Ted walked into the ER and about 20 minutes later emerged and looked at Jim. Jim anxiously asked how I was doing and if I was going to be okay. Dr. Diethrich shook his head; he didn't think I was in good shape at all. He wasn't sure what was going to happen. According to the ER doctors, they didn't think I'd make it through the day. Jim's spirits sank. Dr. Ted looked at Jim and said, "He's pretty messed up Jim; he's got a lot going on. It doesn't look good."

Jim immediately called Paula to give her the troubling news. Paula also spoke with Ted to see if that was truly the case. She told him he had to save her cousin.

Dr. Ted was silent for a few minutes and then said into the phone, "Paula your cousin has no business being alive right now; I don't know how he has survived this long." Paula's heart sank, she was devastated. And now she had to call my sister Karen to relay the disturbing news. My sister stood on the other end of the phone back at my parents' house in Hanson numb and in disbelief.

Jim stayed for a while longer but had to leave for a business appointment though he called back throughout the day to check up on me. He then returned to the hospital later that day and stayed with me off and on till the next day, like a big brother keeping an eye on his younger, defenseless sibling. He wouldn't leave my side until my parents arrived the following day, Friday, June 30. Even though I was in a coma and had no idea what was going on, at that moment, I had a member of my family doing everything he could to make sure I was safe. Damn, family is so important. I owe so much to Jim and Paula.

Jim would tell me later when my parents finally arrived at the hospital it was like passing off the baton. Why is it that some families stop being a family because of stupid, petty arguments and don't talk to one another over such trivial issues as money, a significant other, or internal jealousies? When times or events in our lives are challenging, we need to be able to count on family. What a wonderful relief to know you have family there ready to step in and help. Nothing should ever separate a family! I ask, if you are having struggles with your family or a family member, try and mend things before it's too late.

> When a life passes without closure, a heavy heart remains behind.
> —Andrew Botieri

Life in the little small town of Hanson would stand still for the next 48 hours.

Sister Karen's Story

Below is my sister Karen's recollection from that day.

> It was Thursday, June 29, and I received a frantic phone call from my mother who had just received a phone call from Andrew's co-workers saying my brother had a seizure and was in a coma at a hospital in Phoenix. From what they knew, it didn't look good. I couldn't recall my mother ever being this hysterical. My heart dropped. All I could see was the face of my brother with his mischievous smile. I remember thinking this couldn't be happening. I bolted out the door, jumped into my car and raced over to my parents' house which is only a few minutes down the street.
>
> As I ran into my parents' house, I could see the despair in my mother's face. We immediately hugged, cried, and consoled

each other for what seemed like an eternity. After we separated, I called my father at his barbershop which was just down the street.

When I called, his partner, Mike, told me he had gone across the street to the pharmacy to get something. I raced down to the CVS and waited for him in the parking lot. My mind was racing. I was sick to my stomach. My little brother was thousands of miles away, and I couldn't be there for him.

As I began to say a prayer, my dad came out of the store. He looked at me and could tell something was wrong. He said. 'What is it? What's going on?' I explained to him the phone call Mom had just received and that Andrew was very sick and we didn't have much more information, but from what we were hearing from Phoenix, it didn't sound good.

We hopped into my car and raced back to the house. As we made our way inside, my mom and dad embraced and we all started to cry. I was at such a loss. I had never been so scared in my life and had never seen my parents so upset and distraught. As I looked at my parents and looked around the house, all I could picture was Andrew walking around as if he was there with us. I kept thinking. This couldn't be happening, not to my brother.

Still feeling confused and overwhelmed I began to think of people I needed to call so I could let them know what was going on. I immediately called my younger brother, Michael, and then my older sister Carol. Carol lives nearby and she came right over. Unfortunately, Michael lives in Rhode Island and wasn't able to make it up right away, so he'd receive updates from us when we heard any news.

I then called a friend of mine, Nancy, and explained the situation to her. She worked in the medical field so I thought she'd be able to help our family with all the medical terms that were being thrown at us from the hospital in Arizona. Nancy had been on her way to Hanson, although she would tell me later at the time she didn't know why she was headed that way. How ironic! She was about ten minutes from my parents' house, so we anxiously waited for her to arrive.

After Nancy arrived she contacted the doctors at the Arizona Heart Hospital and tried to get some updated information for us. The hospital would not give her any information about my brother because she was not a family member. I had her call back again and pretend she was me, Marie, which is my middle name which my brother Andrew always calls me. What an appropriate name for Nancy to use.

She finally got hold of a doctor and he told her it appeared to be the scleroderma Andrew had contracted the previous year that shut down his kidneys and put his blood pressure through the roof which led to his brain hemorrhaging and coma.

The reports from the doctors in Phoenix weren't encouraging at all. Things didn't look good for my brother. God how could this be happening? Was this a bad dream?

After my sister arrived, Nancy and I headed over to our girlfriend, Pat's house, to tell her about Andrew. Nancy then called a friend of hers, Dr. Sam, who worked in scleroderma research at a local Boston hospital. Sam also was going to try and contact the doctors in Phoenix to see what he could find out. Nancy was unbelievable; she kept phone calls going back and forth between the doctors in Arizona and Dr. Sam to help us understand what Andrew's prognosis was.

My next phone calls went to other family members and friends. I called cousin Paula in Plymouth to let her know what happened. Paula said she'd contact her husband Jim immediately to let him know what was going on. She would later tell me he happened to be going to a meeting at the hospital with Dr. Diethrich. Another example of Divine Intervention? I was so grateful Jim would be there for Andrew. Jim would sit with him holding his hand and praying. Andrew wasn't aware of what was going on. But at least now we could get direct information about his condition from Jim and Dr. Diethrich.

In between the phone calls from everyone, I'd had to check on my own family. Though I didn't know how much help I'd be to them. I couldn't think straight. I could only think that if I went outside and mowed the lawn that would keep my mind occupied; I didn't want to think of the worse.

In the early evening Nancy received another call from Dr. Sam in Boston, who had just hung up the phone with the doctors in Phoenix and conveyed to her that they didn't think Andrew would make it through the day. She was so upset she drove over to Pat's house to tell her. They decided to drive over to my house to tell me the disturbing news.

They pulled in my driveway, got out of their car, and walked toward me in a slow deliberate way. I was standing in the doorway watching them walk up the front walkway—I knew it had to be bad news—my face turned white when I saw them. I starting yelling and screaming and ran into the kitchen; I didn't want to hear what they had to say. They came in behind me, but I stayed in the kitchen fidgeting with whatever I could find. I finally came back into the living room, and we stood around staring at each other.

Nancy was the one to break the news that Dr. Sam had given her; it didn't look like Andrew would make it. I felt like someone punched me in the stomach and I couldn't catch my breath. I remember crying out of control and banging the wall saying, 'No, God, please, God, no.' I ran into the bathroom and got sick.

They all stayed with me till I calmed down and helped me contact my parents and sister to give them the news. Moments later I placed a call to my brother with the same information. We now had to pray even harder than we had ever done before. It was after 11:00 p.m. East Coast time, and Nancy kept conversing with doctors and nurses to see if there was any change regarding Andrew's condition. He was still critical and all we could do was hope and pray he'd make it through the night. Everyone eventually left to go to their own homes. This had been a very emotional day for everyone. All I could think about was Andrew.

I didn't sleep well, as you can expect. The next morning I went over to Pat's house where she would tell me of an incredible occurrence that happened that night.

After Pat got home, around 11:30 p.m. that same Thursday evening, she was sitting alone at her kitchen table leafing through her *Daily Word,* which is a prayer book she receives and looked in the booklet for the message of the day. This was something she did every night. After she was finished reading the message, she started to close the booklet and noticed a telephone number to a prayer-line. The prayer-line connects you to an individual who would help to pray for someone you knew. As she dialed the number she lit a spice scented candle on her table.

Pat had never called a prayer-line before, but decided this was the best time and place, but she didn't know what to expect. She was mentally exhausted from the entire day and when the receiver picked up on the other end she told the man she wanted to pray for a friend, who was dying from a very rare disease. The man said, 'Do you want to pray for his passing?' Pat said in a loud voice, 'No, I want to pray for his recovery!'

He proceeded to recite a prayer over the phone of which Pat only heard the first few words, because as he began to speak she immediately started to think about Andrew lying in his hospital bed. She felt weird. She felt as if she was being transported to his room at the hospital thousands of miles away. All of a sudden in some type of vision, she saw Andrew lying in his hospital bed by a window and then to her surprise, she saw what looked like the back of a man in a long, white robe standing over Andrew. The figure came into clearer view; the man was holding something in one hand but she couldn't make it out. His right arm was going over Andrew's body from head to toe as if a magic trick was being performed. She was transfixed. The figured turned and looked at her. He looked Christ-like.

While Pat continued to see this vision, she smelled the aroma coming from the candle she had lit earlier, though the smell was not that of the burning candle's fragrance, but it had a musky scent, like that of a man. As her vision began to dissipate she came back to the person still saying a prayer over the phone only to hear his last words, "He will be healed." Pat was stunned and all she could say was thank you and hung up the telephone. The very next day Andrew came out of his coma. Coincidence? I think not!

Friday morning came and Nancy drove over to my house to contact the hospital to see if Andrew had made it through the night. We all shouted, cried and jumped for joy! Our prayers at least for now had been answered. We were so relieved; however the doctors said he still wasn't out of the woods yet. My parents would arrive in Phoenix and get to the hospital late Friday morning just as Andrew was being moved to another hospital.

As Friday turned into dusk I had to keep myself busy, so I continued to mow the lawn in the dark, while I listened to some of Andrew's music he had composed, sung, and recorded. I needed to hear his voice to help me get through this. His voice and lyrics helped soothe me, and I kept those songs close to my heart and soul. I could've never made it through this ordeal without praying to God, and having my family and friends around—especially Nancy and Pat.

One of the hardest things I had to do on Saturday was tell my grandmother, Noni, who was 95 years old at the time and in a local nursing home. I didn't want to tell her he was critically ill. I wouldn't tell her how bad he was until he started getting better. She said, 'We need to pray a lot and he will be alright,' and right she was, thank God.

There was one very funny experience toward the end of all of this. When Andrew felt better and started talking to his nurses, they told him how smart (medically) Marie was. Andrew's comment was, "who's Marie?" He knew it couldn't be his sister Karen. We all had a good laugh.

As I look back on this whole ordeal and what Andrew went through as well as our entire family, I realized how our family bond was strengthened throughout this whole crisis. I've never been that religious before, however I found out over those few days that prayer does work and my faith in God has been reinforced. The doctors say Andrew shouldn't have survived that day, but he did. Thank you God.

CHAPTER 4

You Have Sclero What?

The first question you're probably asking yourself is the same one I asked when I finally found out I had contracted this disease. What the heck is scleroderma? I had no idea. I couldn't even pronounce the word in the beginning.

So where did scleroderma come from? Nobody knows how long it's been around, though scleroderma comes from two Greek words: *scleros* meaning hard and *derma* meaning skin. The hardening of one's skin is the most visible manifestation of this disease. According to the article, "A Brief History of Scleroderma," by Walter Coyle, ancient authors might have alluded to scleroderma in one of the earliest possible references which came from Hippocrates (460–370 BC) who stated, "In those persons in whom the skin is stretched, and parched and hard, the disease terminates without sweats." Hippocrates described an Athenian, "Whose skin was so indurate that it could not be pinched."

At least 20 different names have been applied to scleroderma over the centuries, though around 1945 a South African physician, named R.H. Goetz, proposed progressive systemic sclerosis to replace scleroderma since the disease affects not only the skin, but also the internal organs. At one time scleroderma was also known as stones disease, because the victim's skin would appear to become hard as a rock.

The first known alleged case of scleroderma was a written medical description in 1753 by a Neapolitan physician named Carlo Curzio. Translated, the report was entitled, "An Account of an Extraordinary Disease of Skin, and Its Cure." A young girl from Italy was admitted to a hospital in Naples. The skin on her face looked like a "tight and leathery mask." She had "an excessive tension and hardness of her skin over all her body." Her skin was so tight she lost the ability to form facial expressions and her mouth resembled an "immobile hole that exposed her teeth." Within a year she recovered. In 1865, P. Horteloup described 30 cases of scleroderma in his doctoral thesis and credits Elie Gintrac in Bordeaux for coining the name sclerodermie in 1847 and describes a personal communication from his colleague, Maurice Raynaud, regarding a patient with cold-induced "asphyxia locale." This is the first description of the Raynaud's phenomenon in scleroderma.

The first reports of scleroderma in a child was in 1842 in London which told the story of an 11-year-old girl who had Raynaud's and skin thickening for six months before she saw a physician.

The first American documentation of scleroderma was published in 1869 by A.B. Arnold in Baltimore who described three cases of localized and limited scleroderma. The first report of progressive systemic sclerosis in America was published in 1870 by W. Day in New York who described a 37-year-old man with severe progressive scleroderma.

The first biopsy obtained from a scleroderma patient was described by M. Kaposi in 1874. The observation that thickening of the skin is due to increased production of extra-cellular matrix components such as collagen and was first published in 1896 by P.G. Unna.

In addition to the skin, scleroderma can also affect internal organs such as the heart, lungs and kidneys ("Scleroderma Renal Crisis," Steel). The first discussions of scleroderma involving these other organs were in the 1860s when kidney involvement was reported in 1863 in a 29-year-old patient who developed scleroderma and who had abnormally elevated levels of protein in his urine, headaches, vision loss, and convulsions *(these are the same symptoms that happened to me the morning I went into crisis)*. Many patients don't survive. The kidney involvement in scleroderma was initially considered coincidental and unrelated. The discovery of hypertension along with kidney involvement was first reported in detail in 1957 in Pittsburg, Pennsylvania.

In the late 1800s some doctors also thought scleroderma affected the heart and lungs and these assumptions were eventually corroborated. In 1924, a doctor described five patients with systemic organ involvement including lung, gastrointestinal tract, and kidney involvement. *In my case, my gastrointestinal tract and esophagus has been affected by the scleroderma which causes bouts of acid reflux.*

In 1952, H.C. Moore and H.L. Sheehan described three patients with scleroderma who died as a result of kidney involvement thus the link between kidney involvement and scleroderma was established.

As for the involvement of collagen, it is released throughout the body as its defenses try and fight off an invader. The occurrence of calcinosis (calcium carbonate deposits) under the skin of scleroderma patients was first described in 1878. The patient was a 40-year old Swiss woman with "painful lentil sized swelling in her fingers." The acronym "CRST syndrome" was coined in 1964 in Baltimore, MD in patients with calcinosis, Raynaud's phenomenon, scleroderma and telangiectasias. In 1973 the acronym was changed to CREST to indicate the existence of esophagus damage and deterioration. I still take acid reflux medicine to reduce my chances of continued esophagus deterioration.

Collagen is a major structural protein, a kind of natural glue that holds together everything from bones to our skin. Does the word collagen sound familiar? Nowadays, collagen is used by cosmetic surgeons to enhance the size of both female and male body parts including lips, cheeks and jaw lines, artificially.

This protein continues to over-produce in a scleroderma patient's body and since it has no place to go, it settles into the low density areas of tissue throughout a person's body, normally starting in their fingers, hands and feet. The collagen then begins to thicken and harden in the afflicted areas, often interfering with the normal function of that body part, like circulation. Once it gets into the body it moves progressively throughout affecting arms, legs, mouth and facial areas and even works its way into major joints. As a result, a person's joints and limbs can become stiff, sore and painful to move. That's why it is usually misdiagnosed as different types of arthritis.

In 1941, scleroderma was linked to a family of connective tissue diseases that include Lupus and Fibromyalgia.

These diseases were grouped under systemic diseases of connective tissue. Scleroderma, or systemic sclerosis, is a chronic connective tissue disease generally classified as one of the autoimmune rheumatic diseases. These conditions are characterized by the common occurrence of antibodies (proteins which are part of the immune systemic designed to combat foreign organisms or chemicals), which are directed against self-antigens (an especially common one is antibodies to nuclear antigens or anti-nuclear antibodies-ANA). Autoimmune diseases are basically conditions in which the immune system goes out of whack and turns against its body's own healthy tissues, rather than a foreign invader of the body. This stimulates the overproduction of the collagen.

Scleroderma is not contagious, infectious or cancerous nor is it directly hereditary. There is, however, a broad genetic association with the disease, as there is for the other related autoimmune conditions such as lupus or rheumatoid arthritis. Evidence of the genetic association is further strengthened by the observation that the identical twin siblings of individuals who have scleroderma have a much higher risk of developing the disease than individuals in the general population. This risk is not 100 percent however, so genetic influences are only part of the explanation. Presumably, an unknown environmental factor, perhaps a viral infection or trigger may occur in a genetically susceptible individual. Also it is not known which genes in combination are those which are critical for disease development. And as of the printing of this book, there still is no identified cause or cure for this deadly disease.

Scleroderma is difficult to diagnose in its early stages as many of its manifestations mimic more common diseases like rheumatoid arthritis or lupus. *I was misdiagnosed with rheumatoid arthritis for many months initially.* Scleroderma is a disease where the symptoms may be external in appearance, as in the hardened skin or it may result in internal organ involvement such as the lungs, kidneys, heart, esophagus and intestinal tract.

There are two different major classifications of scleroderma, localized and systemic sclerosis. Localized scleroderma, like its name, is found only in a few places on the skin or muscles, rarely spreads and is the milder form of the two types of scleroderma. The internal organs are rarely affected and it is highly unlikely that the person will develop systemic scleroderma. With localized, waxy patches of skin of various sizes, colors and shapes appear and may thicken and harden underneath. These are called morphea. Another form of localized scleroderma is linear. This type of scleroderma starts as a line or crease of waxy skin on an arm, leg or forehead and is localized to that area.

I am afflicted with systemic scleroderma, which affects the external (my skin) and the internal, my kidneys. Although kidney failure is relatively uncommon in scleroderma, when it does occur, it can come on without warning and can lead to rapid, severe renal (kidney) failure. When this occurs, as in my case, the only advanced notice is the onset of severe headaches, visual disturbances, the cessation of normal urine flow and an extreme rise in the blood pressure to dangerously high levels that can lead to a stroke. In the past, this renal failure had been considered irreversible and unless patients received a kidney donor or promptly went on dialysis the prospects for survival were not encouraging.

As an autoimmune, connective tissue disease, scleroderma is triggered when the body's immune system, which is designed to provide your body protection from illnesses like cancer or invasions from foreign organisms, thinks it is under attack and to "fight off the invader" the body over-produces a number of proteins in your system, one of which is *collagen*. The others consist of what are called matrix proteins, and these, with collagen form part of the connections between cells in the skin and other organs. Collagen is also an essential component of scar tissue, so scleroderma in a sense is the result of overproduction of scar tissue.

Most scleroderma patients get the disease in their hands and fingers, however, some get it so bad their fingers begin to "curl" inward from the tightening skin caused by the collagen buildup. This leaves fingers with limited dexterity for use in simple everyday tasks. This is known as the *claw effect*. Even simple tasks like buttoning or unbuttoning a shirt, tying shoes or opening a jar can be a challenge. *(I went through these same challenges for many, many months, though I tried to hide the disability from those I worked with.)* In rare cases, the hardening skin can encase its victim's body in a mummy-like coffin, causing eventual death. Other patients' skin around their mouth gets so tight they can't move their lips to drink, eat or even speak. The skin begins to pull back like a bad face lift exposing the upper gums of their mouths. Some will end up being on a feeding tube and hydrated intravenously. Most will succumb to the disease. Bob Sagget's, (of *Funniest Home Video* fame), sister Gay died from scleroderma. A movie called *For Hope* documented her struggles and eventual death.

Another casualty of most scleroderma patients is a condition that is found mainly on the fingers and toes, called Raynaud's phenomenon. It is caused by the constriction and narrowing of the blood vessels in those affected areas due to cold or stress. Raynaud's is usually present in about 90 percent of scleroderma patients and it tends to be present in the fingers and the toes. The resulting disturbance in circulation of the blood causes a series of color changes in the skin, turning the finger tips or toes a purplish blue color. I get this on cold days.

How serious is scleroderma? Any chronic disease can be serious. It can be life-threatening, as in my case, if the symptoms are not identified and treated within a reasonable time period or as in other cases it can be a mild case. The seriousness depends on what parts of the body are affected and the extent to which they are affected. Of course prompt and proper diagnosis and treatment by a specialist may minimize the symptoms of scleroderma and lessen the chance for irreversible damage.

So who develops scleroderma? The disease affects an estimated 150,000 to 250,000 people a year in the United States, including 80,000 to 100,000 with the systemic form and the rest with localized. Statistically, 80 percent of them are female, mainly between the ages of 25 to 55. (I tell people, "Sure I had to go out and get a chicks disease.") Though, some cases show infants and elderly having contracted the disease. Some books I read early on in my research stated that almost half of the female scleroderma patients would die within ten years of being diagnosed with the disease. Keep in mind, these statistics do not accurately paint the true picture of scleroderma, because it's a newly identified disease, so people have died from complications of scleroderma, never realizing what type of disease actually took their life. International incidence is unknown, though it has been reported worldwide.

Factors other than sex, such as race and ethnic background, may influence the risk of getting scleroderma, the age of onset and the pattern or severity of internal organ involvement. The reasons for this are still not clear. Although scleroderma is not directly inherited, some scientists feel there is a slight predisposition in families with a history of rheumatic diseases.

Scleroderma has always been difficult to treat and survival rates have been historically low. But it can be effectively treated in many cases today, thanks to better medicines and new therapies. While there remains no effective treatment for the overall disease, treatment of the complications has advanced considerably. Not long ago, patients with scleroderma had a very poor prognosis: 30 years ago, the five-year survival rate was about 50 percent for the healthiest category of patients (those without lung, heart or kidney manifestations). For patients who had either pulmonary or cardiac involvement, only about one-third survived five years and almost everyone who developed acute renal disease died within six months. Now the picture is quite different, with five-year survival rates of well over 80 percent for patients without lung, heart, or kidney involvement. Kidney involvement is now effectively treated and even prevented with medication and sometimes dialysis if needed. Both cardiac and lung involvement may be treated effectively with medication, especially if detected early.

Fortunately for me, in the last decade or so, drugs called angiotensin-converting enzymes (ACE) inhibitors have been proven capable of slowing down and reversing the kidney failure. I continue to take ACE inhibitor blood pressure medicine,

> **ACE inhibitors** not only saved my life but enabled me to restore most of my kidney function.

and only God knows if my kidneys will continue to improve or not. As of the publishing of this book my kidneys have gone from zero percent functioning to about 60 percent!

So how do doctors manage scleroderma? Well it's not easy seeing it presents itself differently in every patient and is unpredictable in its course. Though there is no cure for scleroderma, there are medications and physical therapy programs that can retard or slow down the diseases progressive and aggressive nature, though there is no universally accepted way for treating the disease. Some treatments also help relieve the stiffness and soreness patients feel in their hands, fingers and major joints in their body. I was told several times by doctors that I had to, "Let it run its course."

Another aspect of the disease that isn't visible is the emotional scars that are created for both the patients and their family and friends. When one first learns of being diagnosed with this deadly disease, which has no cause or cure and as your visual appearance can be unsettling, the emotional and traumatic event can be overwhelming.

Much of the information in this chapter comes from my reading the booklet, *Understanding and Managing Scleroderma*, by Maureen D. Mayes, M.D. M.P.H and Khanh T. Ho, M.D., published by the Scleroderma Foundation.

Today, researchers are discovering many new medical breakthroughs that are encouraging in finding a cure for scleroderma or at least medicines that can slow down the progression of the disease. Also the medical information available today for patients and their families is more informative and encouraging. The first books I read on the subject of scleroderma were full of doom and gloom regarding this debilitating and sometimes fatal disease. What's worse, my family and friends were reading the same books as I had, and their concerns over my health and my life were definitely heightened. The disease is getting more attention but not enough. Jason Alexander of Seinfeld fame has been the National Chairperson as his sister is afflicted with scleroderma.

On a sad note, the doctor whose care I was under, Dr. Joseph Korn who is one of the top scleroderma specialists in the country at Boston University Medical Center, died in the Spring of 2005 from cancer. If anyone cares to donate to scleroderma research, please forward your tax deductible donations to: Scleroderma Research, Boston University Medical Center, 720 Harrison Avenue, Boston, MA 02118. And thanks if you do!

CHAPTER 5

The Power of Miracles, Part 1

June 30, 2000

Growing up Catholic, you learn through reading scripture, Psalms, the teachings of the Old and New Testaments of the existence of miracles. Throughout the Bible are eyewitness accounts of miracles occurring throughout the ages. I believe in those miracles, from Jesus changing water to wine (John 2:1–11), raising Lazarus from the dead (John 11:1–46), the healing of the Centurion's servant (Luke 6:6–11, Matthew 15:32) and of course God raising Jesus from the dead and His Ascension into Heaven.

I once read an account where a person standing in front of parked car looked up to see a car raging out of control heading towards him. Just as the car was about to crush him against the parked vehicle, he felt "someone" push him out of the way averting sure death, only to look back where the car made impact to see no one standing there. Who could've pushed him out of the way? Could it have been his guardian angel? Or some positive force?

In all these incidents, the individuals involved seem to have an air of Divine Intervention. I believe behind each blessed miracle lies the power of faith and prayer in its foundation. It's my faith that plays a major role in my beliefs, which lends itself to the possibilities and realities of miracles.

Even some baseball pundits will say the 1969 amazing Mets season and their World Series win over the Baltimore Orioles was a true miracle. Miracles don't seem to discriminate; they appear to happen in all walks of life regardless of race, creed, or color, and they don't occur geographically either. And for reasons unknown to us, miracles do make themselves present in our lives.

My miracle occurred on June 30, 2000 at about eleven o'clock in the morning.

The day before, when I was in the emergency room at the Arizona Heart Hospital, my guardian angel Andrew was there. Around 11:00 a.m. on Friday the thirtieth, I began coming out of my drug induced coma. I recall how heavy my eyes were as a bright and blurry room came into focus as I slowly gained consciousness.

It felt more like a bus had run me over. Where was I? What the hell happened? I had no idea where I was. My body ached and I tried to take an external inventory of my body parts to see if they were all working. As the cobwebs faded from my head I saw tubes and wires sticking out of what seemed every part of my body. In the background, I heard the sound of machines competing with each other with their blips and bleeps, as if in chorus with one another.

I was groggy, almost to the point of feeling drugged. I couldn't put the whole picture together of my surroundings. I realized I had on an oxygen mask and assumed I was in a hospital. The only consolation at this point was I appeared to be alive. That was the good news. I knew there must be some bad news around the corner somewhere.

I felt so confused, as I lay in bed looking around, I tried swallowing but my throat felt like I had swallowed a handful of razors. It was raw and sore. The pain was so intense I had to grab the side rails on the hospital bed. The clock on the wall was close to 11:00 a.m. Funny the things you remember. But what day was it? More important, what the hell happened to me?

As the room came into focus, a shadowed figure to the left of my bed approached and introduced himself as Dr. Moffit. I'll never forget his words, "Young man, welcome back. You've been through quite an ordeal." He then stopped me in my tracks by saying, "You're lucky to be alive."

After the initial shock of his response wore off, he said before he got into the details of what happened and what the next steps would be, he had to ask me some questions and perform some simple neurological tests.

> **Dr. Moffit Describes Intubation**
>
> Intubating or tracheal intubation is a procedure where an ER team sticks a large round hollow tube, about a one-quarter inch in diameter, down the critical care patients' throat so they can get oxygen to their lungs and breathe with the assistance of a breathing device. It also protects the airways from blood, vomit, and secretions.

Seeing my discomfort from swallowing, Dr. Moffit instructed me to answer with simple yes or no nods. I nodded my head. He explained my throat was sore because the ER doctors had to intubate me so I could breathe.

I'm sure he saw the fear in my eyes after he finished with the description.

He asked if I knew what had happened or how I got into the hospital. I struggled to recall anything from the day before, but there was nothing, no recall at all. I shook my head no. His face flashed with concern. He told me my parents had been contacted and should be arriving sometime this morning. He then asked if I knew my name.

What? That should be simple, but I struggled within my disoriented, medicated head and then a feeling of alarm crept in. I shrugged my shoulders and shook my head from side to side. No, I didn't! His eyes now showed deep concern. He wrote something down in my chart. He could see I was tensing up with anxiety from not being able to recall my name. I mean how can you not remember who you are? I lay there thinking, "This only happens to other people."

He said don't worry, "You've been through a lot of trauma in the last 30 hours, and rest is the best medicine for now."

He then took his pen light and flashed it across each eye to check my pupils' reaction. He told me they looked good, considering. He did tell me my reactions to the light were a bit slow, so they'd be keeping an eye on it. I was experiencing extreme weakness in my eye-hand coordination from the trauma. I first noticed it when I went to scratch my head and my arm wouldn't move for a few seconds after my mind commanded it to, as though on time delay. It was so strange and scary.

Dr. Moffit was such a caring and compassionate man, which at this moment as I lay in my hospital bed all alone, gave me a feeling of calm, a feeling of safety and reassurance.

The doctors at the hospital were concerned with my slow response on my motor skills and memory loss. Dr. Moffit said they'd be transferring me to Barrow Neurological Institute (BNI) across town in West Phoenix. Their concerns were my stroke-like symptoms and they wanted to check out every possible angle.

As they were prepping my transfer, Dr. Moffit leaned over my gurney. He pointed to his left, and asked if I knew the woman standing near the doorway. I looked over and as my eyes came into focus, I said, "That's my mom. What's she doing here?"

I started tearing up at the sight of her especially when I saw the fright in her eyes. Hell I was scared too. A nervous smile formed around her mouth when she saw I was alive and conscious. I smiled back. At a time of such confusion, the mere presence of her relaxed me. I felt safer now. I glanced back at the doctor and saw relief in his face. My mom rode in the ambulance with me to the Barrow Neurological Institute at St. Joseph's Hospital.

Mom's Story

Here's how my mother remembers it:

> When we finally arrived in Phoenix, a friend of the family picked us up at the airport and rushed us off to the hospital. We hurried into the hospital in a frenzy. At last I was going to see my son. The only problem was I didn't know what shape he was going to be in. My faith kept me going.
>
> When we got there, Andrew was in the process of being transferred to another hospital. The doctors feared he might have suffered a stroke and wanted to give him the best possible care. When I saw him for the first time, he looked so bad, so sick. "My God, don't let him die," I said to myself.

All I could think was this couldn't be happening to my son, not Andrew. A doctor was speaking with him and as I looked around all I could see were tubes and IV lines sticking out of him. I was so scared. As they were wheeling Andrew out, a doctor pointed over in my direction. Andrew looked over at me and said in a very weak voice "That's my mom." I started crying.

I found out later, when Andrew first awoke from his coma, he didn't know who he was and had a hard time remembering things. It seemed his memory loss was due to extreme high blood pressure. I kept praying for him. It was all I could do. How scary. How scary for him to be going through this all alone.

When they finally got him over to the neurological hospital, my husband and I stayed with him throughout the afternoon until he fell asleep. He looked so vulnerable. For the next 13 days while he was in the hospital we'd come and visit a couple times a day. Some days were good for him and others were not. The doctors said he needed to get as much of his strength back to help his chances of pulling through.

Several times my husband would take Andrew by the arm and walk him up and down the hallways of his hospital floor when he felt up to it. And each time they'd come back from a short walk, Andrew would fall asleep in his bed. He looked so weak, so thin. He was skin and bone.

Once the staff at Barrow Neurological Institute (BNI) placed me into the intensive care unit, Dr. Moffit informed me and my parents the coma was caused by extremely high blood pressure from the renal (kidney) failure brought on by scleroderma. They were going to run several tests to keep an eye on my condition, but for now rest was what they recommended. It would be a long day for me, in and out of sleep, trying to put all the pieces together. Then he left.

Mom and Dad were by my side, though they didn't say much. In retrospect, what could they say? Heck, I didn't know what to say either and didn't feel up to talking much because of my sore throat. All we knew was I was alive; I think in my parents' minds that was enough for the time being. But we didn't need to say anything to each other. Just knowing they were within earshot and handholding distance was sufficient satisfaction. There would be time for talking later.

As my parents sat next to my bed, it hit me. My poor parents! I began to understand their quietness. Not having any children myself, it didn't hit me for a while. I can't imagine what goes through a parent's mind when one of their own children, they brought into this world, is lying in a hospital bed on the brink of dying. My God, their anxieties and fears must have been churning in their stomachs like a corkscrew into a bottle of wine.

Between this and their delayed flights at the airport, standing over me must've given them tremendous relief even though none of us knew what to expect from here on out. I mean, gosh, to get a call out of the blue and told your son, who is 2300 miles away, has been rushed to the hospital and the doctors don't think he'll make it through the day. Parents aren't supposed to outlive their children; it isn't supposed to happen that way.

A few minutes later Dr. Moffit came in to check up on me and after he left, a younger doctor came in. He introduced himself as Dr. Kris Mooresheidan. He was a small-framed, young man, about five feet four to five feet five, who reminded me of the actor-singer Bobby Sherman or even musician Jackson Browne. I'd find out later he was also an accomplished concert pianist and a very bright man. You could sense his great bedside manner, yet he seemed serious about my situation. He looked at me, grinned, and said, "You, my friend, are very lucky to be alive."

I smirked and said, "So I'm told." Dr. Kris, as he liked to be called, asked me if I remembered Dr. Moffit coming in earlier? I shook my head yes. The doctors had some concerns they weren't quite sharing with us yet, that being possible brain trauma brought on from my hypertensive crisis during my seizure.

Dr. Kris said in a matter-of-fact way I looked a lot better than I did yesterday. I looked at him inquisitively, almost with a blank stare; I wasn't sure what he was talking about. He said it was at his office where I collapsed as Rob wheeled me into the office. As I mentioned earlier, the last thing I remembered was Rob wheeling me into the kidney center as I slumped over in the wheelchair. What I didn't know was as I collapsed, I went into a seizure in their waiting room.

My original appointment had been with Dr. Laurel, an associate of Dr. Kris's at the AZ Kidney-Hypertension office that Thursday. Dr. Kris told me I had gone into severe convulsions in their office and a nurse dialed 911. He had accompanied me in the back of the ambulance to the Arizona Heart Hospital just up the street. He continued sharing his story, or our story, how the EMT's recommended giving me a particular medication through injection, which my situation called for to help bring my blood pressure down. Knowing my seizure was brought on by scleroderma, Dr. Kris insisted on giving me a different type of medication he found worked better with scleroderma and kidney failure.

He might have been a man of about 5 feet 5 inches, but he was tough. He said he took control of the situation because he was confident his approach was the right one. The ace-inhibitor he gave me helped drop my blood pressure quicker. All I could do after he finished his story was to look at him in awe and say, "Thank you, thank you for saving my life."

I wanted him to share more, but he insisted I get some sleep, and he'd tell us more over the next few days. My parents sat there stunned after hearing the story. They stayed for a while, but I insisted they go to my Aunt's house and get some rest.

The "in and out" of doctors and nurses seemed to be endless as the hours went by. They were prodding, poking, injecting, inspecting and writing in my chart and asking every time how I was feeling. I joked with them that I was always tired because they continued waking me up throughout the day and night.

On Saturday morning July 1, Dr.'s Moffit and Kris came in and asked how I was feeling; my parents had just arrived as well. I told them I still felt awkward and had trouble making my arms and legs do normal commands, which was frustrating. I still didn't understand everything that had happened to me over the past two days since coming out of my coma. Dr. Moffit said he'd get into all that after he performed more neurological tests on me.

Their main concern right now was my slow response rates to certain neurological tests they'd taken the previous day. My blood pressure was 270 over 170 during my seizure when I arrived to the ER. Dr. Moffit said "not many people would survive a hypertensive crisis like that. With this elevated blood pressure most peoples' hearts explode." That didn't sound like something I wanted to sign up for. They also said I had some hemorrhaging in my brain due to the intense blood pressure; so they were watching my brain and heart for swelling. They even cautioned us about possible paralysis in some areas of my body due to my slow motor skill responses.

Dr. Kris concluded the scleroderma most likely attacked my kidneys and by suffocating them, caused the complete shutdown of my kidney function. He said my lungs began to fill up with fluid because the kidneys weren't excreting any liquids which led the ER team to intubate me to keep me alive.

As both doctors were speaking, I lay there in my intensive care room stunned. Wow, did I really go through all of this and come out alive? Did all this really happen, or was I in the middle of a strange dream or a nightmare? I kept thinking to myself, "My God, how close I came to dying!" Anxiety and fear shot through my body.

The neurological tests continued; one test caused a rare lighthearted moment. A doctor came in and asked me to place my arms straight out to my sides while lying in bed; like a police officer administering a field sobriety test. I joked with the doctor: "I've done this before." I exclaimed, insinuating the police had asked me to perform the test in the past. We both laughed.

He asked me, "Did you pass their test?"

"Of course," I said. As we chuckled, I realized that my mother was in earshot and didn't look amused.

> *Optimism and humor are the grease and glue of life. Without both of them we would never have survived our captivity.*
> —Philip Butler, Vietnam POW

He turned and asked her, "Does he always joke around?"

"Yes," she said.

The doctor felt encouraged saying, "It is a good sign." It signaled I was starting to regain some normal behavior, something they were observing for. Laughter. I'd found throughout my life that humor is such a great medicine, and if it worked for me in the past, it was going to work for me now. I knew I had a big struggle ahead of me; the doctors reminded me every day, and a dose of humor was something I'd take daily.

So he began his coordination examination. He asked me to bring my hands toward my face and touch my nose with the tip of my index fingers. As I brought my right arm up, my arm and hand floated right up over my head missing my nose by a good foot. The frustration and angst of not being able to do a simple command like this was quite unnerving. About five minutes into the test the doctor could see my frustration and said, "Rest now, I'll be back later to perform some other tests."

One test they had to perform was a biopsy of my kidney. But before that took place, I needed to have a dialysis catheter surgically placed into my chest. This was how I'd have dialysis administered to me. I realized there were going to be many more tests I'd be going through, so I prayed and reached deep down to muster up the strength and positive attitude to help get me through these tests without getting angry or feeling frustrated. It wasn't going to be easy. I had to keep telling myself even though my tolerance level would rise and fall; I had to participate in my healing process. They're the doctors; I'm the patient; shut up and go along for the ride!

The next day I was wheeled into a surgical room to insert my catheter. Everything was moving along nicely until the doctor performing the surgery informed me he'd have to "put me under" to insert the tubes into my chest wall. "What!" I shouted. I panicked and froze.

"You're going to put me to sleep? Over my dead body!" I explained I'd just come out of a coma and wasn't about to even take the chance of being put to sleep again. I feared I wouldn't wake up from this procedure. I could feel my pulse rate pumping rapidly through my veins. With fear in my voice, I asked him, "What are my alternatives?"

There was only one. He could numb the right-side area of my chest with local anesthesia and insert the tube. However, he said I'd feel the tubes being pulled underneath my skin during the procedure, and it would be painful. I didn't have to think twice about it, "Go for it! Anything is better than the fear of not waking up!"

Before he started he asked, "What type of music would you like to listen to as a distraction?" I asked for and got some Led Zeppelin.

After the anesthesia set in, he made two small incisions above my right nipple. Then he inserted a tunneler on my neck line at the jugular vein. This allowed the catheter to be pushed downward under the skin toward my lower chest area. The catheter was shaped like an upside down Y. I could feel the catheter being pushed down through my skin; it was such a weird feeling. After he pulled the two tubes through the two holes, he then attached two port lines with clamps, one red and one blue.

The red one (arterial) would draw my blood out through the tube, go through the dialysis machine where my blood would be cleaned of its toxins that had built up inside of me and remove excess water out of my body that I couldn't remove naturally from urinating. The blue clamp (venous) would return my purified blood back into my body minus the toxins and water. Once the blue and red lines are connected to the dialysis machine, it worked its magic. The marvels of medicine! I pretty much felt the entire operation, but it was worth the pain. When all was said and done, I was now set up for a daily or weekly regiment of dialysis.

There were now three open wounds, one at my neckline and the other two in my chest. These wounds never completely healed while the tubes protruded from my body, but they were constantly sore and crusty. After each session the nurse dressed the open wounds and it hurt like hell when she'd have to pull off a piece of the crusty skin to keep infection out. I wasn't even allowed to take a shower, just sponge baths. For the short term, dialysis was a frequent event and most mornings a nurse came in, wheeled me up to the dialysis unit where I'd lie in my portable bed for three to four hours, have my breakfast while my blood got an overhaul. Initially with the renal failure, I had zero kidney function. It was so strange to drink liquids throughout the day and not get the urge to pee.

For those who aren't familiar with dialysis, here's a quick description. The main reason you go on dialysis is to clean and purify your blood and rid your body of the deadly toxins that seep into your bloodstream and vital organs. Your kidneys act as your body's filtering system and when those kidneys become diseased or injured, the kidneys lose their ability to filter toxins out of your body, through urination.

The next ordeal was getting a kidney biopsy. This was one of the most uncomfortable procedures I've experienced, except for the catheter being inserted into my chest. They wheeled me down from my room on a gurney because I still didn't have the strength to sit in a wheel chair for prolonged periods of time. I'd get lightheaded and nauseas every time the nurses tried. As with the other doctors, this one also gave me a step-by-step narrative as he proceeded.

This was what separated these doctors from others I've experienced in the past. They educated their patients. The end result was a higher degree of trust, which put me at ease and I was being educated

---

Dialysis

There are two main ways of receiving dialysis. The first way is the procedure I had, inserting chest tubes directly into an artery, vein, and one into the jugular vein in the neck. The second is through a fistula, tube-like object which is surgically implanted under the skin near the wrist or lower arm. A small vein and a small artery are joined together using very fine stitches through the fistula and inserted in the arm. The nurse then pokes a needle with a line (thin tubular tube) attached to the end through the skin and into the fistula so blood can be drawn through the dialysis lines. The painful part is the nurses don't always get the needle inserted on the first try and may have to poke several times into the skin to get a good connection flow. This can cause the patient's arm to have large black and blue marks around the forearm area. It looked painful and from some the patient moans, it sounded painful. Once the line is in it gets connected to the dialysis machine.

about the procedures being administered to me. Just like anything in life, if we know what's going on around us, we can create a path of understanding of how to deal with it. It's when we don't know, because we don't ask questions, we create roadblocks and obstacles to our success.

The doctor explained he needed to extract a piece of kidney so they could test the tissue to see if my kidneys suffered serious damage or if the episode just brought about acute renal shutdown. The difference, he told me, was if there was kidney damage, then the prospects of my kidney function returning, was limited and not very likely. But on the other hand, if it was acute failure or as one doctor called it "your kidneys just went to sleep," then there was a good chance of regaining some kidney function. He said you only need a small percentage of your kidneys functioning to live a full life. As the doctor finished up his explanation, I said a prayer to God and my guardian angel, Andrew, to keep my mind and body strong.

As I lay stomach down on the gurney, the doctor showed me the long needle he'd be inserting into my lower back. I said, "You gonna stick that big ass needle into my back?" The needle had little teeth at the tip which grabbed a piece of my kidney for the biopsy. Whew, I guess I was ready.

As he inserted the needle I could feel it penetrate and punch through the skin of my lower back and then cut through the muscle tissue. The pressure he was putting on the needle to puncture skin and muscle was very heavy. He said, "You'll feel a little pinch," as the teeth grabbed a piece of my kidney to tear it away.

It did and I winced in pain, "Ouch, that hurt!"

After he extracted the needle he said, "You may see some blood in your urine but do not be alarmed." Shortly after, I was wheeled up to my room where I fell asleep in exhaustion from the long morning.

By the end of the next day the lab results came back and the biopsy showed it was acute renal failure. The doctors felt relieved with the news. They said it was a good sign. At least now we knew what we were dealing with. My parents and I had tears in our eyes as this was the first positive news we heard to keep our hopes and spirits up.

Though only time would tell if my kidneys reacted positively to my dialysis treatments.

Each day in the intensive care (IC) unit seemed to blend from one to another. Every day was a daily dose of needle pricks, medication, dialysis, and visits from Mom and Dad.

For the next seven days, I'd stay in intensive care at St. Joseph's Barrow Neurological Institute where my only visitors could be immediate family, which were Mom and Dad; though my cousin's husband Jim was allowed to visit. My folks shared with me that everyone back home kept calling to check how I was doing. After getting off the phone with my folks, my sisters then made their calls to let family and friends know what was going on. Even my co-workers called and told me clients were checking up on my health status and sending along their thoughts and prayers. Though I was still in tough shape, I was beginning to clear out some of the cobwebs in my head and piecing together more loose ends that led up to my medical crisis.

After seven days in the IC unit, I was moved to a private room on the fifth floor. It was so wonderful to get out of IC, as this was a big benchmark in my recovery. Though like the nurses in IC, the nurses here still were coming in almost hourly to poke, prod, take blood, and check my vitals. I remember telling a nurse, "Now I know what a pin cushion feels like." Even at 3:00 a.m. when the nurses came in and woke me up, I tried to greet them with a pleasant smile or a "Hi."

Okay there might have been a night or two where I wasn't all giggles, but in general I'd joke around with them. They do have a tough job. One nurse, Susan, told me she couldn't believe how cooperative I was being throughout my ordeal. Most patients on this floor had a sort of *edge* to them depending on what they were there for. Most of the patients were recuperating from major surgeries and were in severe pain so many of them weren't in the best of moods. She commented, "You always have a smile and something upbeat to say."

I told her, and this is a lesson for all of us, "Life deals us the cards, and we have to play the hand we're dealt or you fold." I wasn't about to fold. I never had in my past endeavors, and I wasn't about to at this critical junction of my life. I realized if I didn't continue to fight back against this disease and my kidney situation, I could end up being on dialysis for the rest of my life. Or the scleroderma could return and this time take my life. Neither one of these outcomes was an option in my mind. If I was going to get better and get back on my feet, I better let the experts do what they get paid to do. I was the patient and I better be patient! Again, it came down to choosing my attitude each day in the hospital as I did prior to getting sick. I figured if I started copping a bad attitude or being uncooperative with the nurses and doctors, it wasn't going to help my situation. So I didn't, because I chose not to. The way I looked at it, I had two weapons at my disposal: a positive attitude and perseverance.

Our lives at any moment can change direction and be taken away from us in a split second. I can attest to that. I know we all face challenges, but what matters is to take control of our situations. Because if we don't, don't expect anyone else to. We all have issues with confidence or self-esteem, it's only natural, we're only human. Most of these issues can be resolved by working through the roadblocks we've placed in front of ourselves. By changing our attitude and then doing something about it. Take action. Don't just talk about it. Do it! Stop letting the past control your future. Each day you have the ability to change the direction of your life, no matter what your circumstances are. You can't live in the past. Bring yourself to your present and new future.

> *Our efforts and rewards are solely derived from our actions.*
>
> —Andrew Botieri

One of the easiest ways to discipline your subconscious mind is through repetitive positive affirmations. You know those little motivational saying or reminders we have around our house or office. It's really that simple. Just like in goal setting, it's an exercise of keeping those positive affirmations or goals in front of your eyes every day and reading them aloud. Positive affirmations work! Give it a try. Don't let inaction hold you in the past. Learn to discard the negative energy given to you by others or even yourself.

My favorite affirmation, I've had on my bathroom mirror and day planner for many years, is simple, yet very powerful to put thoughts into actions:

> If it's to be, it's up to me.
> —Unknown

Lying there in the hospital, I knew I had to bring my A game every day or it would slow down my healing process.

We all have the ability to choose our attitude every day. Many of us call forth our positive thinking and attitude without having to think about it because it's become such a part of who we are and what we are. I believe it's through the power of our subconscious mind, to discipline our conscious thoughts to help us choose a positive and bright outlook on life. Obviously, outlook is another word for attitude. Unfortunately, many people decide to choose an attitude that is negative, unproductive, or complacent. They complain about how unfair life has been to them, they become self-defeatists. They become victims.

They say *it* (positive thinking) doesn't work. Nothing works. They give up too quickly, give in to what others tell them, and they listen to their own negative self-talk. We all do! You

> I think, therefore I am.
> — Rene Descartes,
> Seventeenth-Century Philosopher

know that little voice in your head? Silence that little negative voice. You are great! You are special and unique. Start acting like it! If you think it, it will be.

Food Adventure

As a lover of good eating, the food selection at the hospital was not the best. Let's face it, they offered your typical three-square-a-day hospital food, and I was limited in what I could eat. They put me on a renal diet because of my kidney situation. I could only have about 16 ounces of liquid a day, which included foods with high water content. This helped reduce my water buildup in my body. I had to eliminate most foods with high protein or high potassium levels, which could store up in my kidneys and create further damage.

The funniest story of my whole stay in the hospital resulted from an overdose of Swedish meatballs. It was the second day in a row I was served Swedish meatballs with lumpy, sticky white rice. Yuk! Now, I don't mind Swedish meatballs that my mom makes, but let's be real; this is hospital food. I took about two bites, threw my fork down on my food tray and said, "That's it!" No more Swedish meatballs! (Okay, here's one incident where my positive attitude didn't work.) So now what? I was starving. I began to plot.

I remember my parents coming into my room during their visits with different snacks from a cafeteria on the first floor. Ah, the cafeteria, they must have foods other than Swedish meatballs. I had to escape my fifth floor room and seek out real food. It was either that or starve to death. I slowly got out of bed, shuffled to the door, and peeked out at the nurses' station. Good it was empty. I was still very weak, but food trumps anything! It was time to make my move. I shuffled across the hallway, past the nurses' station, to the elevator doors, pressed the button and waited for the doors to open. I glanced behind me to see if I had been spotted. No nurses. As the doors closed behind me, I felt light-headed because I hadn't walked so far by myself. I hoped I didn't pass out in the elevator; that would have been impressive. Food trumps pain!

In a few seconds, the doors opened, and I peered outside. It seemed safe so I shuffled into the hallway. I was wearing hospital scrubs, a pair of hospital pants, and a short sleeve top, a regular Mr. GQ. No hospital Johnny for me, thank you. I immediately saw the cafeteria sign and slowly made my way down the hall. As I walked into the cafeteria, people began staring at me. I must have looked like crap, and as I looked down I realized I had my heart monitor on, a dead giveaway I was a patient. Oh well, I got in line, looked at all types of scrumptious foods and then I saw the meal of my dreams, a slice of pepperoni pizza. Yes, finally some good food. I ordered a slice of pizza and a Sprite. I then realized I had no money, so I asked her to charge it to my room. Almost as good as room service. I took my first bite, I was in heaven. Boy do I love pizza! It's got all the major food groups!

After a few heavenly minutes I finished off my cheesy pizza and ice cold Sprite and thought I should head back to my room before they notice I was missing. I shuffled to the elevator and hit the button for the fifth floor. I was feeling great, full, and content...until the doors of the elevator opened. In front of me was not one, not two, but three nurses standing with their hands on their hips. They didn't look happy. One nurse scolded me, "Where have you been?"

I told them of my adventure to find something other than Swedish meatballs and told them how good my pizza tasted. One nurse said the whole floor was frantically looking for me. Unknown to me a few minutes after the elevator doors closed, my heart monitor alarm went off at the nurses' station, as it only operates on the fifth floor, and they sprang into action thinking I was having some type of cardiac arrest. They all dashed into my room to find it empty. At this point, they ran up and down the halls looking in and out of rooms for me. Oops. I looked down at the ground like a little puppy that knew he did wrong. As they helped me back to my room, they told me I had to stay on my renal diet and pizza or more specifically red sauce was not part of the diet. I said I couldn't do the Swedish meatballs anymore, it was patient torture. They laughed. I asked if they could call Dr. Kris and see if it would be okay for me to have pizza on occasion. He said it was okay. Sweeeeet! I'm not sure if the nurses liked being overruled, but I had to have my pizza!

Later, spurred on by my field trip to the cafeteria, a nurse came in and gave me a sheet of paper which spelled out all the food items I could and couldn't eat as part of my renal diet. I had to keep protein and potassium to a minimum. I could eat small amounts of meat for protein (hence the very small portions of Swedish meatballs). I had to avoid high potassium foods which come mainly from fruits and vegetables. Even large servings of low potassium foods can raise your level higher than it should be.

Here are a few of the items I was forbidden to eat: chocolate, bananas, pears, oranges, coffee, milk, beets, asparagus, peanut butter, potato chips, french fries and tomato sauce* to name a few. They also instructed me when I got home to wash all vegetables, to soak them in water, drain, rinse again and drain. This helps to wash excess potassium from the vegetables. I was restricted from drinking coffee, which is high in potassium. So over the next six months I could only drink tea. I had to do what I had to do. Much of what I learned came from the "Fresenius Medical Care Nutrition Education Fact Sheet," 2000.

Why is protein a potential problem? Most protein in moderation is good for you but too much protein in the diet of a renal patient can slow down the recovery process of the kidneys and place a lot of stain on that organ.

Why potassium? Potassium is a mineral found in most foods. We need potassium to keep our hearts working. If your kidneys do not work well, potassium can build up in your blood. In renal patients, this can cause diarrhea, nausea, weakness, and trouble breathing. It can also cause your heart to stop. So to keep minimum levels of potassium in my blood, I had to stay on this renal diet.

One thing amazed me, the amount of medication I was taking on a daily basis. At one time, I required about 19 pills a day: various blood pressure medications, Phoslo, a phosphate reducer due to renal kidney failure (because retaining phosphate can cause soft-tissue calcification), acid-reflex medicine (because my esophagus had deteriorated from the disease), iron pills, antibiotics and pain relievers. I was also given OxyContin for pain, but chose not to take it.

> **Dangers of Excessive Protein**
>
> "When you eat too much of protein, a byproduct of protein metabolism called urea (blood urea nitrogen or BUN) is formed in your liver and excreted via the kidneys. The kidneys have to work overtime to eliminate the excess urea which has accumulated in your blood. This can lead to kidney damage especially in older people whose kidneys function less efficiently or in people with preexisting kidney damage. If you take in more protein than is needed, it is excreted because protein is not stored. The way it is excreted through the body is through the liver. The liver has to increase its activity…. As a result of the filtering of the urea and the protein, kidneys enlarge under this high-protein load that we eat.
>
> Excerpt from "Dangers of Eating Animal Proteins,"
> —Dr. D. P. Atukorale

Some days in the hospital were better than others. With all the prodding, poking, and jabbing going on, I had to remind myself I had to be patient during my healing process. The way I look at it: There are two types of people, those who fight back and those who give up. Too many people, in my opinion, accept what happens to them, and they give in without trying to make a difference. They never even exert a little bit of effort to see if they can fight their way out of a particular circumstance. I believe deep down inside everyone there's the ability to win at life with a positive go get 'em attitude regardless of your lot. When people don't try, I have to ask, "Why were you put here on this earth?"

What is your purpose and reason for being, for living? I truly believe each one of us has a purpose. How can you find out what yours is if you never stretch your abilities and capabilities to find out? I knew I had those two weapons at my disposal: attitude (positive thinking) and perseverance, and I called on them when I needed reinforcements. Don't get me wrong, I had times in the hospital where I doubted whether I could beat or overcome this deadly disease. I'd find myself buying into the lack-of-hope comments from some doctors about my chances for kidney recovery. Or reminding me the scleroderma could come back. How's that for encouraging news.

What was my future going to look like? Would I have limited or no kidney function, limited use of my hands because of the claw effect setting in with scleroderma. I didn't know. However, Dr. Kris and Dr. Moffitt kept encouraging me to fight, to take care of myself, to push myself at various tasks while in the hospital and when I got home, so I could continue building up my stamina. I think I'd rather listen to them than the other doctors.

Positive Thinking Amid Frustration

The toughest days in the hospital were the visits to the dialysis unit. The whole idea of being hooked up to a machine to survive was overwhelming, not to mention the fear, confusion, and the numbness of contemplating why I was there. As you sit in the dialysis chair you truly understand and appreciate the power this machine has. At the moment, this was my new reality. I'd lie in my hospital bed at night thinking about the prospects of being hooked up to this machine for the rest of my life. If I wanted to travel anywhere in the country or the world, I'd have to make sure a dialysis unit would be available at that destination, or I couldn't go. I couldn't live without a dialysis machine.

Though in my mind, the question was not if I would get off dialysis, but when. I realized I had the power to will myself off this machine, but I had to get tough, I had to fight back, I couldn't give in. It took so much strength to get through my treatments. Whenever I did feel depressed or was having a pity party, I preferred to be the only one who dressed for the event.

When my parents came to visit, I'd always have a smile on my face, even if I didn't feel good. I didn't want to worry them. I had several of those days. I knew there was a long road ahead, and I made up my mind that day in the hospital to do whatever it took to get out of the hospital and to beat this disease. Positive thinking brings about positive results; negative thinking brings about negative results.

I've always seen a correlation between competitive sports and success in life and business. To be a successful athlete you must possess discipline, a hard work ethic, and keep yourself in tip-top shape. To be successful in life or business, you must also possess discipline, a strong work ethic, and have the ability to learn to keep your skills and talents in "shape." The only difference is your uniform and playing field.

I know as an athlete and a successful business professional if you put your mind to something and believe passionately about it, you can change the outcome of any situation. Again, it comes down to making the right choices and following your convictions. Plain and simple: struggles in life can't be sugarcoated. Make a plan and be disciplined on your plan of attack. Don't look at a situation and throw up your hands; approach each situation with a strong positive attitude and look at that situation as one more challenge in life to deal with. As they say, what doesn't kill you makes you stronger.

> It's not whether you get knocked down; it's whether you get back up.
>
> —Vince Lombardi

As each day passed in the hospital, I started feeling more coherent and was gaining back some of my strength, not much, but enough where fatigue wasn't keeping me in bed all day. I still had trouble walking by myself, so when my parents came to visit, Dad would take me by the arm and walk me around. I had just enough energy to make those trips, my feet shuffling beneath me. It felt as though I was learning to walk all over again.

My first couple ventures were a bit frustrating. My steps consisted of only four- to six-inch increments as I tried to place one foot in front of the other. Dad was right by my side giving me words of encouragement. I reflected how he must have done that 39 years ago when I first learned to walk as an infant. After about a 75-foot stroll around the fifth floor, I was too exhausted to go on, so we'd turn around and head back to my room. I couldn't believe how a short walk could wear me out. But it made me realized how much of a shock my body and organs had gone through. I knew it was going to be a while before I would feel like my old self.

One of my biggest frustrations and concerns was struggling with my ability to recall much of what happened before I got sick. At first I didn't know my name. I had no recall of events the first few days at the hospital; everything seemed like one long trip of confusion. Memories from my past that should be second nature, ingrained since childhood, I couldn't recall. Events, people's names, or even recalling places I used to live or work seem to take a while to come into my memory. In my mind's eye, I could see the faces of childhood friends or friends I'd made around the country, but I couldn't put names to those faces. It was unsettling. I found out later many friends called me at the hospital to check up on me, expressing joy in being able to talk to me over the phone. I don't recall any of those conversations. The doctors told me with time most of my memory should be restored.

> *Except for forgetting what I had for dinner the other night, my recall seems to be okay today. However it took about nine months after my coma for it to come back. Today though, I do have bouts of ADD.*
>
> —Andrew Botieri

Hospital Stay Recollections

Here are a few other recollections from my 13-day stay at the hospital.

There was an older gentleman, a senior citizen volunteer who delivered flowers, cards, and gifts to the patients in the hospital. It seemed everyday he'd stop by my room and dropped off some flowers, plants, or get-well cards. Reading the cards from family and friends with their notes of encouragement made me choke up and weep like a baby.

It was crazy. I felt like Pavlov's dog, with each card I read I'd get more overwhelmed. One day the volunteer stopped by to deliver a few more gifts. He said in all his years of delivering items to patients, he could never recall delivering so many items to one person. He asked me, "Are you somebody important or famous?"

I chuckled and said, "I don't think so." But as I looked around the room, saw the outpouring of love represented in all the plants, flowers, balloons, teddy bears, and cards that decorated my room, I began to think about what he said.

I knew many people around the country and had built many wonderful friendships along the way, but as I gazed around the room his question had been answered. I must've had some effect on the lives of these people, who in my hour of need were there, thinking and praying for me.

> My lovely Stacy would later relate an incident that sent a chill down my spine. Shortly after being placed in the drug induced coma, Stacy was standing by my side holding my hand to comfort me while having a one-way conversation with me. She asked the doctor, "Can he hear what I'm saying?"
>
> He replied "No he's in a drug induced coma and won't be able to hear you." At that moment, while I lay there unconscious, I reached my arm across my body and placed it on Stacy's hand. Stacy and the doctor looked at each other in amazement. *I guess I don't always listen when people tell me I can't do something.* The power of love and friendship at its finest. I wish I'd remember that moment, but obviously I heard Stacy.

I guess you don't realize how you've touched someone until something traumatic happens in your life. Think about your own life. How are you making a difference in the lives of others?

To this day, when I make my bed (yes I do that), I place a teddy bear given to me by two co-workers, Marcia B. and Natalie D. on my bed and think of them and smile. I remember reading somewhere you can tell a person's wealth by the number of friends in their life. In my case I felt like the richest man alive. A heartfelt thank-you to all who prayed for me and kept me in their thoughts during my ordeal.

Throughout my stay at BNI, Dr. Kris filled me in about what happened during the hours of my coma. About an hour after slipping into my coma in the ER, the doctors were trying to get my crisis under control and I began coming out of my coma. They said I became very irritable, aggressive, and began pulling tubes and medication lines out of my arms and chest. He said it's a normal occurrence because many patients become disorientated from their ordeal, and they don't realize what's happening to them and lash out. So they had no alternative but to place me into a drug induced coma.

For the next 24 to 26 hours I lay unaware of my surroundings. Dr. Kris said it was critical the doctors stabilized me as quickly as possible because time was of the essence! If they couldn't get my blood pressure under control from my hypertension, they feared my heart could explode. This occurs in most fatal heart attacks. I am so glad I wasn't conscious for that.

As I began to feel stronger, I started receiving telephone calls from family and friends more frequently, but no call was more powerful than the one from my cousin Paula back in Plymouth. Though she was on the other side of the country, I heard she had been so helpful in assisting our family with all the doctors in Phoenix, the medical terminology, and explaining the different medical procedures I was undergoing. She's like a third sister to me. My phone rang in my room, I picked it up and heard that all familiar, "Hey cuz," it was Paula.

After I heard her voice, neither one of us could say another word except to cry, and we wept nonstop for a few minutes. That's all that came out, no words only tears. After a few minutes without a word being spoken through our tears and crackling voices, we whispered, "I love you cuz."

Then I told her, "I have to hang up the phone." It was too emotionally draining. She'll always hold a special place in my heart.

One day my mother mentioned my 95-year-old grandmother, Noni, who was in a nursing home back in Plymouth. She had been asking why I hadn't called her lately. I'd usually call her a couple times a week, and since being in the hospital recovering, I hadn't had a chance. Mainly, I didn't want to alarm her. After a week, I placed a call from my hospital bed. I tried to muster up all my strength to get through that phone call without breaking down. I told her I'd been real busy but was planning on coming home in a few weeks. I told her I was a little sick and was resting, but I was fine. I was tired from working too much.

She scolded me as she did many times for not slowing down. I promised her I would. We laughed about a few things. I always enjoyed making her laugh. I said I'd call her next week to say hi. As she always did, she told me to be careful and told me she prays for me all the time. I told her to keep on praying because it does work.

It wouldn't be until I traveled back to Massachusetts in late August that I visited her in the nursing home for the first time since my crisis and told her face-to-face what had happened. I'll never forget the look on her face, the sadness and fright that surrounded her. I told her I was fine and was going to beat this disease. Looking at her motivated me even more. I joked that between her and her three sisters, who say their rosaries about ten times a day, how could I not be cured?

Throughout my stay, many of my nurses told me I was their best patient; they didn't have many patients who'd keep them laughing as much as I did. I was always giving them and the doctors a hard time (in jest) to keep things lighthearted, and a few told me they pulled strength from my positive outlook and great attitude. Some even said they'd stop by my room when they were having a bad day so I could put a smile on their face. What a great compliment. I was very flattered. Could this be another purpose or reason?

As friends continued calling the hospital they relayed stories of me being on prayer lists in churches and synagogues all over the country; apparently hundreds, if not thousands, of people were keeping me in their thoughts and prayers. Let me put you all on notice. Prayer works!

Leading up to this point, I spent many hours rehashing in my mind everything that had happened since being admitted to the ER nine days ago. Most of my thinking took place at night, between visits from Mom and Dad and the flurry of doctors and nurses throughout the day, which ate up most of my thinking time.

It had only been a couple days since I'd regained some semblance of a coherent mindset. In the beginning, most thinking brought me great pain. I kept visualizing dying on the way to the hospital or if I didn't wake up the morning of my doctor's appointment would I have died in my sleep? I imagined the feeling of not being able to say goodbye to my family and friends. I wondered how my death would affect them. How would my parents cope? My siblings? Would they do anything different in their daily lives? How would they say I lived my life? In nightmares, I'd see family members reacting to the news of my death, then the calls to our other relatives. Oh my God, my Noni. How would she take the news? One night I dreamt of my funeral, which was so surreal with a tinge of reality. How could you, in the blink of an eye, not exist? It's surely strange where your thinking time can take you.

I hadn't yet fully considered why this happened to me. Was there anything to read into it? At this point, I just knew I had to change direction, change my lifestyle, and change my status quo. I looked back and saw all the hours I'd put into my career, which I truly loved, but along the way some sacrifices occurred, mostly personal. It was in this thinking time I realized I'd become a workaholic and something had to change.

As I continued thinking about my future, doctors prepared me for my release from the hospital. I'd have to go on dialysis three times a week and would need someone to drive me back and forth. So what now? I wasn't dating anyone at the time, and I couldn't ask friends to work around my schedule. I missed my family. I wanted to see them, spend quality time with them, hang out with them, and not just twice a year for four or five days as had been the pattern. I knew I had to take a breather from this fast-paced environment. On the night of July 7 as I lay in bed, I knew there was only one direction. It was time to give up the corporate rat race and move back home where I grew up. As I drifted to sleep, I couldn't wait to tell my parents the next morning. Though the doctors didn't have to tell me, I knew I was still pretty sick.

It was that night I decide to leave the corporate world for a while. I realized it wasn't about the work, the big salary, the promotions, and the power. It was about health of body, mind, and soul. It was about work to live, not live to work. It was about trying to bring a balance into my life.

Mom's Story Continued

Here's my mom again.

Some mornings after Andrew had his dialysis treatment we'd visit and he'd either be sleeping or out of it from the effects of his treatment. But he'd go when they came for him; he never complained, and even though he'd come back exhausted, he always carried his smile with him. It seemed to rub off on other people. His nurses loved him, and doctors were impressed by how he listened to them and the questions he'd ask. We still didn't know how he was going to come out of this. I knew my son was strong and knew he had an incredible attitude about life, which had given him success over the years. I was hoping he could do it again. I kept praying he'd pull through this horrible ordeal.

After 13 days there were many memories, some good and some trying, though one day I will remember more than others. My husband and I went to visit Andrew in the late morning, and he looked a little bit better. He said he was feeling stronger, though he had lost so much weight, he was still not where he should be. He said he'd been doing a lot of thinking about everything, his life, his dreams, and as he continued to speak, he looked up at me from his bed and said, "It's time to come home." I began to cry. After 17 years my son was finally moving back home. As a mom, I couldn't have been happier. Andrew's always been a free spirit; he's always had incredible confidence, even when others didn't believe. So it is a blessing to have him back home.

CHAPTER 6

Growing Up in Mayberry

Some say when you have a brush with death or a near-death experience, you'll see your life roll by in front of you like a movie; others experience some type of spiritual event. My health deteriorated so quickly, I didn't have time for a movie or a spiritual experience, but the event of June 29, 2000 would change my life forever.

While lying in my hospital bed over the next 13 days, I had a chance to look back and reflect on the events and the first 48 hours. What had brought me to this major turning point? I needed to take an assessment of my life, where it had been, how I got here, and what lay ahead.

My mind raced everywhere, thinking of the many what if scenarios. I knew one thing for certain; I was very lucky and thankful to be alive. However, my mind kept falling back on what if. What if I didn't make it that day? How could the accumulation of my life's efforts come to such an abrupt ending? An ending where there was no chance to say good-bye to family and friends. I thought of home, of my little hometown of Hanson, my family, and childhood. At this moment everything that was important seemed to rush through me like a large wave crashing in against the shoreline. It truly felt like a movie where visuals of people and events all came to me at once. The following is a recollection of that movie.

I've been very blessed to have lived in many wonderful places around our great country from Scottsdale, to Southern California, San Francisco, and Philadelphia. People always ask me where my favorite place was. Well, they all were in their own special way. Each new city, each new job opportunity, each new group of friends were like new chapters in my book of life.

However, what I reflected on most during my stay in the hospital was growing up in my little town of Hanson. It gave me a feeling of comfort and security I wasn't experiencing at the hospital. Thinking of home made me feel rooted, knowing my family and friends were thinking and praying for me.

Hanson is a very typical, picturesque little town in Massachusetts located on the South Shore about 45 miles south of Boston and about 15 miles northwest of Plymouth, America's hometown, and the home of our forefathers, the Pilgrims, and Plymouth Rock. Okay, no Plymouth pebble jokes! (People visiting the first time expect the rock to be much larger than it is.)

Hanson was incorporated in 1840 and was originally a rural farming area, along with being a large cranberry producer with bogs scattered throughout the town, like so many of the surrounding towns. Hanson's claim to fame was it once housed the headquarters of the Ocean Spray Cranberry Company. If you've never seen a cranberry bog before, they're usually square or rectangular in shape and from the sky look like disarrayed patches on a quilt laid out over the countryside.

Best Things About Hanson

One of the best things about cranberry bogs is the annual fall cranberry harvest. Workers called bog men flood the bogs from a nearby water source. This process is called wet harvesting. As they flood the bogs, the cranberries float to the top of the water because they have a hollow cavity inside that makes them buoyant. As the berries float to the top, a machine with long thin arms, like a straightened rake, shakes the berries loose from their vines. Then the berries are corralled by solid nets, fed up a scoop escalator, and then dumped into waiting trucks. It's a great event to watch. Many people sit out with a blanket by the edge of the bog and have a picnic while they watch this New England tradition. I highly recommend it.

The second best thing about bogs is after the harvest most remain flooded so the cranberry vines will be covered and protected underneath the coming ice which acts as insulation from the cold harsh winters. In many areas the water is only a foot or two deep so they freeze very quickly, in some cases within a few days, allowing us to skate early in the winter season. When it snowed, we'd come equipped with shovels to keep the snow off our ice.

We skated all day, whether it was at a bog or a local pond. Our mothers dropped off lunch and then picked us up before dark. Some parents even put up flood lights for nighttime skating, while others brought hot cocoa and sandwiches to feed us and keep us warm. When we got thirsty and ran out of our jugs of water, we'd kick the edge of ice with our skate tips, break open a hole and quench our thirst; never worrying the water was full of chemicals. But you know what, no one got sick or ill. Today we're still all fine. Kids today are afraid to even drink out of a garden hose. What's up with that? Oh and there was always a bon fire. It was a magical and wonderful time to grow up. It was like the fictional town of Mayberry, portrayed in the '60s sitcom *The Andy Griffith Show*. It was priceless.

> There was something very special and almost fairytale-ish about the neighborhood I grew up in. There were four houses (one being my parents') side by side with large front and back lawns with acres of woods behind.
>
> Now stay with me here; one parent in all four homes grew up together on the other side of town. Amazingly, years later these childhood friends would all get married, move across town to create a new neighborhood and build their homes side by side. Pretty cool, hey? It was like a second generation neighborhood. That's what helped make it magical. Today, all of us "kids" from these families remain close.

I know a lot of people say this about their small towns, but it's true in my case; we had only one stop light, which was at the intersection of Routes 58 (north and south) and 27 (east and west). The milkman made weekly deliveries of fresh milk to our doorstep and gently placed the ice cold bottles inside the insulated galvanized milk box that sat on our red brick steps.

We had a Sheriff Andy Taylor type, our police chief; we even had our very own Otis the drunk. He was harmless, like Otis in the television show, so no one bothered him much. He would get his little buzz on and walk up and down our street and then take a nap on the stone wall at the front of the cemetery. We also had Floyd the barber, who was none other than my dad. His loyal patrons either called him Don, Mike, or years later Guido. Hanson had its cast of characters.

Remembering Mac and Passion for Life

One such character Mayberry didn't have was Mac or Cam (his real name was Cameron) as some called him. He was our town rubbish collector. While making his rounds through the neighborhood, you'd hear him whistling as he went house to house, belting out his favorite tune. Some days, he'd stop and shoot basketballs with us kids or toss a baseball before moving on to his next neighborhood. Good ole Mac was my dad's best friend growing up. They were like brothers, almost inseparable. They played baseball and hockey together. I'd sit and listen to the two of them as they weaved their baseball and childhood stories like a grandmother knitting a sweater for her grandchild. Most tales had some degree of embellishment, as you'd never hear the story told exactly the same way twice. I think it's moments like this that made me realize how powerful our childhood friendships, memories, and experiences can be.

Sadly, years later, Cam passed away from a sudden massive heart attack and is so missed, especially by his wife Shirley. The thing I remember most about Mac, he was always upbeat and took the world on with a smile, a wink, and a twinkle in his eye, while always displaying a mischievous grin. He had an incredible passion for life and wanted life to be fun and simple. Whether he was collecting trash or tossing a baseball with the neighborhood kids, he always had a smile on his face. A simple, yet talented man, he put effort into his job whether he loved it or not. I'd think of Cam during my business career when things got a little crazy and stressful. I could hear him whistling as he came up the street, reminding me no matter what you do in life, do it with passion and a positive attitude. Thanks for the lessons Mac!

How many people do you know, like Mac, who possesses that level of passion for life, regardless of the work they do? Answer this simple question: are you having fun at what you do? Do you wake up in the morning and look forward to going to work? Do you strive to make a difference in someone's life? Take time to reevaluate what you're doing; ask yourself:, do you love what you do? Not that you have to love your job every day, but the essence of joy and satisfaction needs to be present. If you don't, you need to decide whether a change will be good for you. In most cases it will be. Life is too short to work at a job you dislike or carry a chip on your shoulder because you feel like a victim.

Think about this: we're the only animal on this planet that God gave free will to. Face your fears and insecurities and make a positive change in your life and get on with living. Living the life you were destined to live. When I think of these words it reminds me of the scene in the movie, *Shawshank Redemption* when inmate Tim Robbins says to Morgan Freeman, "Get busy living or get busy dying." What great words of wisdom!

Our Playground

We grew up across the street from Fern Hill Cemetery. It's both an old and current cemetery with headstones dating back to the late 1600s. As you pass through the 20-foot granite archway, large patches of sprawling lawns and rolling hills come into view. A meandering set of dirt and paved roads leads you to the back of the cemetery, where the beautiful and tranquil Wampatuck pond unfolds before your eyes as you approached its edge. An 18-foot gradual decline places you at the water's edge. Wampatuck stretches out to your left about 200 yards to the banks of the town hall and to your far right in the distance are two small canals that lead to the town reservoir. An old duck blind sat partially hidden 200 yards directly across from where you stand. In this spot in the fall you can look out over the pond and see the reflection of the brilliant shades of reds, yellows, and oranges as the leaves explode with color as they begin their journey. It's breath taking.

I know this may sound a little weird and eerie to some, but the cemetery to us neighborhood kids was an extension of our playground. The large hill which sat in the back left corner of the cemetery was hallowed ground to some of its oldest headstones. These graves were scattered from the back part of the hill across a rolling green taking their place in history. The boundary of the cemetery was marked by an old two-foot high stone wall that separated the cemetery from the woods and water's edge; the stone wall acting as though it was a gateway between the living and the dead. From an aesthetic viewpoint, it's a beautiful site.

This hill was where we'd go sledding; skiing, or tobogganing after any snow storm and it also became part of our battle ground for neighborhood snow ball fights. The cemetery was more than a winter playground; it was also the scene of our summer evening episodes of flashlight tag. Our games were full of fun and anxiety as you anticipated a hand reaching up from under the gravestone to grab you by the ankle. These memories help us to revisit and to reconnect small, but significant events in our lives that are part of our foundation and our growth as an individual.

We also learned from our parents that the cemetery was to be revered, to be respected and to appreciate the sanctity the holy grounds deserved. In fact, my Italian grandparents are buried in Fern Hill, resting side by side. If I had not survived my medical crisis, I would've been laid to rest next to them. (During the writing of this book, my father Don Botieri, passed away from Alzheimer's and lies beside his parents. Love you Dad!)

On a side note, my first real job of my working career, at the age of ten, was raking leaves at Fern Hill for a whopping $.75 cents an hour. It's all relative, but I thought I was rich!

To me, old cemeteries have such a magnetic draw: they possess so much history with an incredible story to tell. Whether it's a founding father, a Revolutionary War solider or a Civil War hero, the history of our country and our ancestry lie in these cemeteries. Do me a favor? There are hundreds if not thousands of old cemeteries scattered around our country, calling out to the present not to forget who they are and what they stood for. Next time you go on vacation do a little online search and see what old cemeteries you can find along your travels and make a point to stop by and explore. If you live near an old cemetery take your kids. They'll learn to appreciate and experience our history.

Life today is so fast paced and crazy. We forget we can tap into our fondest memories to rejuvenate our tired and weathered souls. Don't underestimate the power of these positive events to get you back to your "center," the center you had before life got to be so crazy. While lying in my hospital bed, I thought back to these days when I'd get into a funk or rut in my corporate life. I'd think of my little town and my humble beginnings. This helped put things back into perspective for me.

IT'S ALL ABOUT FAMILY

I grew up blessed with a wonderful family full of love, surrounded by all four grandparents and a host of childhood friends. Since returning to Massachusetts in 2000, I spend quality time with so many old and cherished friends, while making new ones along the way. It's such a wonderful feeling to reconnect with people who had such an influence growing up. Then what happens? The years and miles get between us and then 5 years becomes 10, becomes 20. I continue rekindling friendships, some going back to infancy. Unfortunately, our busy lives and the "controlled" chaos we operate in keeps us off balance at times. Granted, it's hard today, but if you want to stay in touch you have to make the effort. Remember, those old friendships are part of our makeup, our foundation.

Our family was of modest means. As I mentioned, Dad was the town barber in Hanson for over 58 years and my Mother, like most moms back in the '60s and '70s, was a stay-at-home mom. She stayed home until we were all in school, then got a job at my school working in the cafeteria. Unfortunately, I always had to be on my best behavior, especially during lunchtime in the cafeteria. But I'd still manage to get myself in trouble every once in a while for talking too much or goofing around. "What? Me in trouble for talking too much? No, not me! Though when I'd get in trouble during lunch, I'd have to stand with my face against the cafeteria wall, isolated from everyone else. I didn't even have to look; I could feel my Mother's eyes piercing down upon me like a hawk eyeing its prey on the ground below, and of course, I'd hear about it when I got home.

It wouldn't be until years later I'd appreciate and understand how important it was to have a parent around when you came home from school. I know it sounds like a cliché, but not that long ago this was the typical family scenario. When you look around today, you see the adverse effects in our children and in our society with fewer parents home to raise and nurture their children. Well, in my humble opinion, raising children is the most important responsibility a parent should have. Like anything else in life that's important, it takes effort, but the benefits and payoffs are priceless.

> I know today economically both parents need to work, that is unless one is making a modest six figure salary. Today, too many people keep score based on their materialistic rather than important achievements like personal development, helping those who are in need, or raising children to respect adults and authority. I look around today and ask myself, "What happened?"
> —Andrew Botieri

I was one of those fortunate kids growing up with both sets of grandparents and even a great-grandmother and grandfather. We always visited relatives on both sides of our family and you could always count on seeing a relative almost every weekend. It created a very close-knit extended unit which truly was one big happy family. My favorite was either the Sunday cookout or the famed Sunday family dinner at 1:00 p.m. When did these traditions get replaced with computer games and sport seasons that blend into one another creating no family time for kids to be kids? Where is that close knit extended family unit today? If you still do this, my hats off to you and thanks for carving out the time. Too many people say they *have* no time. Is that the real story or is it they don't *make* time? It's important to keep your family traditions alive. For when they're gone, they vanish, like footprints washed away in the sand by a retreating wave back into the ocean.

My grandparents (Antonio and Ida), on my dad's side, came over from Northern Italy when they were young children. My Noni (or Ida, as my sister and I affectionately called her) came from a little farming town called Saint Agostino, north of Bologna and Gramp's family came from Cento. Though both are now deceased, fortunately I've been blessed to possess many cherished moments with them, many wonderful memories in which they taught lessons about life, faith, and family.

Being Italian immigrants, or for any immigrants coming to America in the early 1900s, life was very tough. But they worked hard to become Americans, unlike today, immigrants come here to live in America and not assimilate our values and language. My grandparents had a very simple yet strong value system; belief in their God, a hard work ethic, and fostering a close family and community environment. These values were instilled in me at an early age. Their lessons have shaped me into the person I am today. Thanks, Noni and Gramp!

Noni was one of four Italian sisters, who all reached and surpassed the 96-year mark. We called them the aunties. Noni passed away in November of 2001 at the age of 96 years and 6 months, followed by her oldest sister Julia in September of 2002 at the age of **99** and 6 months. And two years later, Aunty Florence passed in July of 2004 at 98. While I was writing this book, the youngest of the four sisters, my Aunty Dolly, passed away in December of 2008 at **99** and 2 months. What incredible genes. When I told Dr. Kris about the age of the aunties, he said luckily I had a strong heart like them.

Even in their old age, it was amazing to watch the aunties get around their kitchens where they'd cook up great Italian meals from scratch, like homemade Bolognese (meat sauce) and pappardelle pasta, homemade tortellini, squash tortelloni with Bolognese. Of course, all us cousins watched and learned. Everything the aunties made was authentic northern Italian quality, better than any restaurant you'll ever eat at. It was such a joy to watch them cook together, where they'd engage in sibling arguments, in a friendly way of course, on how much of this or that spice went into a recipe. We'd all sit back and admire the free entertainment.

Talk about a typical Italian tradition; as wedding gifts each aunty received a four-foot long rolling pin, about an inch and three-quarters in diameter. They would flip the rolling pin around in the air like a pair of nunchucks as they kneaded the dough and rolled out homemade pasta. I now possess Aunty Dolly's rolling pin, its worn-out weathered look, with remnants of flour stuck inside the aged crevasses. I'll treasure it for as long as I live.

We were so blessed to be in the aunties' presence for all those years. It was incredible to listen to the stories of their early childhood. Like coming to America, living hand-to-mouth, working for pennies a day, living through the depression, The World Wars and getting married, even though their mother didn't approve of any of their husbands.

One of my favorite Noni stories was as a child her mother would make them (pre-child labor laws) go berry picking for a local blueberry company. They'd walk four to five miles to get to the patches and receive five cents for each pint of blueberries they picked. After their long walk home from a back breaking day they'd give their mother (Little Noni) all the money they made, and she in turn would give them each a little something for their efforts, usually only a couple pennies. How many kids would do that today?

Boy, have times changed. It's amazing how much did change in their lifetime. They grew up with more horse and buggies on the road than automobiles. The aunties have had such a profound and positive impact on their grandchildren and great nieces and nephews. To this day when the cousins get together, we always talk about the aunties. We laugh and cry as we recall so many precious moments, and we pledge to continue our wonderful family traditions. Many of us cousins are great cooks today because of the aunties. My family even makes homemade Italian sausage from my grandfather's recipe, usually about 80 pounds at a time.

I don't think the aunties realized the powerful impact they had upon us. What was truly magical was we didn't learn just from our own grandmother we learned from all four sisters. We all admired, respected, and loved each sister as if they were our own grandmother.

As I lay in my hospital bed in Phoenix, their faces and stories came alive. Aunty Julia, Noni, Aunty Florence. and Aunty Dolly. We love you all and thank you for enriching our lives and making us the individuals we are today!

Mom's side of the family also has an interesting history. Her lineage can be traced back to the Pilgrims and the Mayflower. Her descendant, William White, only survived a short time after the Pilgrims set foot in Plymouth and was buried in Cole's Hill cemetery overlooking Plymouth Harbor. My mother's younger sister, Aunt Laura and I have researched our family tree that was started by my Little Aunt Barbara before she passed away. We found a series of biographies about each of the Pilgrims who traveled over from England in 1620 and in William White's biography, the last name Richardson appears in the index of his book as a family line, which is my Mother's maiden name.

My mom was one of five siblings who had a tough life growing up. Her Dad died when she was 12 from a freak accident so she hardly knew him. He'd been painting the famed wooden rollercoaster at Nantaskett Beach near Hull, Massachusetts, which used to be one of the largest amusements parks in New England. While he was up high near the top of the rollercoaster, someone sent cars around to dry off the track, not knowing my grandfather was up there. The cars knocked him off and he fell to his death. Back in those days there was no life insurance, so my grandmother, Nannie, was left on her own to raise five children. Needless to say, they struggled and lived hand-to-mouth.

I have many fond memories of Nannie and our family cookouts, which occurred almost every weekend during the summers. I learned at a young age the importance of a close family and the strength it brings; the importance of living within your means, to be resilient and not take anything for granted because life will throw you curveballs. Be ready to take the challenge head on and give it your best whether you succeed or fail. These lessons and the lessons from Noni and Gramp, I'd take into the business world and would use them when dealing with scleroderma. When faced with so many challenges and hardships in dealing with this deadly disease, I thought back on the challenges Nannie faced as a widow. I realized how easily she could've given up, but she didn't. Neither would I! She raised her 5 children and was blessed years later to enjoy 16 grandchildren and several great-grandchildren. Nannie was the epitome of perseverance. What a great role model she was, even though at the time I had no idea what a role model was. Who are your role models from your past? If you have one in your life, good for you. If not, continue searching.

Another great childhood memory was our family Christmas Day get-togethers at our house or those of my mom's siblings. During these get-togethers, Nannie's longtime friend, Grampa Tony as we called him, would dress up as Santa Claus and sit each child on his lap, as we gazed at him in awe. He would hand each grandchild a small present from his big red Santa sack. At the time we believed in Santa, and this visit by Grampa Tony made our whole day, as we thought Santa had come all the way from the North Pole just to visit us. We'd be playing in the house and all of a sudden we'd hear the sound of sleigh bells jingling which signaled Santa would be arriving soon. We'd all run around the house screaming with excitement. But as with most childhood innocence, once we got a little older, Santa started looking a lot like Grampa Tony. Looking back it's sad when we begin losing our innocence as kids. Today, it seems children lose that innocence way too early in life.

After Nannie and Grampa Tony past away, this Christmas tradition went by the wayside. Years later my mom and her siblings decided to rekindle the Christmas get-together. For this special occasion, my sisters asked me if I could write a little speech and dedicate it to Nannie and read it out loud at our Christmas celebration. As I started to pen my talking points something began taking shape. Just like in many of the songs I've written over the years, the words seem to flow through me as if Divine Intervention had taken hold. The short speech I began to write slowly began to turn into a song about my Grandmother and her life. The lyrics to that song which I titled, "Dreams from a Garden" follow.

Dreams from a Garden

She takes her morning walks through her little downtown,
Lonely wind a blowin' but it never knocked her down.
Five strong kids, with sixteen grandchildren,
Enough to make you crazy and little bewildered.
She grew up in hard times, living hand-to-mouth,
Never once complained and she never gave out.
She dreamed of a day a break would come from above
She knew all she could give was her undying love.
(Chorus): But in her garden she'd get lost in her dreams
   Best laid plans don't always happen as they seemed
   Everyday she'd place her pansies in a bright row
   Now that she's gone, who'll help her garden to grow?
Watching her game shows with a smile on her face
A charm for each grandchild, she knew this was her place.
Everyone in town all loved her, who knew her
Remember the day she pulled Chipper from the sewer
(inside family joke)
Grampa Tony in his Christmas Santa suit
Remember us kids thought we heard reindeers on the roof.
Santa's little helper was the love of his life,
It's really too sad he never took her for his wife.
(Chorus): But in her garden she'd get lost in her dreams
   Best laid plans don't always happen as they seem
   Everyday she'd place her pansies in a bright row
   Now that she's gone, who'll help her garden to grow?
We took her for her last ride, though her little downtown.

As we sat around the living room, I passed around the lyrics to everyone and began playing my new song. A few even joined in on the chorus. Most listened and read along to the words that so described their mother, mother-in-law, and grandmother. As I played, I looked up at my sisters, my mother, and her siblings, and tears started welling up in my eyes. Practically everyone in that room was crying. But the tears everyone cried were happy tears as each person reflected on their own memories of Nannie. I've always been accused of tapping into people's emotions. I plead guilty! Once again, the importance of family connections and traditions.

What are your special memories you carry around from your family traditions or have you forgotten or don't practice those traditions because you don't have time? How passionate are you about embracing your family history? Or, are you letting them burn out like a candle at the end of its wick? You owe it to yourself and your children to carry on these traditions. This is your only link to the past, your past.

The most exciting prospect of finding out about and uncovering your family past is being able to trace back hundreds of years of family history and see a concrete connection. Wouldn't it be exciting to find out if you carry around certain characteristics and traits that your ancestors had 500 or more years ago? How amazing would that be? Maybe a hand gesture or laugh you have is the same as a descendant of yours had hundreds of years ago. Or maybe you resemble a distant relative from centuries ago. How powerful is that?

Why wouldn't you want to know or at least explore the possibilities of your past and the lineage of your family? To me, it gives a sense of perpetuating your future. If you've been procrastinating about doing a family tree, go do it and stop with the excuses. In business as in life, execution is the key to success! If you live in the area you grew up in, go to the local library and see if they have a genealogy department (my Plymouth Library has an incredible genealogy section), and research your family and build your family tree, or go onto geneology.com and see what you come up with. And if this doesn't work, ask a grandparent or an old aunt or uncle about your family's past. One way we can prepare for the future is to have a better grasp on our past.

Roots in Italy

Along this line, upon returning home to Massachusetts, I got the address of a cousin on my Noni's side in Bologna, Italy. My Aunty Florence had been writing to her family in Bologna after she accompanied my grandmother, my parents and her son and daughter-in-law, Howie and Mal in the mid-eighties to Italy.

After connecting with my second cousin or cugina, Beatrice, I got her email address and we began emailing each other. Shortly after, I decided it was time to go to Bologna to meet my Italian family. I flew into Rome and made my way to Bologna, where my grandmother's family was from. My cousin Giordano, Beatrice and her parents Benito and Piergiovanna met me at the hotel. I was a little nervous and could tell they were too. But it's family and shortly we were all smiles and hugs.

We drove to a restaurant owned by Benito's childhood friend. All the authentic foods we ate were the same dishes my grandmother taught me to cook over the years. While sitting at the table they kept saying to me in broken English: "Coris. Russia. Andrew. Plymouth." I looked at them with a puzzled expression. Beatrice, who was the only one who spoke good English, explained they were trying to convey that I resembled an uncle of theirs, who would've been my Noni's first cousin. They pulled out a photo of him, and it felt like I was in the Twilight Zone. It was an old black and white photo, but the resemblance was remarkable. We could have been twins.

From what I gathered, Coris fought with Mussolini against the Russians during World War II and was part of the Julia Brigade, which roamed the snowy mountains in Eastern Europe on skis. They were snipers whose mission was to pick off the enemy combatants they came across, more specifically, going after those who appeared to be leaders. Coris was only 25 years old when he went off to war and was never heard from again. Whether he was captured by the Russians or died in the mountains, we'll never know. He left behind two young boys who never got to know their father. Unless I had made the effort to reach out to my relatives in Italy and sat down to break bread with them, I would've never known about Coris.

Before I left Bologna, my relatives gave me that picture of Coris, which I still have today. We are all connected to our past, and we can learn so much from that past. I have spoken to so many people who have traveled to Europe to meet distant relatives and how those meetings changed their lives forever.

When was the last time you called or visited one of your relatives regardless of their age whom you haven't spoken with for a while? If your grandparents are still alive or maybe an older relative, how often do you sit with them and ask about their life story, their journeys, their funny moments, and their stories of hardship? Everyone has a story; don't think your life is too busy or to important not to listen and learn. We can learn so much. Please find the time. Go out of want and not out of guilt or because your mother or father told you to. Visit out of love and connectivity because if you don't you'll be losing a big part of your family history and your own history when older relatives pass away. Once they die, their history does as well.

> When the elderly die, the library closes.
> —Andrew Botieri

Don't procrastinate. Do it now, tomorrow may be too late! In fact, right now, write down those relatives and make that call! You'll thank yourself for doing it. There is nothing better than the warm smile or an instant connection created from sharing old memories with a trusted relative or friend. Surprise someone you know, just because.

Life and Baseball

During one of my parents' visits in the hospital, I asked Dad how the Red Sox were doing. I wasn't in any condition to read a sports page, and my hospital room TV didn't have ESPN. Plus being in Phoenix, a national league market, they don't talk much about American League teams on the local news. His response, "They're being the Sox," which is a familiar retort Red Sox fans have made every year since 1919.

I thought, "Oh my God, baseball!" The game I loved to play and watch with passion throughout my early life. Growing up, anything and everything to do with baseball was part of my life, whether it was my grandfather's love of the game, the Red Sox, or my dad's involvement with our town's Little League organization. It was such a fabric intertwined within my family for three generations. Many of my discussions early on in life with my grandfather (Gramp) and my dad were about baseball.

Both of them were exceptional ballplayers. They had dreams no different than any other kid who's ever picked up a baseball, a bat, or a glove and yearned to make it to the big leagues. They both played semi-pro baseball, and I later strove for the same. I love baseball and wanted nothing more than to follow in their footsteps. After my dad mentioned the plight of the Red Sox of 2000, I thought of Gramp, who'd always been my hero and my eyes began to well up.

Baseball was like a religion where I grew up; some of you will understand that statement and others may not. Growing up in the '60s and '70s baseball meant consistency, a way of life; baseball meant tradition; you ate, slept, and drank baseball. It was a time when ballplayers stayed with the same team until they retired. Not only was baseball consistent and orderly, but our lives seemed to follow that same path! We'd play ball every day in our neighborhood when we got home from school, even if it was raining. It was that entwined in our lives.

Baseball was the one thing you could always look forward to each spring. When it came to baseball, there were three things you could always count on:

1. The smell of spring in the air. The smell of everything coming back to life after the dormancy of winter. Think back. Hear the chirping of the birds, smell that warm light spring breeze blowing gently through the trees, and hear the excitement of kids' voices playing baseball in the backyards.

2. Getting excited as the Red Sox began a new season and...

3. Once again being disappointed by yet another wait-again-till-next-year season by our boys in red stockings.

So why is baseball so important? Aside from being a big part of the Botieri family's life, it was in our blood. The blood of baseball also runs through the veins of our society. Baseball is such the complete sport. I hear people say it's boring. If you've never really played the game, you'll never truly understand the mystic and excitement that baseball possesses. Baseball was and still is a spiritual experience for me, my family, and every Red Sox fan that has ever lived.

And then there's Fenway Park, the fabled ballpark of the Boston Red Sox, with the storied Green Monster the towering wall in left field. The park opened in 1912 the same week the Titanic sank. Whether it's a local ball field or Fenway Park, nothing compares to the musty smell of the damp dirt of an infield, the aroma of fresh-cut green grass, and the sight of the dusty white baseline outlined in chalk. These all say, "Let's play ball."

I remember reading a quote by Bill "the Spaceman" Lee, who pitched for the Red Sox in the '70s. He said, "Baseball is the belly button of society; straighten out baseball, and you straighten out the rest of the world." Even as a Sox fan after having our hearts and hopes ripped out as our Sox lose another close championship series, we still looked forward to every spring training and opening day as the new season of hope that our Red Sox would win the World Series, which had been denied us since 1918. Between 1915 and 1918 the Boston Red Sox were the most dominate baseball team in the American League. 1918 would be the last year Babe Ruth played for the Boston Red Sox which would bring about the Curse of the Bambino.

Never heard the term "Curse of the Bambino?" The owner of the Boston Red Sox, Harry Frasee, was in dire financial straits and needed to raise quick cash to support his vaudeville show, *No, No, Nannette*. So what did he do? He traded the most dominant player of the time, Babe Ruth, to the New York Yankees (or the evil empire as some Red Sox fans call them) for $110,000. And almost overnight the fortunes of both teams changed. The Yankees were not that good a team before Babe Ruth came to play for them. After that, the Yankees amassed the most championships in the history of sports, and the Red Sox built the biggest legacy of sports disappointments. So because of that trade, the Boston fans felt the "baseball gods" and Babe Ruth had cursed the Red Sox thereafter.

But that trade would only be one of many major bloopers and disappointments the Red Sox and their fans endured. As an avid fan, it's like being left at the altar during your wedding, like about six times! My generation and two generations before me have watched the Boston Red Sox go to the seventh game of every World Series they played in since 1918. They lost in 1967, 1975, and 1986. And then there were the "should've been" years of 1978, 2000, and 2003 and probably a few more. Oh, how painful! People in and around the Boston area said when their dad or grandfather passed away, it was the Red Sox who killed them.

But fortune and fate helped "reverse the curse" in 2004, when the Red Sox mounted the biggest comeback, not just in baseball but in sports history, coming back from losing the first three playoff games to the New York Yankees and then taking the next four games to win the American League Pennant. They went on to sweep the St. Louis Cardinals in four straight to become World Champions. The curse of the Bambino was broken! For game four of the World Series my sisters and I went to my parents' and watched the game with Dad. After the final out we jumped up and down, hugged and cried and opened up the door and began yelling out into the neighborhood. Other neighbors joined in. It was a momentous event.

The next day my sister Karen and I went to my grandfather's gravesite and placed a Red Sox championship pennant upon his headstone. As we looked around the cemetery we noticed we weren't the only ones who had visited. Many deceased Red Sox fans now proudly flew banners by their headstones. They finally got their championship!

Over the years people have tried to describe what baseball is and what it's all about. One of my favorite movies of all time is *Field Of Dreams*. The following dialogue takes place when Terrance Mann, played by James Earl Jones, remarks after hearing that Ray, played by Kevin Costner, is going to lose his farm because he wasn't producing crops or income after turning his cornfields into a baseball field.

> Ray, People will come, Ray. They'll come to Iowa, for reasons they can't even fathom. They'll turn up your driveway, not even sure why they're doing it. They'll arrive at your doorstep, as innocent as children, longing for their past. They'll walk out

to the bleachers, sit in their short sleeves on a perfect afternoon. They'll find they have reserve seats somewhere along one of the base lines, where they sat when they were children and cheered on their heroes, and they'll watch the game, and it will be as though they dipped themselves in magic waters. The memories will be so thick they'll have to brush them away from their faces.

People will come, Ray. The one constant through all the years, Ray, has been baseball. America is ruled by it like an army of steam rollers, it's been erased like a blackboard, rebuilt and erased again. But baseball has marked the time. This field, this game is a part of our past, Ray. It reminds us of all that once was good and it could be again. Oh, Ray, people will come. People will most definitely come.

Every time I watch this movie I cry. It moves my soul and reminds me of playing catch with my grandfather.

My dad, with a handful of other dedicated men, took time out of their daily lives to develop and build one of the best run and most organized Little League organizations on the South Shore of Massachusetts in the 1960s, in my humble opinion. Not only was my father president of the Little League, he was also a Little League manager for decades. For four years he was my manager. He knows baseball inside and out and every year he claims he could manage the Red Sox better than their current manager. Sometimes I think he may have been right.

I mentioned my dad was our town barber. His barbershop was a sports museum with photos, articles, championship T-shirts and pennants hanging all over the place. He had the team pictures of every team he'd coached up on the walls; along with his tribute to Ted Williams; pennants of all the Boston sports teams: the Sox, the Patriots, Celtics, and the Bruins. Also there were articles, photos of local high school sports teams, and local news stories of kids who had gone off to prestigious colleges or into the military. Long before ESPN, Dad's barbershop was the original sports center. And what's cool and so Mayberry is the way all this memorabilia is scotch taped or tacked to the walls. Not a speck of wall can be seen by the naked eye. It's truly a local phenomenon.

In 1986 the town honored Dad for his selfless dedication to our Little League. On opening day of the Little League season, they unveiled a new scoreboard in right field that read, "Donald A. Botieri Field." He was quite taken aback by this gesture and became very emotional, something I've rarely seen in my dad. The rest of the family was there with him, and I know his father was watching from heaven with a proud smile on his face as well.

What an incredible honor for a man who gave up his days off to work on the Little League field and three others in town. It was a very proud moment for the Botieri family as the town honored him while still alive to enjoy his hard earned efforts. I once asked him why he dedicated himself to baseball and the fields. He said without pause, because of his love for the game and because he wanted, "To give the youth a place to go to learn the game," he so loved and maybe help them realize their dreams of becoming a professional baseball player like he and my grandfather had. I am so proud to be his son.

My Grandfather, Antonio Joseph, or Nino as his friends called him, was and is my hero and role model. He was warm, loving, a practical joker, who loved his family and baseball. Gramp played semi-pro baseball in our area and was an outstanding player who, according to the locals, had the talent to go to the pros.

In the Spring of 1933 at the age of 28, he had plans to try out for the St. Louis Browns baseball team, later to become the St. Louis Cardinals. He was home nursing a hamstring pull from an earlier ball game. He was outside mowing his lawn with a push mower. No power mowers back in those days. A couple guys approached from the ball field down the street and asked if he'd umpire for them as the original ump couldn't make it. My grandfather hesitated because his coach told him to rest his leg for an upcoming game that week. Even my grandmother told him he shouldn't go. She would later say she had a premonition that something might happen. He couldn't let the other ballplayers down. That's how he was.

So he went to the field and as the teams were warming up, my grandfather yelled out to toss the balls in so they could start the game. One guy didn't quite get the message and threw the ball in just as my grandfather turned. The ball hit him squarely in the eye. He dropped to the ground like a sack of potatoes. He would spend the next three months in the hospital and to his dismay; he'd never regain the sight in that one eye. If his accident had happened today, the doctors could have saved his eye.

The news crushed him, his family, and it extinguished his only true dream, to be a major league ballplayer. I can't imagine how he felt. So sad, for the few dreams one had back in those days, to have something he wanted more than life itself be taken away because of a stupid throw from the outfield. But his faith and the love and support of my grandmother kept them going. Old-timers in the area would tell me if my Grandfather hadn't lost his eye he would've made it to the "big dance," to the major leagues.

Brother Michael and I played catch with Gramp every chance we had when younger and despite his bad eye he'd never cease to amaze us especially when he'd catch the baseball behind his back. I'm sad I can no longer have that toss with him.

It brings back another scene in *Field Of Dreams* when Kevin Costner realizes why he's built the baseball diamond in the middle of his corn field. As the movie goes on, we find that Costner's character, Ray, had a falling out with his father as a teenager and never spoke to him again. His dad, who had played professional baseball before Ray was born, died never making amends with his son. Ray's desire to make good with his dad was the force that brought the best ballplayers from yesteryear to appear from the cornfields. At the end of the movie, Ray recognizes a young catcher, it's his late father. His father, not realizing who Ray is, thanks him for building the field and asks if he can come back and play again.

Ray says, "Sure," and as his father begins to walk out toward the corn stalks, says, "Hey Dad, do you want to play catch?" The movie ends with them tossing a baseball as a long line of cars make their way to the magical ball field. Yes Ray, they will come. That scene gets me right to the bone. I wish my grandfather could reappear like that so I could have one last catch with him. Now that my father has passed away I wish he could join us too.

My desire to play pro ball was not only for me, but also for my dad and grandfather. Though I was an above average baseball player, I didn't have the size, the power, or the year round playing time to do anything more than dabble in single A baseball where I played up until the final cut. Oh well, it was still an exciting opportunity and learning experience.

As I lay in the hospital not knowing if the scleroderma would come back again with devastating results, I thought of my grandfather and how he dealt with adversity, and I knew I was in for the same type of fight. In my head, I kept hearing the doctors say, "You have a disease that has no cause and no cure."

My Gramp died when I was 14 of prostate cancer, which was a very painful death for him. To this day when I have a success to celebrate or a failure to contemplate, I look up into the sky and ask Gramp for guidance. I know in my heart of hearts he is listening and observing my life and the lives of his family here on earth.

CHAPTER 7

My First Guardian Angel

Growing up I always felt a little special. No, not that kind of special, though some may differ with that assessment. I wasn't too sure why, but as I lay in the hospital, I started to put more pieces together in my life and began to see an interesting pattern emerging. For me it began six months before I was born. My dad's first cousin, Andrew Louis Balboni, died tragically at the young age of 18. Against his mother's wishes (my Aunty Dolly) he went swimming at a local pond with his girlfriend on an early evening in July. He was swimming just off shore, and his girlfriend later remarked, "He just went under." He was found shortly after, he had drowned. Andrew was purportedly a very good swimmer, so it was even harder for everyone to understand how this could happen.

Andrew died on July 26, 1958. How it must have pained and crushed Aunty Dolly and Uncle Louie to lose their only child. My dad told me years later Uncle Louie was never the same after Andrew died. How do people get through something like this? I know it was their strong belief in God that helped them cope and move on without Andrew. I know a day didn't go by that Aunty Dolly didn't think about Andrew, as she mentioned him often.

Six months later on December 19, 1958, I was born and out of respect for Andrew's memory, my parents asked Dolly and Louie if it would be okay to name me after their son, and also asked them to be my Godparents. Dolly and Louie were delighted to have me carry on the name of their beloved son. Maybe that's why I felt a little special. Not that I felt I was better than anyone else, but because I felt there were certain expectations since I was carrying around the name of someone in their honor. January of 2000 Aunty Dolly added her loving husband, Louie to her thoughts and prayers as that month he passed away.

> **Your Name**
>
> A mentor and great friend, Tony, would present me with a plaque when we worked together in Scottsdale, Arizona. The plaque was very simple, yet powerful. It truly exemplifies how I felt in being named after Andrew. The plaque has my last name on top of it and the inscription reads:
>
> *You got it from your father; it was all he had to give. So it's yours to use and cherish, for as long as you may live. If you lose the watch he gave you, it can be replaced. But a black mark on your name son, can never be erased. It was clean the day you took it and a worthy name to bear. When he got it from his father, there was no dishonor there. So make sure you guard it wisely, after all is said and done. You'll be glad the name is spotless, when you give it to your son.*
>
> Now, isn't that powerful!

I believe in God, the Father Almighty, His son, Jesus, and the Holy Spirit. I have faith in this higher power yet I also believe in a spiritual realm, the powers of our universe. I believe we can each spread good and positive energy or karma to others and have that energy reciprocated. I believe in a special energy, maybe it's an energy of nature and of God, that each of us possesses, whether we know it or not. It's an intangible energy. To me it makes sense when someone's physical body passes; their spiritual energy remains behind, as we've read about in stories of ghosts, apparitions, and visits by deceased family members. If that's the case, then doesn't the possibility exist of someone's spiritual energy passing from a dying body into a new body and being a part of that living body as their spiritual guide or guardian angel? The question I contemplate: is a guardian angel predestined for us? Interesting. What do you think?

So with that said, even though I was in my mother's womb only four months, I feel Andrew's sudden and unexpected death made it possible for my arrival into this world. Maybe he was born to be my protector, my guardian angel. And with the half dozen close calls I've experienced so far in my life, I know someone has been keeping an eye on me from above. You can't prove it, but you sure can feel it and know its guidance is there.

This is one of those forces of nature, that cosmic mystery. Do you know what I mean? Have you ever felt this yourself? It could be a premonition. Or when a coincidence you experienced wasn't a coincidence at all. Do you realize it happens more than you know? Think about that coincidence and reexamine it and ask yourself if it was supposed to happen. Was it part of your life's blueprint? Have you experienced an almost tragic event that was about to happen or should have happened to you, and you felt as though someone, something, came down and placed their hands on you and pulled you from the depths of tragedy or despair?

Our universe is endless. Let me repeat, our universe is endless. We only know what's in and around our solar system. Scientists have no idea what's out there, and they're the experts. To think as you look around that this is all there is to life, in my opinion, is so shortsighted. We don't know what's out there. Who's to say God didn't bring life to other planets that are at the farthest reaches of another universe? Does it really make sense that we're it, end of subject? There's more to be discovered and unveiled. There is magic in the universe, God's universe. And after my experience in June, I know deep down in my soul this was supposed to happen to me. It was supposed to be. It was part of my blueprint.

A Visit from the Other Side

My grandfather's untimely death was the first tragedy I'd face growing up as a child. It wouldn't be my last. Today, with advancements in prostate cancer treatments, my grandfather would've had a better chance of survival. How sad!

Death is that inevitable ice cold splash of water on our face we'll all have to encounter at some point in our lives. For the first time, it places mortality squarely in front of you, and you don't know what to feel or how to feel. It's hard to know how you'll react and most important how to deal with easing the pain, the loss, the void. All you know is that you'll never see them again. It's especially hard when that person was your hero, like Gramp was to me.

Unfortunately, while my grandfather was sick, all four kids were kept in the dark about the severity of his cancer and ultimate fate. I guess that's how it was done back then, trying to keep kids sheltered from anything upsetting or traumatic to help us keep our innocence. I suppose my parents were trying to shelter us from death. But after my grandfather died, I became angry at my parents' decision. None of us got to say our final good-byes to Gramp. I would hold that anger against them for over two decades and hated how it made me feel. It would be about 25 years later, when I'd finally find a way to forgive my parents. Why'd it take 25 years? I guess it took a spiritual event during a dream, which I believe was not a dream, but an actual visitation. The following is that dream:

> When I was living in Philadelphia working for HPC Apartment Guides, I would think about Gramp on a weekly basis and talk with him as if he was right there in the room with me. I always hoped he was standing by listening. Many of those moments were usually reserved for when I'd do something stupid and laugh at myself and say, "Hey Gramp, did you see that?" But over the years I truly missed him, telling him I wish I had a chance to say good-bye.
>
> One night my grandfather came to me in a dream. He had been in other dreams over the years, but this time it was different. It felt different. Usually in my dreams some things don't make sense, very disjointed, where faces or dialogues are a little vague or fuzzy and recalling details seems difficult. My grandmother was also in the dream. She was still alive at the time. Noni and I were sitting at a kitchen table and from a darkened doorway in the corner of the kitchen my grandfather walked in, in a very nonchalant manner. He walked up and began teasing Noni about drinking her second glass of wine. Growing up as kids, he would always tease her and she'd laugh her "Ida laugh." She looked up at him and gazed with the love of a faithful wife.
>
> Gramp then walked over to me and as I stood he gave me a big hug, I could feel his presence, his affection as he hugged me. As I gave him a bear hug, I could feel his strong embrace and the smell of his Old Spice aftershave. It was all so real. I immediately started to cry, and he looked at me and said he was sorry. Sorry, I never got the chance to say goodbye to him be-

fore he died. He told me the reason he'd come back in this particular dream was so we could finally and officially say our goodbyes. I continued to cry; I was weeping. I told him how much I missed him as he nodded knowingly. I looked up into his eyes and I could sense he was proud.

Gramp held me by my shoulders at arm's length and looked me in the eyes. I can see that look today. I couldn't believe he was there. After several moments he told me his visit was near an end and he'd have to go back soon. I didn't have to ask him where he was going. I knew. I looked up at him, tears still flowing down my face, and asked him, "Can you stay a little bit longer?"

He said, "I came so you can say goodbye and finally rid yourself of the pain you've been carrying around."

We hugged again, tears still flowing. I looked at him once more, "I love you. I miss you."

He said, "I know. I've been keeping an eye on you all these years."

As he walked away, I bid him a goodbye. He turned, looked back at me with a smile, then walked out of the door by the kitchen and was gone. My grandmother looked over at me with a smile, as if she was in on it. She was happy he came back so I could finally say goodbye.

I awoke that morning, my pillow case soaking wet from my tears. A smile came to my face as I recalled my grandfather's visit. But something else was very noticeable. The anger I felt towards my parents for all those years disappeared, gone, as if lifted from my soul. Thanks, Gramp! And you will always be my hero! This is one of the most uplifting events in my life.

CHAPTER 8

The End and Beginning of a Journey

The day finally arrived; July 12, I was going home from BNI after spending a total of 14 days in the hospital. It was a bittersweet moment. I became attached to the doctors and nurses who took care of me, especially Dr. Kris, who saved my life. You build a special bond, a connection with these people who nurse you back to health, especially in an extreme situation like mine. Only you and they understand; you have an intimacy with them like no one else.

I slowly got ready, pulled together my belongings when Dr. Kris stopped by to wish me good luck. He expressed optimism my kidneys could possibly kick in if I keep building up my stamina. Through a cracking voice and tears in my eyes, I thanked him for everything. "Dr. Kris, you saved my life, and I'll never, ever forget that. Thank you." He smiled shyly and said, "You're welcome, good luck." We'd keep in touch for a while after I left the hospital and to this day when I think of him a grateful smile comes to my face. Several nurses and doctors came to see me off as well. With tears still in my eyes, I thanked them all and in a strange way, I was going to miss them, except for the Swedish meatballs. But it was time to move on, and heck, I was excited about going home.

I was still too weak to walk under my own power so a nurse brought a wheelchair and said, "Time to go." As I dropped down into the wheelchair, I looked around the room to soak up the events of the last 14 days. What really happened here? What was the lesson? What was this all about? And I also thought, would I be back? I had a lot of time to think over the course of those days, thinking about my future.

Did I have a future? How would my life be different? I knew I had to make some key changes in my life and think about how I'd live from here on out. At this point, I had no answers.

With Mom and Dad at my side, they wheeled me to the elevator. As we waited, nurses and doctors continued to stop and say goodbye. I kept tearing up; I couldn't help it. I felt anxious and excited all at the same time. We entered the elevator facing the door. As the elevator doors began to close, a few more nurses waved their last goodbyes, remembering my last elevator episode didn't go so smoothly.

A few moments later the doors opened into the parking garage. Wow, my first time in two weeks out in the fresh air. Okay, don't forget I'm living in Phoenix, it's July, and the temperature is about 107 degrees. I forgot the feeling of experiencing a Phoenix summer cold turkey. It felt like being hit in the face by an old blast furnace. You know that feeling you get when you open up a hot oven door too quickly?

As I tried to acclimate to the hot air, the blaring heat cancelled out the initial exhilaration of being freed from weeks of captivity. Though with the excitement came a feeling of uneasiness in my soul. I was still sick and had several mountains to climb before I was out of danger. One chapter of this ordeal was about to close, but another one would open, and I'd have to face what lay ahead. Quick let's get to the air-conditioned car!

As we pulled onto the street I looked behind me and saw the hospital disappear and fade. I continued to absorb the last 14 days and hoped it would be the last time I'd have to visit this or any hospital for a long time.

As Dad began to drive out of Phoenix, he was asking directions to get on the US 202 Freeway. Now my dad, I love him dearly, however, he is not the best of drivers. Maybe back home in Hanson, but this was Phoenix, lots of traffic congestion and confusing street signs. As I mentioned, he's not a very good driver, and he missed the road I was pointing at to the highway. He stopped, then moved on slowly, and abruptly pulled into a gas station to turn around. Cars behind him were honking their horns. He could've caused a minor traffic accident. For those who know my dad, you're probably laughing right now. I was a little nervous, and thinking, after everything I'd just gone through in the hospitals, I was going to die in a car accident, driven by my dad! My nervousness turned into humor as I poked fun at him about how his bad driving was elevating my already high blood pressure, and he might have to turn around and bring me back to the hospital.

We finally made our way to the freeway heading toward North Scottsdale. I was now feeling a little better about the drive and the driver. As I looked out the window of the back seat, I couldn't help but realize the landscape I'd looked upon for so many years took on a whole new appearance. It's hard to describe what I was seeing. It was as if I was experiencing these views for the first time. It was strange because I'd lived in Scottsdale three different times dating back to 1987 when I first laid eyes on this desert landscape. I drove this freeway to work in the mornings and realized I hadn't been watching this desertscape as I commuted. Had I been that focused on work that I missed this each morning? Not a good sign is it?

As I continued looking out at my newfound surroundings, I felt an inner peace move through me like the warmth of a cup of hot cocoa. I felt so connected to my surroundings, the colors, the landscapes, the desert vegetation, and with my spirit, my inner-self, than I had in a long time. I then gazed out at the Superstition and McDowell Mountains lofting in the background. I looked to the bright blue sky and thanked God over and over for giving me a second time to see His artwork. Each view like a painting in vivid colors. Though in the back of my mind I kept thinking my disease could come back at any time and the next time it could be fatal. As we got closer to my house, anxiety kicked in. I realized everything I was now seeing was truly a gift. If it hadn't been for the Grace of God, I might've never seen His works of art again.

Home from the Hospital

The anxiety increased as we pulled down my street, into my driveway, and then into the garage. I was overwhelmed. As the car came to a stop, I wasn't sure I could get out of the car. As I sat in the back and looked around the garage, a sudden rush of emotion hit me as I realized how close I came to never laying eyes on this home again. Wow! My dad came around, opened my door and reached in to help me out. He slowly pulled me out and got me upright. I felt so weak I had to put my hands on the back fender to keep from falling over.

I could see the concern in his eyes, and he said something I hadn't heard from him in a long time. He looked at me and said, "I love you son." You see my dad is from the old school where they keep their emotions to themselves, especially when it comes to taking about love. Some of his generation, though they love their children and show it in many ways, have trouble saying, "I love you." Hearing him say that was momentous. I was so glad he did. I think he was as well.

As I looked around, the emotions of the moment kicked in and I began sobbing uncontrollably. Everything hit me at once; my poor parents weren't quite sure what to do. My mom, with alarm in her voice, asked, "Are you okay?"

I told her, "These are tears of joy, Mom," the joy of coming home from the hospital and being given a second chance on life. Oh the joy of being alive! The last 14 days flashed back through my mind like a high-speed movie, and I was too overwhelmed to handle it.

My dad took me by the arm and led me through the garage into the house. I looked down the hallway into my bedroom, where 14 days earlier it all began. I could've died right in there. The tears flowed even more. My dad held on tighter so I wouldn't fall. This whole experience has sensitized my emotional state. Today my emotions come to the surface much easier and quicker than they have in the past. Whether it's an emotional story somebody emails me or even a touching commercial on TV, my eyes water up. I have to say, I've always been a compassionate person, though not at this level where so much touches my soul.

As we walked through the house I kept looking around, touching things, from my guitar to gazing at picture frames of family and friends remembering how special each person was to me. It seemed each room I entered brought on more and more tears. Even a piece of stupid furniture! How instantly a life can be taken away in the snap of a finger. Everything I was seeing, touching, hearing, and smelling was truly a gift. It's amazing how easily we take things for granted!

Here's my mom again:

> The day finally came when Andrew was discharged from the hospital, and we could bring him home. Finally! It seemed like he was in the hospital forever. Though there were many emotional times during this period, the one that frightened me the most was pulling up to his house, from the hospital. He got out of the back seat with the help of my husband, and he broke down crying. He said he never thought he'd see his home again. I was crying right along with him.
>
> He was quiet for the first few days; not saying much. I was sure he was doing a lot of thinking about what he'd gone through, and we didn't know what to say, so we let him have his moments to think.
>
> God answered our prayers. I found out later there were people praying for my son all over the country. I didn't realize how many people knew him. Thank you. I know prayer works. My son is living proof!

As I sat around the house resting, I began to ponder crazy stuff about what could've been. One place I wish I didn't go was visualizing my nonexistence: the thought of never attending a family cookout, watching a baseball game with my dad or brother, not even being able to witness a sunrise or a sunset, not being able to exist and experience. One day you're alive and the next day you're dead. From that moment on, everything took on a different perspective and still holds a different meaning than it did before I got sick. That's why I go out of my way to make every day special, to turn an ordinary day into a wonderful eventful experience. You also have the ability to create a wonderful, fulfilling life by choosing your frame of mind (attitude) each day. What's keeping you from making your choice?

I don't think my parents understood what I was going through. Heck, it was all new for all of us to deal with the experience of almost losing a child or a sibling. In most cases, I felt like I wanted to go through this part alone because I wasn't sure what was going on inside my own head. I wasn't sure what emotions I should be feeling.

For most of my adult life, living away from home and family, I rode out most of my challenges by myself. Even sharing things in your day-to-day life by phone or email 2300 miles away doesn't lend itself to the proper intimacy.

My dad walked over to me as I sat in the chair and put his hand on my shoulder and asked what he could do. I grinned and said I needed some quiet time to take it all in and reflect. So for the rest of the day and night the three of us sat around dealing with our own private thoughts.

I went to bed early that first night. The best part was sleeping in my own bed for the first time in two weeks. As I lay there in bed, I felt the catheter port tubes sticking out of my chest and thought how crazy the past two weeks of my life had been. I began weeping and through tears I again gave thanks to God and Jesus. Yes I am alive! As I dozed off, I thanked Andrew for being there by my side. I also recalled the promise I made to myself in the hospital: if I was going to beat this damn disease I was going to have to have a strong faith in my God, in myself, and faith in the power of attitude and persistence. I couldn't give up!

The next few days consisted of soul searching, TV, shooting a little pool, sticking to my renal diet (most of the time), talking with Mom and Dad, going to dialysis up the street, sitting in my pool, or lying down resting. Though several friends came by to visit, I never felt like having company. The joints throughout my body still hurt and even the easiest of tasks seemed difficult. But I was home and in familiar surroundings.

My biggest frustration and concern was the crippling claw-like effect in both hands caused by the scleroderma. As the skin on my fingers began to tighten my fingers started to curl under my palms. They were always stiff and sore. I couldn't open jars, bottle tops, button a shirt, tie a shoe, or more important play my guitar. Anytime I wanted juice or soda I'd take the bottle, place it on the counter and as hard as I tried I wasn't able to get my fingers around the top of the cap tightly enough to unscrew it; I'd have to call my parents for help. Other days I was too weak to go out and walk around the neighborhood like the doctors had insisted. So my dad would walk me around inside the house.

With everything else going on around me two more things were adding to my reflective journey. I began dealing with the realization I might not be returning to HomeStore, or for that matter, if I'd be able to perform at the same work level I had before. In addition, I was trying to find closure from a romantic relationship that had recently come to an end. This made some days tougher than others, and I had to dig down even deeper to pull myself out of those funks. Over the next few months, I fought bouts of depression and anxiety brought on by my crisis and a failed relationship. I choose to fight these battles alone and not let others, especially my parents, know what was going on. They had enough dealing with their own emotions.

It was now time for Dad to head home. As he got ready to leave for the airport, we embraced. I thanked him for being there for me. As we hugged his words brought tears to my eyes, "Son I'm so glad that you're here, alive, and I love you." That was another moment I'll never forget. It was so great to have my family close at that moment unlike the last 17 years of being far away from home. I felt overwhelmed as I pondered how close I came to never seeing any of them again and more important not having the chance to say good-bye. I immediately thought of Gramp. I thought about how that affected me for all those years until he appeared in that dream. I have a request for everyone reading this book: please appreciate and tell those around you how important they are in your life. You may never get a second chance.

Later that night Dad called to let us know he had arrived home. A day later my brother flew out from Rhode Island to stay with me and Mom.

Mom's Story Continued

Here's Mom again:

> My husband stayed for about two weeks and flew back home to take care of things in Hanson. As he flew back, my other son, Michael, flew out to stay with us. After a couple days, Andrew started being the Andrew we all knew. He laughed a bit, joked about incidents in the hospital but there was a reverent silence about him. I am sure his mind was still processing what he went through. The three of us would pass the time watching movies, making Andrew his special foods, and helping him walk around to get his strength back. Many times my son Michael and I watched TV as Andrew slept. We took turns driving him back and forth to dialysis, which was just up the street. We didn't know what to say the times he'd get frustrated when he couldn't open a bottle or jar because his fingers wouldn't cooperate with him. We were glad to keep him company and thankful he was alive.

My dad updated everyone back home. Over the next week he kept calling to say so and so, "Came into the barbershop and asked how you were doing." His barbershop became the Andrew update center.

It now became my brother's job to walk me around the house to build up my stamina. I was beginning to feel stronger and thought it might be time to go outside and get some fresh air. Holding onto my shoulder my brother walked me into the garage. The temperature outside was around 105 degrees and as the garage door went up the roaring heat unfolded under the door. It was so intense it buckled my knees. Luckily, my brother was holding me up. So much for the walk outside. I decided to confine my short walks to inside the house.

I had lost a lot of weight in the hospital, in total over 25 pounds. I lost so much I could zip up my jeans and pull them down over my hips without unbuttoning them. It was a little concerning but the doctors said I should regain my appetite. We continued to spend most days inside the house, resting, reflecting, shooting pool, and watching movies. It would've been very challenging trying to recuperate on my own, so I was glad they were there while I mended.

A very emotional moment occurred when I asked Mom and my brother to take me to my favorite church, St. Maria Goretti in Scottsdale. Aside from my treatments at the dialysis center, this would be my first time going out in public since my crisis. After what I went through, I felt a strong desire to go to church. To give thanks and praise to God and Jesus for saving my life. It was also an opportunity to contemplate and reflect on what was ahead of me. I didn't think it would be that hard to attend Mass, but it was.

As we entered the church I felt uplifted and my spirits grew. As I slowly got to my knees to pray I looked up at the altar and saw Jesus on the cross. It hit me again how lucky I was, how close I came to dying. A warm flush of emotion swept over my body and I started to cry in the pew. My brother put his arm around me, but I couldn't stop weeping. I was in the house of the Lord, the One who saved my life. It was overwhelming. I knew I couldn't make it to the end of Mass; it was too emotional. Before communion was administered we walked out and went home. Even though I didn't finish Mass, as I walked out, I felt a renewed energy. I felt spiritually stronger to fight this disease. Other things were becoming clearer about why I was going through this. It seemed like a large puzzle, and I was slowly trying to fit the pieces in. As we drove back to the house, I thanked them for taking me and looked up into the blue sky and thanked God. I was still trying to process why me?

Going Home to Family

My first trip home to Massachusetts since my crisis was late August to partake in our family's annual lobster clambake at my parents' house. My brother was still in Scottsdale, and he accompanied me on the plane ride back. It was a trip full of reflection. Like a movie playing in my mind, I kept thinking about what could've been. I had such a great life up until this point, and how would it be changed moving forward? I felt blessed to have lived in many great places like Scottsdale, Southern California, Philadelphia and San Francisco and all the friends I'd made over the years. How would I feel about moving back home? Would I fit in after being gone for so long?

Heading home I didn't know what to expect. What would my emotional state be like when I see other family and friends face-to-face for the first time since my crisis? Before I left, I had to coordinate with a dialysis unit in Weymouth, Massachusetts as a transient patient to receive my weekly dialysis treatments.

We landed in Providence, Rhode Island. It felt great to be back in familiar territory. A few family members met us at the airport, which was very emotional. After getting our bags we drove to my parents' house in Hanson. As we turned up the street I grew up on, I saw all the places I spent my childhood: the town hall pond, the cemetery, and my old neighborhood. My brother helped me into the house, and I started weeping. This was where it all began, 40 years ago, my house, the house I grew up in, the house and family environment that shaped and molded me into who I am today. How surreal it was knowing I might never have seen my family, friends, or old neighborhood again. Wow, I guess I came pretty close to death. Still crying my brother walked me over to the couch to lie down; I was exhausted from a full day of travel and quickly fell asleep.

After I awoke from a short nap, Mom told me everyone was calling the house seeing how I was doing. They wanted to come over to say hi; I wasn't sure if I was ready for that. Emotionally I wasn't ready for this at all. I didn't know what to expect. But at some point I'd have to find the emotional strength to see family and friends. My oldest sister, Carol, and my brother-in-law Phil (or F-i-l-l as I call him) were the first to come by. I'd spoken to her on the phone from the hospital and my home, but this would be the first big test for me. Their car pulled into the driveway. I took a deep breath and slowly walked outside to greet them. Before my sister and I even embraced the tears were flowing from our eyes. We hugged and held on tightly as if it was the last time we would ever see each other. With our heads buried in each other's shoulders we sobbed like babies. We separated just long enough to look each other, then right back to sobbing. We kept saying how much we loved one another. I told her I thought I'd never see her again and that just made matters worse.

Each encounter I'd have with family members and friends would be about the same outcome, long tight embraces and lots of tears. For the next three weeks I would lay low as I didn't have the strength for much else.

Three days a week Mom or a sister or friends took turns dropping me off and picking me up at dialysis which was 25 minutes from my parents' house. My good friend Nancy Hickey was always there to chip in with a ride or keeping me company. This dialysis was no different than the Scottsdale unit. I knew it was going to be a while till I felt a semblance of normalcy. I had to stay tough, I had to stay mad at this disease; if it pissed me off I'd fight back harder. The one constant was my positive mental attitude and perseverance. Every morning I'd wake up and set my mind to summon up the mental and physical strength to get through the early days. This reinforced my belief that we choose not just our attitude but the *altitude* we'll allow our *attitude* to soar.

The nurses and doctors at the Weymouth Dialysis Center were great, just like the ones in Scottsdale. Unfortunately, like Scottsdale, most of the patients were in varying degrees of depressed states. Upon entering the unit you'd hear the same moaning and groaning I heard in Scottsdale. One lady in her early fifties had both legs amputated and was on dialysis from what I assumed was diabetes. She kept moaning that all she wanted to do was die. "Let me die," she said over and over.

At times I must admit it was hard not to feel depressed and frightened. I went through some of these feelings at both locations, especially when I realized I could end up like her. Fortunately that feeling of desperation only lasted for a while, and I'd dig down deep into my soul, my being and will my attitude to take over and get me out of these occasional funky moods.

I recall when two childhood friends, Angel and Robin came to pick me up one day at the Dialysis Unit. From my chair I watched them get out of their vehicle and walk into the waiting area. I had finished my treatment, and the nurses had put clean bandages on my open sores where the catheter ports protruded from my chest. I began walking up to the front to meet them, and they walked right into the unit, not knowing what to expect. As they looked around their eyes widened and their jaws dropped as they saw all these patients sitting in their chairs. Both their faces turned white. Later that day at lunch, Angel asked me, "How can you go through all that?"

I responded, "What choice do I have?" I told them I planned on beating this disease and this episode is just one in a long string of medical challenges until I achieve full recovery. Their reaction was not much different than the others who either dropped me off or picked me up. I don't blame them, however, and as I've done for most of my life, I had to find opportunity in this chaos. As the saying goes, "Failure is not an option." My survival depended on it.

So just like in Scottsdale, I took it upon myself to stop and say hi to the patients as I walked to my chair. The older men and women seemed to enjoy my short visits and our lighthearted conversations. Most of them commented on why an energetic young man could be on dialysis? I would sit, and we'd share our stories. Some shared the years they've been on dialysis. A few were waiting for a kidney transplant. I could feel dread in the pit of my stomach as I wondered if I'd be part of those statistics. I had to push those thoughts to the back of my mind and not give in. I constantly reminded myself that if I didn't approach each day with a renewed sense of self and faith, I could be sitting in a dialysis chair for the rest of my life. That was not going to happen.

Other friends and family stopped by throughout the weeks to say hi and to see how I was feeling. Many said they were still praying for me and asking everyone they knew to keep me in their prayers. With each story like this my eyes began to water and I had to make a big effort not to break down. Once again it became apparent how many lives I'd touched. I think if we all truly looked around we'd see how we've touched the lives of many people.

Cemetery Visits

The doctors continued to encourage me to take small walks whenever I felt up to it to build up my stamina and strength. Seeing I lived across the street, the town cemetery would be a great place to start. It was quiet and had a great view of the pond where I could sit and reflect. It wasn't the walk I was dreading, from an emotional standpoint, it was the visit to Gramp's grave.

I'd only been back for a few days but had this overwhelming feeling to visit him and talk with him. Sister Karen offered to go with me, but I needed to do this on my own.

I made my way past the first couple of houses down the street, crossed over and through the stone gates of the cemetery. As I approached the Botieri gravesite, anxiety shot through my body; I felt as if it was a dream. I dropped my hand onto the headstone as my legs felt weak. I began sobbing. I knew my grandfather had been there for me during my crisis, and he, along with my guardian angel Andrew, guided me through this ordeal.

As I looked at his name and the dates etched in the back of the headstone, I had an illusion or a delusion. I saw my name and my dates flash up on the back of the headstone: Andrew L. Botieri, 1958–2000. It was so eerie and surreal. I pulled back from the stone until I came back to my senses.

I continued to sob. Would that be all I'd be about, a name and a date etched on a headstone? My knees got weaker and I collapsed next to the grave holding onto it for support. For a moment I pictured my body being shipped back home to Hanson from Arizona. Family and friends peering into my casket during my wake, then visiting my gravesite, laying flowers nearby, crying they never got a chance to say good-bye. It was so surreal, yet so real. I sat next to the grave for about an hour, talking to Gramp and thanking him for being there for me, and I cried a little more. I prayed and asked him to watch over me because I still wasn't out of the woods yet.

About a week later, I made another trip to visit the grave of my guardian angel, Andrew Balboni in Plymouth. This trip I also made solo. When I reached his head stone, all I could think about was how Aunty Dolly and Uncle Louie must of felt when Andrew drowned at such a young age, and how they lost their only child. What would my parents have gone through if I had died? I got down on my knees and placed my hand on his stone marker as my tears dripped on his name. I thanked him for being there for me, for being my guardian angel, for saving my life. I know he was there that fateful morning.

I stayed in Hanson for a few more weeks feeling the comfort of family and friends. I'd spend my time walking around the old neighborhood, stopping in to see Uncle Roy and Aunt Lorraine who lived next door. Though not blood relatives, they were just as close and important growing up as my real aunts and uncles. It was so nice to sit with them and talk; they were like my second parents growing up. They were glad I was home. We reminisced about the good ole days and laughed at the things we did as kids. Sitting there brought me back to the early days, and I took comfort from that. Maybe I was looking for that feeling of a time when things were simple, easy, and safe, especially after what I had been through. We had many fond memories growing up in our *Leave It to Beaver* neighborhood. Sadly, during the writing of this book they both passed away from cancer.

My time for this visit was coming to end, and I knew I had to be getting back to Scottsdale. A few friends offered to fly back with me, but this trip I had to make alone. I was still trying to deal with the whole emotional experience of facing death. I did have the consolation of knowing I was going back for only one reason. After 17 years of moving around the country, it was time to come home permanently, back to my roots.

Readjusting in Phoenix

About two weeks later, I flew back to Phoenix by myself and had a friend pick me up. When I arrived home it was so surreal as I reflected on the last 30 days. My whole life had changed and would never be the same. My home seemed so empty without my parents or brother around. From here on out I had to rely on the help of friends to pick up the slack from shuttling me to and from doctor's appointments and dialysis. It wasn't always easy finding someone to drop you off at dialysis and then pick you up three hours later.

I'd continued to struggle with most common tasks that involved my hands as the "claw" was becoming more pronounced. But I held my own. There were a couple times when friends couldn't pick me up, or I didn't want to bother them, so I drove myself. Thank goodness those days were easy dialysis days. The doctors and nurses strictly prohibited dialysis patients from driving themselves home in the event they passed out.

It was nice living on my own again, I wasn't use to anything else, but I realized for the first time in a long time how much I needed those around me to be there for me, and they were. Thanks to all of you who were there when I needed you the most.

A few weeks later sister Karen came and visited. She'd never had the opportunity to visit when I lived in Phoenix or Southern California, so I was glad to share in the wealth of my surroundings. This was a bittersweet visit as it was one of the last times I viewed these same sites before I moved back to Massachusetts. Over the next couple days, Karen and I went to a Diamondbacks baseball game, kicked around Old Scottsdale, took a trip to Sedona, the Grand Canyon, and spent time with cousin Paula. It was a great bonding experience. It was great spending quality time with Karen as she was the one back home keeping everything together while I lay in the hospital 2300 miles away. Six days later I returned with Karen back to Hanson where I stayed for about three more weeks.

Reflection

My post-crisis recuperation, which lasted about 12 months, allowed for many hours of self-reflection and contemplation about my life, what direction it had been going in and what direction it now would take. I reflected on the successes I'd experienced, the failures, the joyous moments, the sadness, and the professional and spiritual growth I accumulated along the way. I realized in a short period of thinking time I'd reached many of my professional goals I'd written down earlier in my career, but was I happy in what my purpose had been? At this time I wasn't sure what the answer was.

As I looked back on my life, I definitely saw the characteristics of an overachiever like many of those I worked with and met throughout my career. I knew I'd worked way too many hours to get ahead, to get a jump on things. I guess the old saying; the early bird gets the worm rings true. Since stepping into the corporate world, I'd been that way; it was a conscious choice to get ahead. I assume it's a choice many successful people make. It becomes easier when you truly love what you do. I knew I had to be honest with myself in assessing where I'd go from here. I realized I'd become a workaholic and had been that way well before I got sick. I feel strongly my work habits, and hence, long hours, not taking care of myself, not eating properly, not exercising, and not fulfilling my spiritual needs allowed my stress to build up, unchecked, which facilitated the onslaught of scleroderma. Picture a balloon and keep blowing it up. Eventually the balloon gets very taut, and then it explodes. In a nut shell that's what happened to me.

CHAPTER 9

A Cat Has Nine Lives

Surviving my medical crisis was in every way a true miracle. As I mentioned, the emergency room doctors on that fateful day didn't think I'd make it. However, when I did, some quickly nicknamed me the Miracle Boy of Phoenix, a badge I wear with humility and honor. Even now when I go to my nephrologist (kidney doctor) for my annual check-ups, he'll review my medical history from the past and shake his head. I'm glad he reminds me how lucky and blessed I was that day. His reminders reinforce the positives I've taken away from this experience and the better choices I continue to make in my life.

As I began to pen this book, thoughts about having a guardian angel watching over me became stronger and stronger. I never thought about it that much until I was lying in the hospital or the dialysis chair for hours on end reflecting. I saw a pattern of events that seemed linked together. Was Andrew Balboni keeping watch over me since my birth? Was there something going on that kept me from harm's way?

They say a cat has nine lives; well I guess I've used up a few of mine. Thankfully, I do have a few left. My triumph over scleroderma wasn't the first time in my life where a potential crisis or major catastrophe had been averted. We don't know how many close calls any of us have had in our lives, whether from a disease or from potential harm that never comes to fruition.

The first incident happened in Vermont at St. Michael's College. In 1979 I was visiting a grade school friend of mine, John Puleio. We were pretty tight back in high school where we attended Cardinal Spellman. John and I were Frisbee fanatics, and as far as I know, we may have invented the infamous toe throw. Frisbee is the ultimate game. It truly enhances your senses and helps to increase your motor and reflex skills. If you have children, get them into throwing a Frisbee and watch their eye-hand coordination increase as well as their spirit, as they become one with the Frisbee.

So back to the story: John had invited some classmates from Spellman up for the weekend. We had a blast catching up. After a night of "college" partying, we got up a little hung over and went to get some breakfast. After breakfast we headed over to the rock quarry just off the grounds of the school campus.

The quarry was surrounded by 75- to 90-foot cliffs towering above a flowing river. As we know when you're 18 or 19 years old you feel invincible; nothing can hurt or harm you. In fact, if you look closely sometimes you can see the Superman cape on your back in your reflection. Well, what did I do? Something a little stupid, I must admit. I decided to free climb the cliff. Why? Who knows, maybe it was my testosterone or maybe for a challenge. So after taking a few deep breaths and cheers of encouragement from the guys, I carefully guided myself from one rock to another as I cautiously crossed the river. The rocks formed a rock bridge that traversed from the quarry bank to the edge of the cliff. Okay maybe it wasn't all about invincibility; I am open to the possibility some stupidity may have played a factor.

So I began my assent up the jagged cliffside. Did I mention I had absolutely no climbing equipment or any real experience with free climbing cliffs? Okay I want to be clear. I was moving along at a decent pace, as suggestions and encouragement rang from the bank across the river. I was about 50 feet up and was moving along fairly easily. As I ascended higher, the climb began to get a little more challenging. In hindsight I began to think this was a big mistake. Then at about 70 feet it didn't take me long to realize I was stuck. I couldn't move left or right, I couldn't descend or climb up. I was stuck! As I looked around for my next move, all I could see was a 70-foot drop on either side of me straight down. I knew if I fell it meant at least severe injury or even death for the only thing between me and the running river were many large sharp and jagged boulders to break my fall. My legs started to shake from fear. I knew I had to calm down and focus if I was going to get out of this crazy stunt without injury.

After a few minutes, I got composed by talking myself into a calmer mindset. I looked around for options, of which there weren't many. I glanced above and just out of my reach was a large tree root about two inches in diameter and about a foot long growing out of the side of the cliff. I was pondering my other options aside from the fire department coming to my rescue. I eyed the tree root, and decided, with the help of a quick prayer, I'd take a leap of faith from the rock I stood on and grab the questionable looking root. All this time, my friends were on the other side trying to direct me to safety, but they soon found out as well, there weren't many options. I just had a feeling everything was going to be okay.

After whispering a Hail Mary, I took a deep breath and jumped up from my foothold and grabbed the tree root with my right hand. It started to give way just a bit, and a rush of panic hit me as clumps of dirt fell away into my face. The tree root held. After rocking myself over to my left side, I quickly grabbed a protruding rock with my left hand and swung myself over to a large ledge enough to get a good foothold. I then pulled myself up to the next level and climbed about four more feet to another ledge. I stood there in amazement; my legs still shaking. After a couple more maneuvers, I climbed up the rest of the way to safety.

Needless to say, that was my one and only venture up the side of a 90-foot cliff. Once on solid ground, I lay back and replayed the whole crazy scene in my head; how my legs were shaking and trembling, how I thought I might fall. But I also remembered a calmness; a feeling that, "It would be okay." Was my guardian angel watching over me? This was not be the first time Andrew had intervened on my behalf and fortunately it would not be the last.

I couldn't believe what I'd accomplished. I was more upset for how stupid I'd been for wanting to scale that wall of rock. Though, I guess it shows when you put your mind to something, you can make anything happen. I would see this scenario play itself out in so many of my business endeavors where focus would play such a crucial role. The ability of a person to focus on a goal and not give up until it's accomplished is such a great attribute to possess. So many people give up without trying, without ever giving it a fair shot. Whether it's in your personal life or business, positive mental attitude and perseverance are the keys to a successful life. These two weapons you have at your disposal each and every day.

The Three Town Chase

I was out one Friday night with two friends, Chris and Bobby. Chris and I played men's softball together and Bobby was a local heartthrob drummer, who we affectionately called Keith, because he resembled Keith Partridge of the Partridge Family.

We left an area restaurant bar sometime after 11:00 p.m. As we were heading home a car swerved into our lane and smashed into the back of Chris' 1972 Chevy Impala convertible. It was a mint condition vehicle, which I believe had a 454 engine, a very powerful engine. Chris pulled into a parking lot and waited for the other vehicle to pull in behind him. But the car sped off through a red light and headed into downtown Rockland. We finally caught up to the car, which had pulled over to the curb. I jumped out of the car, ran over to the vehicle and started yelling at the driver. I approached the driver's window and could see he was drunk as he bobbed his head and slurred his words. He said it was his girlfriend's car and was sorry for hitting us. My instincts told me not to trust him. I told him he wasn't going anywhere until the police arrived. As I reach in through his window to shut off the ignition and take his keys, he stepped on the gas with my arm stuck in the steering wheel. I ran alongside the car for about 30 yards trying to turn off the car's ignition.

He began to speed up to the point where I couldn't keep pace any longer and finally yanked my arm free and rolled about a half dozen times in the middle of the street as he drove away. I lay in the road for a brief second to make sure all on my body parts were working. I shook it off, only sustaining a few cuts and bruises and pulled myself up to my feet. This idiot almost killed us and me! The driver turned around at the top of the street and zoomed right by us. I ran to Chris' car and we looked at each other in amazement at what just occurred. I jumped in and yelled, "Go get 'em!" The chase was on.

Chris spun his car around, tires screeching and chased the drunk driver. It was very dark outside as we headed toward a four-way intersection, and then we lost sight of him. We weren't sure if he went straight, left or right. I remember noticing as I picked myself up off the pavement that one of his tail lights wasn't working. As we sat in the middle of the intersection looking in all directions, I noticed about a hundred yards down the street to our right, a car, after releasing its brakes, had only one tail light. That was him! Chris banged a sharp right, stepped on the gas, tires screeching.

With Chris behind the wheel, his Chevy Impala with the 454 engine pulled up behind our assailant in no time, flashing our lights and honking our horn for him to pull over. He wouldn't stop and began to pick up speed trying to put some distance between us. Our adrenaline was pumping full throttle. We stayed right on his tail trying to get him to pull over but to no avail. We were going about 60 miles an hour in a 35-mile-an-hour zone. Up a head was a familiar intersection and it didn't look like he was going to stop at the red light. And he didn't, he blew through the intersection without hesitation. Chris' mind was thinking hard, his focus on the task at hand. Without slowing down Chris timed a car coming from his left, who had the right of way, and placed his car into a controlled skid and swung around the back of the car as both vehicles went through the intersection. It was amazing. I looked at Chris in astonishment; this guy could drive!

After making it through the intersection, we caught up to the driver and pulled beside him to get his attention. From the passenger seat, I yelled out my open window at him again to pull over. He looked at me with dazed eyes and then without warning turned his car toward us and slammed right into the side of the vehicle. We swerved but Chris steadied the car and the driver slammed into us a second time. This sent Chris' car swerving off the road toward someone's front lawn. Coming toward us at a high rate of speed were three large oak trees that lined the roads edge each were separated by about 40-feet in between. It looked like we were going to crash head-on into the first tree. I looked at Chris and saw a calm and focused look. I didn't say a word. I did say a prayer. Chris put his Chevy into a fishtail spin, expertly placing his car between the first two trees as we rode up on the lawn and then to my amazement he stepped on the gas, fishtailed again directing the front end of his Chevy between the second and third tree and back out onto the road as his tires bit into the pavement and a loud screech followed. Chris straightened out his car and in a few short seconds we were back in pursuit of this lunatic. At some point, Bobby was screaming at Chris to slow down. Chris said to Bobby, "You may be a drummer in a rock n' roll band, but I'm a race car driver." We didn't hear another word out of Bobby for a while.

By the time we caught up to the driver, we were about four car lengths behind, still racing at high speeds. As luck would have it, the Abington police station was approaching fast on our right. As we raced past the station, we honked our horn and screamed out the window trying to get someone's attention. We kept going. We knew up a head the street came to a dead end; only a left or right turn available. As we approached we slowed down and began looking for his car. There across the street, past the stop sign, we saw his car up on someone's front lawn after plowing down a four-foot stone pillar that marked the entrance of the driveway. We pulled up behind him and the intoxicated driver sat motionless behind the wheel. The front end of his vehicles was all smashed up with the stone pillar lying next to him. We sat in Chris' car pulling ourselves together, soaking in the past 15 to 20 minutes of the car chase.

All of a sudden the driver kicked opened his door and started running across the lawn making his way to the street. Chris and I looked at each other and one of us said, "Does he know we're athletes?"

So in a flash the three of us were out of the car running after this guy. About 50 to 60 yards down the street Chris caught up to him, grabbing his shirt. Bobby came in next, and as I got there, I wrapped my arms around all three of them, and we crashed into the road. After a brief scuffle in the middle of the street, the police came and took control of the situation; they must have heard us. We sat on the side of the road giving our statements to the police. I sat on the curb as the police handcuffed and placed the suspect into the back of their cruiser. I lost it. I started yelling at the guy through the window. An officer told my buddies I'd better quiet down or they'd arrest me. I took a step back. I replayed the whole ordeal in my head and realized how crazy this had all been, how close we came to dying and yet surviving with only minor injuries. Was my guardian angel watching over me?

We attended the suspect's arraignment within a few days. We found out the guy (I've decided not to use his name in print) got drunk and took his girlfriend's car after an argument. The most shocking information was he'd been on a work release program from a near-by prison. He'd been doing time for burglary and some other offenses. With his background, the prosecutor charged him with three counts of attempted vehicular homicide, using a vehicle as a weapon, and three counts of attempted murder from deliberately crashing into us and knocking us off the road. He also had stolen vehicle, drunk driving, and several other road violations added to his charges. Because of this incident, the judge added another five years onto his current prison term after the trial. The whole event was surreal. I'd find out a few years later, while on another work release program this guy committed suicide by hanging himself. What a bizarre ending to a strange story.

The Summer Of '79

I mentioned earlier it would not be the last time my guardian angel interceded. It was a Friday night in August and like most Friday nights it was time to go out and have fun with friends. We were just out of high school two short years and two good friends of mine, Doug Cunningham and Jeff King were heading up to Vermont with some friends. Doug and I played competitive baseball for many years including high school. We played on a few championship teams together over the years. Our parents were good friends. Jeff helped me coach an instructional hockey team for six- and seven-year-old boys in a local league. We enjoyed helping the kids learn their basic hockey skills and the many laughs along with it.

On that Friday night I stepped out of a local convenience store. I hadn't seen Doug for a while and was surprised to see him. He asked if I wanted to join him and Jeff with some other friends going to Vermont to party for the weekend. It sounded like a lot of fun and I was tempted. As Dougie told me more about the trip, I said I'd go. But as I did that, I felt an uneasiness. Some call it instinct, others call it intuition. In that instant, I thought I'd made other plans for the weekend; though at the time I didn't know exactly what they were. I felt I had committed to something else, so I told Doug on second thought I take a rain check. But told him next time they were going I'd love to join in. I didn't realize there would be no next time.

The next night, on Saturday, while in Vermont, Doug, Jeff along with two friends were killed when their vehicle slammed into a bridge abutment. Jeff and his two friends were killed instantly. Doug survived till Sunday morning. They had been passengers in the vehicle. It must have been horrific. To this day, I wonder what they must've felt or thought before the crash or did they even see it coming? I can't imagine how their parents felt when the police gave them the disastrous news. My mother told me that morning about the accident. I sat in disbelief. It was hard to imagine my friends had died at such a young age; they had so much to offer the world. I cried. Then it hit me. I was supposed to be with them. I sat in a daze. I still think about that moment, of what would have happened had I gone. I used to see Doug's parents, Judy and Bill, around town and though they always wore a bright warm smile when I'd see them. You know they carry around such a large void inside.

Ironically, I never ended up finding out what my plans had been on that fateful weekend. Though, I feel strongly once again my guardian angel, Andrew, was there that night, sitting on my shoulder and with all his power guiding me in a better direction. Isn't it funny how the mysteries of God work? Or maybe it isn't so funny after all. I think of Dougie and Jeff and hope they are at peace and in a better place. This event was without a doubt Divine Intervention.

Demolition Derby

I was living back in Scottsdale as the vice president of sales and operations for AllApartments. On a Sunday night in December 1999, I was approaching a busy intersection talking on my cell phone. Being distracted by my phone call, I drove through a red light without stopping. I never saw the light pickup truck coming through the intersection to my left.

All of a sudden there was this smashing of glass, crunching of metal and a loud concussion sound as the cars made impact. His truck slammed behind my driver's door. All I remember is my four-door Nissan Maxima spinning around the intersection a couple times and coming to rest in the middle of the intersection heading in the opposite direction. My vehicle was totaled. The back tire on my side was bent in at a 45 degree angle from the impact of the crash. This car was going nowhere. I sat dazed for a few minutes trying to shake the cobwebs out of my head. My back and neck were stiff and my body ached. If that truck had come through the intersection one second sooner he would've had a direct hit on the driver's door. If I didn't end up dead, I probably would've at least been seriously injured. I only sustained minor cuts and bruises. I thanked God and my guardian angel. Could this have been another wake-up call for that overachiever Sagittarian that went unheeded? I spent the next two months going to a chiropractor to help ease the pain and stiffness in my back. If you have to drive and talk on a cell, use hands free. A side note to this story. The guy who hit me had been drinking and had prior warrants out for his arrest. When the police ran his license they arrested him on the spot. And other than that he was okay, but needless to say I didn't make his night any happier. The police thanked me for helping capture him.

And Then the Heavens Opened

My biggest scare up to this point without a doubt occurred at 4:31 a.m. on Monday, January 17, 1994: the Northridge earthquake, in Southern California, which registered 6.9 on the Richter scale. I was recently promoted to oversee the LA/San Fernando Valley Apartment Guide after the Inland Empire Apartment Guide (San Bernardino County). I'd taken a corporate apartment in Woodland Hills because the commute from my house in Upland was over 60 miles one way. My girlfriend Julie and I would drive up to Woodland Hills on Sunday afternoons, stay the week at the apartment and drive back to Upland on Friday nights.

That Sunday afternoon, we ate dinner out and went to bed around 10:00 p.m. All of a sudden we were awoken as the bedroom began rocking from what seemed like an explosion; like a bomb going off right next to us. We were jolted from a deep sleep when a picture frame came crashing down on us from above the headboard. It was pitch black out, and all we could hear were loud cracking, crashing, and shattering sounds all around us. It was total confusion as we quickly tried to shake the cobwebs out of our heads and evaluate what the hell was happening. It was horrific. We realized we were in the middle of a big earthquake.

With a mix of fear and instinct we leapt out of bed and onto the floor, and as we did, the floor was rolling under our feet like a wave crashing into shore. The jolt knocked us back onto the bed and I tried a second time to get up only to get knocked back down. It felt like being in one of those dreams where you're trying to run away from the monster but your feet can't move. As the earthquake continued, the bed shook violently like in the movie *The Exorcist*. Julie was starting to get hysterical. I couldn't blame her; I would've probably joined her but I knew I couldn't. This was about our survival.

What to do now? With the earthquake still going on, we lay back on the bed, and I told her to put a pillow over her head in case any of the ceiling fell on top of her. She kept anxiously asking about her cat, if he was alright, but for the moment this was about us getting out of this ordeal, not her cat. The room continued to shake violently back and forth; it felt as though it was rocking three to four feet from side-to-side. I tried putting the lamp on next to the bed, but nothing happened. We realized there was no electricity. This was a much bigger earthquake than we first assumed. As we continued to ride out the quake on the bed we could hear cracking and ripping sounds as the walls began to separate from the door jams and the floorboards. We could hear the glass in the windows shattering under the force of the quake. In the living room and kitchen we could hear glass and appliances crashing to the floor. We had no control. The scariest thing was not having control over our own destiny. At this moment I thought the whole third floor, bed and all was going to collapse down onto the second floor and then down onto the first floor like pancakes. The shaking was that intense! We held hands. I remember saying to her, "Say a prayer. We may not get out of this alive!"

And then all of a sudden everything stopped. The shaking and rocking came to a standstill. What seemed like an eternity had only been 53 seconds. Amazing! Knowing earthquakes come with multiple aftershocks we had limited time to assess what was going on and what our plan of action was. It's amazing when faced with adversity how a person will react. Will you freeze or jump into action for your survival? You don't receive any training unless it's your job like a Marine, a firefighter, or a paramedic. Though things were literally falling down around us and the scene was chaotic, I felt a sense of calm. My thought process seemed to be functioning well as the world around us collapsed. I thought quickly about what needed to be done. So much can happen in a blink of an eye. At one moment I was telling Julie we may not get out alive, and the next minute I was on my feet with my instincts kicking into high gear trying to deduce the best way of getting out of this building alive. It was pitch-black; you couldn't see your hand in front of your face.

The first thing we needed was light. We had no flashlight and no emergency kit. Who knew? We were at a corporate apartment, not at my condo, where I knew where things were. The California authorities always mention to be prepared for an earthquake, we weren't and I guarantee, not many others were either. Before we could assess what shape the apartment was in, we needed light. With no electricity, the only source of light in the apartment was the gas fireplace. I told Julie to stand under the threshold of the bathroom off our bedroom while I made my way to the living room in the dark. As I passed through the doorway, I got down on my hands and knees and began a slow crawl so I wouldn't trip over furniture or debris as I couldn't see my hands in front of me. I knew there was a pack of matches on the coffee table to my right so I fished around the floor with my hands and realized the table had tipped over during the initial jolt. As I was feeling around the floor, I cut the tip of my finger on a jagged piece of broken glass. Ah must be the ash tray, and then beside the ash tray I found the book of matches, but no candle.

I struck the match and watched the room slowly come to life. I couldn't believe my eyes. All the living room furniture, the entertainment center and pictures were tossed around the room; the TV smashed on the floor. The match burnt out, so I lit another and headed across the room toward the fireplace.

My plan was to ignite the fireplace to provide ample light to collect our belongings and get out fast. I was going to turn the gas on, stand around the corner from the fireplace and flip the electrical switch. But wait, there was no electricity. I needed to light the fireplace the old fashion way, by placing a lit match to the gas register under the fake logs. What else do I need to be thinking of? What were the potential dangers? Many earthquakes will rupture gas lines creating firestorms. I had no idea what I was going to encounter. I quickly stuck my head inside the fireplace and smelled for gas, but couldn't smell any odor. Though this was a promising sign, I still wasn't sure if there was a leak somewhere, but instinct and fear can be a great motivator. I told Julie to stay in the bathroom behind the wall in case of an explosion. I sat up against the side wall of the fireplace and collected my thoughts and assessed my next move. I leaned against the wall hoping this would give me some protection in case the gas exploded. I yelled to her to get ready and stay low if my plan didn't work. It was apparent this was a life and death situation, so I said a quick prayer to God to protect us.

Time to act! I lit the match, turned the gas on and threw it into the fireplace and ducked around the corner. In an instant, there was a "poof" sound and presto the fireplace ignited, and no explosions. How we take for granted the ability to turn on a light switch and have there be light. The glow from the fireplace revealed an apartment that had been torn apart. Every picture on the wall was on the ground smashed into pieces; every piece of furniture was turned upside down, the kitchen was a disaster, all the cabinets had opened during the quake resulting in smashed dishes, cups and glasses on the floor. The refrigerator fell forward and crashed onto the breakfast bar that separated the kitchen from the living room. Your typical apartment set-up. Glassware and broken jars of salad dressings and other condiments littered the floor. It was a complete disaster.

The kitchen looked as though someone blew it up with explosives. I needed to get myself back to the situation at hand. The light from the fireplace cast shadows all around the apartment. I called for

Julie to come out and when she walked into the living room, she couldn't believe her eyes. I walked over to her and we hugged very tightly. I looked into her eyes, and all I could see was fear and confusion. I tried best to hide mine. But at this moment there was no time for fear, we needed to act. In moments like this there is no time for hesitation, our lives depended on it. We also knew eventually the aftershocks would hit.

We made a vocal list of what we needed to bring. Julie kept asking about Mason, her cat, who was nowhere in sight. I instructed her to throw our personal stuff into a pillow case, wallets, money, and a change of clothes, the essential things we needed and get the hell out. We began looking for her cat and found him scared to death under a bed in the second bedroom. He was all freaked out; he wouldn't even let Julie near him. With concern and urgency in my voice I told her grab him, she did and he started clawing and screeching at her. Julie had him at one point, but he bit and scratched her out of fear and she let him go. Enough was enough, I lifted the bed up and she was able to grab a hold of him. We grabbed a pillow case, and she placed him inside so he wouldn't bite or scratch any of us. With our minimal personal belongings and cat in tow we made our way out of the apartment.

As we hit the hallway and turned right toward the exit, the first aftershock hit and it was a big one. We were jerked back and forth in the pitch black hallway and scared as hell. Several people in the hallway let out screams. You could barely make out their shapes from out of the shadows. We raced down the hall toward the exit door with our pillow cases over our shoulders.

It was now a little after 5:00 a.m., and light began to make its way under the door. We hit the third floor exit door ready to run down three flights of stairs. But as I opened the door, I noticed some of the support bars that joined the stairs to the wall of the building had come loose because of the massive jolt. You could see the bolts disengaged from the concrete. I kept stomping on it to make sure it was safe. People behind me began to panic, and I told them we'd get out of this, they needed to stay calm. The stairs appeared to be strong enough to hold us for our escape to the bottom, but there were no guarantees.

There were also no other options, for I wasn't going back into that dark and dangerous hallway. As I looked out over the grounds of the apartment community, it was at this point I began to make out dark outlined images of other buildings. My mind was racing a hundred miles an hour thinking not only how to survive this ordeal, but what the heck to do next.

I'd never seen such in-your-face damage, chaos, and destruction as this earthquake created. Everything looked out of place. The first thing my eyes could make out were about a dozen, 40- to 50-foot palm trees snapped like toothpicks and laid out on the ground like the childhood game Pick-up Sticks. It felt as though we were in a Hollywood disaster movie, except in this case, the special effects were real. More and more images were revealed as the sky got brighter. You could now see large cracks running up and down the outside of the apartment walls.

I grabbed Julie by the hand and we began to descend the stairs, anticipating some more aftershocks. Others followed behind. We were about halfway down at the second story when the second aftershock hit. This one was pretty strong; the building began to sway. We were jolted as the stairs began to creak; the stair supports were sliding in and out of the wall. People screamed. Who knows I might've been one of them.

I tightened up with fear. It was at this point I thought the stairs might collapse with us on it, and we would fall two stories and either die or be severely injured. As the stairs were shaking, I looked at Julie and told her to hang on. We both held on for our dear lives. As soon as the aftershock stopped we looked at each other and said, "Go!" as we hustled down the stairs as fast as we could.

When we hit the bottom we got away from the building as quickly as possible, and as we did, we could see over a hundred people walking around slowing, shuffling their feet with a dazed look in their eyes. Many were crying and shaking their heads in disbelief as it was starting to set in: we all had just survived a large and destructive earthquake. Adults and children were crying, people were helping others, some praying out loud, and consoling each other. I was witnessing the human spirit in full action. I grabbed Julie by the hand and put more distance between us and our former home.

The scene around us was surreal. Our plan was to get into my car and drive about 90 minutes southeast to my home in Upland. I realized most of these people had no other place to go. We made our way through the throngs of wandering and dazed people to the car. Once inside, Julie took Mason out of the pillow case and he jumped and hid in the back seat. Okay, let's get out of here!

As we headed toward the gate, along with quite a few other cars, the ground began to shake again, another aftershock. As we pulled into line, we realized with no electricity how the heck was the security gate going to open? Now what? At this point, a small black pickup truck pulled in front of the gate and pressed his front bumper against the gate arm and began to inch forward. The metal arm began to bend far enough out to allow the cars to squeeze through.

As soon as we got out of the parking lot we turned on the radio and listened to the news reports. We knew we needed to call our families, but each time we tried the cell phone lines were busy. You can imagine the many cell towers that were incapacitated by the quake.

Both of our families were back on the East Coast, where it was a little after 8:30 a.m. The news of the earthquake was just hitting the morning news programs back East and to make matters worse news reports showed the epicenter of the quake in Northridge, which is next to Woodland Hills where our families knew we stayed. We calculated we were only two-and-a-half miles from the epicenter. After several failed call attempts, I finally got through to my mom; the first words out of her mouth were, "Are you two okay?"

"Yes, though a little shaken up." I told her our plan and asked her to call Julie's parents in Florida to let them know we were okay.

The scariest part of our drive home was local news reports talking about collapsed roads and vehicles driving off bridges that were destroyed. I drove ahead carefully looking for any road damage. After what seemed like a long drive we made it back to my house in one piece. I stood in my living room, recapping the whole event in my mind and dropped to the floor in exhaustion. We both realized we could've died that morning in the earthquake.

Unfortunately, about a month after the earthquake my relationship with Julie ended, so we packed up a moving truck, and along with her and Mason, drove back cross country and resettled her in Atlanta. She's a wonderful and caring person, and we still keep in touch, usually around the anniversary of the earthquake.

The thing about major earthquakes is after the initial jolt, you'll have hundreds of smaller aftershocks that can still cause damage and death. When I left California for Philadelphia in September of '94, I heard one report that stated over 1500 aftershocks were attributed to the 6.9 Northridge earthquake on January 17, 1994.

CHAPTER 10

The Learning Years

"Accumulation of efforts, brings realizations of success." Are these just words or do they offer us a glimpse into the correlation between hard work and consistent persistent efforts to enable individuals to achieve success? Whatever success may mean to that individual. The key to life is to learn more from our mistakes than our victories and grow from those experiences. If we don't learn and grow we become stagnant, complacent in our personal and professional life. With learning and growth you create a solid foundation to build upon. What efforts have you been accumulating?

JC Penney

My first professional job out of college was working for JC Penney in their management trainee program in Westerly, Rhode Island in July of 1982. Why Penney's? It surely wasn't a starting salary just under $13,000 a year. The reason? I loved clothes; I enjoyed dressing up and really didn't know what the heck I wanted to do with my life after college. I never realized what a great company Penney's would turn out to be.

I enjoyed my newly found freedom, of being fresh out of college, making a mark on the world. We've all felt that sense of freedom and self-reliability upon leaving the roost of our parents' home and making it on our own. It's a huge moment of truth, when for the first time; you're in charge of making your own decisions and choosing your path in life and living with the consequences of those choices. Welcome to "Live on the Big Stage!" I was very excited, scared, and apprehensive about my future and how it would unfold upon graduating. My

God, you mean my parents can't take care of me anymore? Now what? But I grew up quickly. JC Penney helped in that metamorphosis.

The company was founded by James Cash (J.C.) Penney in 1898, and the foundation of his company was the Golden Rule: do onto others as you would have them do onto you. Great words to live by. Too bad our country today seems to have forgotten that practice.

For anyone looking to get into an entry level management position fresh out of college or high school, JC Penney is a great company for that. In fact, I tell those graduating if they aren't sure what they want to do after graduation, try retail merchandising with a national chain, it's a great place to start, a great stepping stone. For me, JC Penney gave me the tools and skill set to enable other doors of opportunity to open. Some of those skills were merchandising, building and working a budget, managing profit margins, advertising, people skills, conflict resolution, and the responsibility of providing a living for your people, or associates, in Penney-speak.

JC Penney is where I'd meet my first mentor, Mr. Dan Antal, my boss, or Mr. A, as I usually called him. He was a towering figure who possessed a hearty laugh and a good natured demeanor. He had integrity, kept life simple, and worked hard. He was a Penney lifer and years later retired with the earned respect of those he worked with. He loved his retail! Right from the start, he took me under his wing and guided and coached me on the "rag business." He felt like my surrogate father since I was away from home. And just like his own kids, if I screwed up, which happened on occasion, Mr. A practiced tough love on me. Those three principals, the power of nurturing and coaching, the keenness of using tough love when appropriate, and enjoying your work were lessons I learned from him.

I'd been on the fast track at Penney's and learned much about the world of fashion, apparel, and retail merchandising. I oversaw children's, infants', young men's, men's, sporting goods, and athletic shoes and tried to absorb as much as I could. My departments did about $4 million a year. I was truly enjoying my job and kept learning as I'd listen and soak up what others at our district meetings were doing and started taking risks on unproven lines I felt would sell in our store. I knew what my customers wanted because I asked them! As my passion grew so did the time I spent in my work mode. I'd bring work home to stay ahead. It was competitive, as you're being compared to similar volume stores in sales and profits. You were accountable for the success or failure of your departments. There's no free ride. Just like in sports if you want to be the best, you have to put the time in. No gain without pain as they say. So I jumped in, rolled up my sleeves and got busy. One of Mr. Antal's favorite sayings was, "You can't sell goods from an empty wagon." Once I overstocked a line of clothing, and to send me a message, he came into my office, broke my pencil, and walked out. He didn't need to say another word.

My team and I achieved the highest sales gains for our district in our young men's department, and all of a sudden, other stores were calling to find out what we were doing. I'd only share so much with them and kept a few safe guarded secrets for myself and Mr. Antal. Shortly after, I was promoted to senior merchandise manager. Things were moving along nicely. One of our merchandise managers went out on an extended leave, and I was asked to take over her responsibilities as well. Initially I didn't complain. I never would; it isn't my style. I figured it was short lived. I didn't mind. I was helping the store as a whole and learning new merchandise lines.

Though after a while, I approached Mr. A about a raise as I was doing the work of two and getting paid as one. He said he'd check with his boss, Ken Miner. Two weeks later after a store visit by Mr. Miner, I asked Mr. Antal if he'd spoken about my raise. He said unfortunately Mr. Miner turned down the request, with no explanation. I was so disappointed and upset, not at Mr. Antal, but with Mr. Miner.

Miner was not very personable to me and very rigid. He even made a fellow associate promoted to his district staff, shave off his beard. No questions asked, off with the beard or no promotion. It appeared he wasn't a big fan of beards. That information would come in handy later.

I was so mad. I knew I had to do something. There always has to be a plan B. After a couple days I decided, as payback for not receiving a raise, I'd take a two-week vacation. This is shunned upon in the retail world, especially when you're the department manager and in-store buyer. I did receive a little flak from Mr. A, but it was the end of

September, back-to-school was finished, Christmas buys had been made so it wasn't that big of a deal. I decided to go out West and visit my Uncle Buzz (my mom's brother) in Southern California and then my cousin Paula and her husband Jim in Phoenix. Up until this time I'd never been west of the Mississippi. I thought, boy what a great trip this was going to be! It would be a trip that set into motion the gears of change, major change.

For the next two weeks, I enjoyed myself with uncle Buzz who lived in Newport Beach, and we had a blast. Going to Balboa Island, walking around Huntington Beach, Venice Beach, and swimming in the Pacific Ocean for the first time. Upon getting out of the water though, you could feel an oily film on your body caused by the oil derricks in plain sight off the coast. I was falling in love with the weather, the sun, and the beautiful women.

After a week there I flew off to spend my second and last week with my cousin in Phoenix. Though I loved both places, I fell in love with Phoenix. My cousin's husband Jim had many business contacts, and he introduced me to two general managers (GMs) from local radio stations. After two impromptu get-togethers, both GMs were interested in hiring me for a sales position, until they found out I lived on the other side of the country. I guess they had a good point.

As I flew back east after my wonderful and restful vacation, all I could think about was Phoenix. For some reason I was being drawn there; I could feel it pulling at me. My mind was being consumed with Arizona. I knew I needed to make a move. I knew I was bound for the Southwest, how I still wasn't sure.

Back home I immersed myself back into life at Penney's. After two weeks I went in and asked Mr. A for that raise again. He looked at me, shook his head and said, "You know what the old man will say."

He asked anyway and the answer came back, "No!"

A few weeks later I called Jim in Phoenix, "Will you set up an interview with those to GMs you introduced me to?" One station was KOY Radio/Edens Broadcasting and the other was a Kool Oldies station, KOOL-FM. So in November 1986, I flew out to Phoenix and had a formal interview with both GMs I'd met during my vacation. Again, they expressed real interest, but at the moment, I wasn't living in Phoenix. If my living situation changed, let them know. I jumped on a plane and flew back to Rhode Island.

A sinking feeling came over me. I knew what I had to do, but it was such a big decision. Was there a sign letting me know which way to turn? My current situation hadn't changed. I was still doing the work of two people and only getting paid as one. More and more this grated on me. It seemed so unfair in my early career. More and more I knew I needed to make a decision to get on with my life and its next chapter.

A few weeks later, Mr. Miner was making his Christmas clean-up store visit. I knew this was my moment of truth, it was now or never. Don't get me wrong, I loved working for JC Penney but I wanted to be fairly compensated and appreciated. Sound familiar? Over the next few weeks the entire store worked hard getting ready for Miner's visit. His job was to walk around inspecting overstocks, ask about hot selling items, marking down "dogs," and then find something to grind you on.

Since I'd come back from vacation and knowing I'd see Mr. Miner shortly, I decided to make a statement, a bold statement some would say. I decided to grow a beard, just for him. Yes the rebel in me was coming out, and I wasn't going to be deterred. Even though Mr. Antal was pleased with my performance and my beard, he shook his head in minor exacerbation at his mentee gone wild. So the stage or showdown was set.

The day came and the store sparkled. Mr. Miner made his rounds with each merchandise manager and Mr. A in tow. Then it came my turn. As Miner approached my departments he walked up to shake my hand and saw the beard. I could see from the look on his face, as he gazed upon my hairy growth, he copped an attitude right away. He seemed fit to be tied. He couldn't even make eye contact with me. I couldn't believe it. I tried asking questions so he'd have to look at me or even look in my direction, but he'd avert his eyes. It was almost comical. But I was prepared. Every question he peppered me with, I answered with confidence, and with the help of my team, our departments looked great, and we passed with flying colors.

As we finished our walk-through, I could tell Mr. Antal was a little uneasy. He wasn't quite sure what I was going to say. He knew I was still upset about being denied a raise for a second time. When the time was right and my tour was ending, now was the opportunity. I turned to Mr. Miner, explained my situation again and ask him point blank for a raise. I said it was only fair. He looked pissed. His face crunched up with a frown. He said he'd already made his decision over a month ago, and he wasn't going to change. I thanked him for touring my departments and walked away. That was the final straw. I had to put plan B in motion.

At the end of the week I walked into Mr. A's office with a heavy heart. He had done so much to help me in my career. I walked up to his desk and handed him my resignation. He was a bit surprised; I was his protégé and he my surrogate father. I think he sort of expected it. He knew it was time for me to spread my wings and fly the coop. He said he was proud of me and wished me good luck. To this day we keep in touch, and when I call, I still address him as "Boss." He gets a kicked out of it. That was December 1986. My next decision would make way for a very significant move and change in my life.

From JC Penney I learned nothing is permanent, that job loyalty is just a phrase. That regardless of how you feel, your company will move on without you. On the positive side if you believe in yourself, you can create your own path to success in your life. Nobody has a better eye out for you than you.

Off to Phoenix

Now I knew where I was going. I was headed to the Southwest, though I wasn't quite sure how. After spending quality time with family and friends, in late January 1987, I packed up everything I owned into my Volkswagen Jetta and headed out cross-country, destination: Phoenix, Arizona.

As I drove out of my parents' driveway, I left with mixed emotions. I'd never lived this far away from my family and there seemed to be a permanency about it. I'd be about 2300 miles away. My family seemed to be happy and sad at the same time. My mom didn't seem too happy at all. I'm sure she had trouble with one of her own moving so far away from the nest. I was heading off to play in the bigger arena of life than I was used to and had no clue what lay ahead. But I knew my metal was going to be tested. I knew success was predicated on how much effort you put into your endeavors. I was ready. Bring it on! What I didn't realize was the stage was set to encounter two new mentors in Phoenix.

My immediate concern was going somewhere new and not having a job waiting for me. That insecurity was frightening and at the same time a motivating force. My plan was to visit the two radio stations I'd interviewed with earlier and see if they'd hold true to their word. As I looked out of my windshield at the road ahead, I felt as though I was looking at my future down the road and was very excited about those prospects.

My cross-country trip was just what the doctor ordered. I traveled down through the Mid-Atlantic states, into Tennessee, up to Alabama, Kansas, over to Colorado, down through the Rockies and into Four Corners. Four Corners is where the states of Arizona, Utah, Colorado, and New Mexico all meet at their boundary points. It's identified by a marker on the ground where you can place your arms and legs in all four states at one time. It's pretty cool. After leaving Four Corners, I drove through Flagstaff and in no time entered the city limits of Phoenix. Wow! Five days on the road. My new home. I'd stay with my cousin Paula for a month until I got my own place.

Phoenix back in the late eighties was a wonderful place to be. It was still early in its growth, and I was glad to have been a part of that expansion. I relaxed for a few days, but in short order I was at the door steps of both KOY and KOOL FM. I got offers from both companies but decided to go with KOY Radio. I had just turned 28 years old.

KOY/ Y-95 RADIO

KOY is one of the oldest radio stations in the country, hence, only three call letters versus the normal four. Former Arizona Governor and US Senator Barry Goldwater and comedian Steve Allen got their starts at KOY radio. KOY is rich in history.

I felt this job would give me the opportunity to break into outside sales and open up more doors of opportunity in the future. In fact, it would be my first outside sales position since selling boxes of candy door to door raising money for our local little league team back in the late sixties and early seventies.

What a shock outside sales can be. I'd come from JC Penney where customers came to us through our front doors. Now as an account executive at KOY/Y-95, I'd be going out and finding new customers to advertise on our radio station with something called cold calling. And if I didn't cold call and make sales, I didn't eat or pay bills. Instead of being paid a salary, I was now on a draw. A draw is when they pay you up front and at the end of each month they take back that equal amount from your commissions. If you didn't make enough you unfortunately ran a deficit, which is not something you want to do for an extended period of time. At first I wasn't sure if I was cut out for this type of sale, though I was far from giving up. I was the first guy on an all-female sales team. The women were great and very supportive, and they also gave me the nickname, Zipper, because I was the only one on the team who wore pants!

After going through their in-house sales training program, which consisted mostly of Gene Chamberlain tapes, my first day of cold calling was upon me. I was excited, though also a little apprehensive because I'd never had to knock on doors before to make a living. I wasn't too sure about this whole cold calling thing, the name alone made me stiffen up.

My local sales manager, Dick Ionnella, asked me, "Are you ready to go out and drum up some business?"

"Could you give me the lead list to work from?" I asked.

He leaned over and plopped the A–M and N–Z phone books on my desk. I looked up at him and said, "Are you serious?"

Though I had confidence in myself, I'd never played this type of game before, and I wasn't sure the best way to do it. As I thumbed through the yellow pages negative self-talk started to creep into my head. What if I couldn't do this? What if I failed? Would I end up moving back home? I thought about Gramp and what he went through losing his eye and what he would say, "Don't give up!"

With words of encouragement from the sales team, I drove off to find my first cold calling victims. I drove to Tempe to a familiar area, pulled into a strip mall parking lot and mentally got prepared to give this a try. I pull out my client contact cards (no automated contact relationship software back in those days) and decided where I'd go first. As I got ready to get out of my car something dreadful happened. Anxiety began to build inside of me, and I couldn't pull my hands off the steering wheel. I froze. What's going on? I looked at my white knuckles clasping the wheel. I didn't realize I was holding on so tightly. I'd never experienced anything like this before. Go figure. I sat in the car for about 20 minutes shuffling papers and trying to get the negative self-talk out of my head. I looked at my watch and noticed it was time for lunch. Saved by the lunch bell!

After lunch, I took a deep breath, put on my conqueror mindset and walked into about a half dozen businesses. It felt awkward at first. Three of the business the owners weren't there but I did chat with some staff, two were polite and listened for a few minutes, and I gave them some sales collateral, and one guy said, "No," in a loud voice. After these calls I drove around and wrote down other businesses to add to my prospect list. After several hours and about 30 prospects added to my list, I drove back to the radio station and started thumbing through the rest of those phone books.

As I sat at my desk, one of our top account executives, Dixie stopped by and asked how my first day in the field went. I told her I didn't think it went that well. I mentioned this outside radio sales thing might not be for me. She looked at me and smiled. What she said next changed my perception on the world of sales. She asked if I listened to our station and our competitor's. I did. She continued, "So you realize there are businesses out there who have said yes to advertising." I nodded in agreement.

She said, "So you agree there are people who want to advertise and as you experienced today there are people who will say no?" I nodded again.

She then looked at me and said, "So what's your problem? Get out there and find people who want to say yes." I looked at her and it hit me like a ton of bricks. That was it? It's that easy? Why was I making it so hard, why was I placing a roadblock in front of me? Fear. Fear of failure. Negative self-talk! I stopped looking at it as something to fear, but more like a game to a larger commission check. It's a numbers game; the more people you get in front of, the more opportunities will present themselves. What great words of wisdom. From that day on I never looked at cold calling the same way. In fact, I began calling it warm calling. The key is: be prepared, know what your message is, relax, be yourself, and don't take yourself too seriously. Wherever you are Dixie, thanks dear!

Y-95 provided me many great opportunities to learn and grow and so did my confidence. I began seeing how important relationships are in building trust and getting commitment for the sale and then that strong relationship to enable you to up-sell or renew. I realized prospects had to "buy" me before they bought my product or service. I'd also learn not to take the rejection of cold calling or losing a sale personally. Again if you play the numbers, you'll come out on top. My other motivator to succeed: I could never go back home to Massachusetts a failure. Changing careers and moving 2300 miles away from home without a job and away from your family, it's tough in the beginning as you have no support system. I knew I'd have to be the one to motivate the motivator and tap into my positive attitude and perseverance to help navigate around challenging moments and obstacles.

Most of the sales team had national accounts and worked the large ad agencies, giving them a great client base and consistent commission checks. I was still working off my yellow pages and new prospects. But as the months went on, I started picking up steam. One reason was I learned how to utilize and sell spec ads. I'd go into a potential advertiser, make mental notes of key areas of their store. Back at the station our production master extraordinaire, JD, short for Jack Daniels (you know those radio guys) who'd voiceover a 60-second commercial for me. I'd take the tape with my shoulder strapped cassette recorder to that store, find the decision-maker, and play the ad for them. It seemed to work nicely. But I needed to find a niche, an industry or business sector I could go after and become an expert in and hopefully cash in on. Isn't that why people get into sales, to have the ability to give yourself a raise with each new sale? As I drove around metro-Phoenix looking for that golden nugget, I realized my niche was right in front of me; I was living in one: apartments and the property management industry. Phoenix was going through an incredible growth spurt and apartments were being developed all over the Valley of the Sun. You never know when that window of opportunity will present itself.

It was 1987 and I happened to be dating a property manager of an apartment community, so if I was going to become an expert I needed to know the ins and outs of the business. I'd spend hours working with her and her leasing team refining their sales and customer service programs. I watched and learned their business sales model. From these experiences, I built several leasing sales modules and implemented them with her team with great success. Most leasing professionals increased their closing ratios by 35 to 40 percent. With this new found niche, I went to my sales manager and asked to attack this industry head-on. I wanted to create an opportunity for me and the radio station in an area not many of our competitors were capitalizing on.

I got the thumps up and began creating unique "live remote" advertising packages for my property management clients to drive potential renters to their door. The advertising packages included on-air personalities at their apartment community with live call-ins by the radio jock asking listeners to stop by. Also included was our cold-air inflatable Y95 tethered balloon, which was about two stories high and last but not least, our exclusive Pepsi Jam Box. It looked like a 25-foot long boom box on a trailer with a broadcast booth in the middle for our celebrities. My manager, Kevin, began calling me the apartment expert of metro-Phoenix. However, I wasn't going to stop there!

To ensure even greater exposure and added value to our clients, I created the Y-95 Apartment Guide Hotline. Where listeners could call into and get the latest information on apartment communities who were advertising on our station with 15-second teasers. The hotline had a counter that registered each incoming call. We'd promote the Y-95 hotline through on-air promos throughout the day. Within the first month the counter was receiving about 25 calls a week, 100 calls a month. Of course I used these results to add credibility and momentum in my selling efforts. Within a few months the hotline was receiving 50 calls a week, 200 calls a month. The Y-95 Apartment Guide Hotline was a winner! I had found my opportunity to break out and create something permanent and worthwhile.

As we added more apartment communities to the live remote packages, I began tracking their results at the property level on the number of leases the on-air commercials and live-remotes were generating and began asking for the all-important testimonial. One property, Towne Square, received 23 leases from our three-hour remote. Other properties began getting similar results. The live remotes became the talk of the market and started receiving calls from other communities and property management companies wanting in. Word of mouth is a wonderful thing. Even the other salespeople were giving me high fives. It goes to show if you look around at your current situation take off your blinders and take chances, you can change the direction you're headed. With this success, I approached the two big apartment magazines in the area, The Apartment Guide and For Rent Magazine to see if one would like to sponsor my Y-95 hotline. They showed no interest. Bad call on their part.

> You can no longer sit back and dream, the moment has come to paint on a broader canvas and create something permanent and worthwhile. Don't wait for fortune to smile upon you, you owe it yourself to find a new purpose and forget about limitations and restrictions, for the only ones that exist are of your own making. —Unknown

Here are some behind-the-scenes stories from the radio world and its competitiveness. Our station had gone through a major format change almost overnight from an adult contemporary format with music from Neil Diamond, Elvis, Babs, and Patsy Kline to a Top-40 format with music from George Michael, INXS, Michael Jackson, and Madonna. At the time we were the seventh most listened to radio station in the metro-Phoenix market as a combination KOY AM/KOY FM simulcast owned by Edens Broadcasting, based in our Phoenix office. Edens were the originators of the morning "zoo" format (chaotic like a zoo), which was cutting edge at the time. The on-air morning teams were not so much outrageous and over the top like Howard Stern, but they were extremely cleaver, funny, and creative, and okay, a bit wacky. Radio icon Scott Shannon was instrumental in the zoo format, and was a DJ for Edens in the Tampa market. It didn't take long for Y-95 to go head-to-head with the number one hit music radio station in Phoenix, KZZP.

Our station had just hired a new morning guy, Glenn Beck, to team up with our current morning on-air talent Tim Hattrick. Glenn Beck's name may sound familiar as today he has his own successful syndicated conservative talk radio show and has a news program on the FOX News Channel. These morning zoo guys did spoofs and parodies so that it was sometimes hard to tell what was real or made-up.

A provocative promotion was the $10,000 scavenger hunt. Tim and Glenn gave clues to the listeners, who'd race around metro-Phoenix searching for the scavenger items; the first to collect all the items would win $10,000 in cash. One time a controversy arose when they broadcasted the next item to find: the toupee of our then Governor Evan Mecham. After hearing his toupee promoted on our station, his office immediately called our general manager and threatened assault charges against any person who tried to grab the toupee off the Governor's head and possible charges against the radio station. Needless to say that particular item was quickly substituted for another.

But Tim and Glenn's coup de grâce, in my opinion, was broadcasting over several weeks from a secret underground amusement park being constructed somewhere in the desert outside of Phoenix. With the sounds of heavy earth moving equipment and other construction noises in the background, Tim and Glenn did their show live from the theme park. They talked with the architect of the park, with investors, and management team. They described incredible never-before-seen rides and games. They kept saying the owners didn't want to disclose their location until the amusement park was built and ready for the public. Our switchboard lit up like a Christmas tree from TV news stations, even our competitors wanting to know where the park was. But the best part was when city and state officials called demanding to know where it was because no building permits had been taken out for this major project. Any project like this needed state permits and oversight. It sounded so real. They pulled this one off to perfection. There was no secret amusement park at all, it was a spoof! It was a classic, "Gotcha!"

With continued stunts and crazy contests our station gained in popularity and in ratings. Some of us thought we needed to do some self-promoting, even if it meant pushing the envelope a bit. We needed more attention. Unlike a restaurant or most businesses, bad press for a radio station still brought new listeners to our station to see what was going on. In radio, it's about the number of ears that listen to you. So our program manager, the morning guys, some from our promotions and sales department, created the unofficial Y-95 Hit Squad. Our job was to, in a nice way, sabotage our competitor's promotions.

Our first venture was Cinco de Mayo on May fifth. It's a huge holiday and celebration in Phoenix and the Southwest. Every major radio and TV station would team up with a local Mexican restaurant or shopping center and do live remotes from these locations.

Now there was an unwritten rule in the radio biz about respecting each other's live remote events, but that rule was about to be tested by the hit squad. Glenn called me to his office and asked where a competitor, KKFR, was holding their Cinco de Mayo event. They'd fenced off an area at a shopping center near our station. The chain link fences were then wrapped with a green tarp around the perimeter so people couldn't look in; they'd have to come inside to enjoy the festivities. We knew one of the local TV stations would be airing their newscast from inside the event. How could we turn this to our advantage?

Late in the afternoon, Glenn and I headed over to the event to map out our strategy. Before going inside, I rolled up ten-foot plastic banner with our station's colorful Y-95 logo and slid it inside my pant leg. I looked a bit funny walking in with a pronounced limp. We walked around figuring out how to pull off our prank. While we were inside, another group from our hit squad placed Y-95 banners on the outside perimeter of the fence. People driving or walking by thought it was our promotion, not KKFR.

Our plan was to unroll our banner live on TV. We got into position, the news anchors getting their last minute touch ups before going live. We waited for the red light on the television camera to go on. Glenn and I walked behind the broadcast platform as the anchors were welcoming their viewers to Cinco de Mayo. Before anyone could react, I pulled the banner out from my pant leg, and we unfurled our Y-95 banner in bright yellow and red for all their viewers to see. Wow, nothing better than free advertising. The female anchor turned around and with anger in her eyes, scolded us and told us to leave. We nonchalantly rolled the banner up and where escorted out by the security personnel. But we achieved our goal and gave our station some free publicity. As we walked out, Glenn and I slapped a high five with big grins and drove off. Mission accomplished. Later that night when I got home, I had several messages on my answering machine from friends saying they saw me on television with our banner.

Another hit squad event targeted our top competitor, KZZP. All month they were promoting musician Richard Marx for an outdoor concert. Tim and others went to the concert venue. Tim's plan was to sneak over to the sound board guy (who I think he knew) and offer him $500 if, when KZZP's morning team of Bruce Kelly and Maggie Brock came on stage to introduce Marx, the sound guy would kill their mics and give Tim a live one. As Bruce and Maggie made their way to the stage, the crowd started cheering, and as they started to speak into their mics, nothing happened, and then from out of nowhere, blasting over the sound system was Tim's voice saying, "Hi, this is Tim Hattrick from the Y-95 Morning Zoo and from the only station bad enough to pull it off. Y-95 presents Richard Marx!"

The crowd went nuts. Bruce, Maggie, and the rest of KZZP's team were stunned, looking around in astonishment. How could this happen? They spotted Tim and his team and chased them from the concert venue. But the damage was done. Back at the station as Tim retold the story we were all on the floor laughing. As you can imagine KZZP was pissed! Their general manager called ours and protested the incident. Though reprimanded, we were not asked to dissolve the hit squad.

Unfortunately the last straw that shut down our operation occurred when the general manager of KZZP was getting married at a local church. While everyone was inside for the ceremony our squad hit the parking lot and put Y-95 bumper stickers on most cars. Even I'd have to admit, that was a bit over the top. Our general manager received a furious call from the GM, who was far from amused. That was the end of the Y-95 Hit Squad. But boy was it fun pushing that envelope.

Our biggest splash at our station, which got us the most press, was hiring the former mistress of Reverend Jim Baker and Playboy centerfold, Jessica Hahn. For those who care, Jessica had an affair with the Reverend who was married to Tammy Baker. Jessica was on two different Playboy covers, one her pre-cosmetic surgery photo shoot and the other was after her cosmetic surgery. So why did we hire Jessica? Mainly for shock value and controversy. Just like the hit squad all that mattered was creating news and getting people to turn to our station from a curiosity standpoint, whether it was positive or negative news, just as long as they listened longer. Jess came on as a small addition to the morning team with Tim and Glenn. They nicknamed her the weather bunny because at first that's all the powers that be allowed her to do. But her name definitely brought attention and controversy. We even had some long-time advertisers pull their ads from the station after hiring her. Those advertisers eventually came back after our ratings soared along with their new higher advertising rates. Let's face it, she was a celebrity, and people wanted to hear and see her.

Since she was famous, I used her on my live remotes. We packed our clients' businesses with listeners, celebrity gazers, and people who spent money. People lined up to have her sign their Playboy magazines as well as an autographed promotional photo of her. My dad was so excited when I had her sign one for him from his "Wild Thing," Jessica.

I also hung out and partied with Weird Al Yankovic after a station promotion. Let's say he's a unique individual. I sat and had a great conversation with Donny Osmond during our Y-95 Fourth of July celebration at city hall in Phoenix. I shared some warm laughs and childhood memories with Spanky McFarland who played Spanky in the old series *Spanky and Our Gang*. Actor Leslie Nielsen; Donna Rice of Gary Hart and Monkey-Business-boat fame; the late musician Robert Palmer; Phoenix Suns star Kevin Johnson, who at the time of this book is mayor of Sacramento, CA; and football greats Bart Starr and Lyle Alzzado were others I met. The most important thing I learned from mingling with these celebrities was like me, they put their pants on one leg at a time, and they were really no different, though their pants were probably a lot more expensive than mine.

The most pivotal event during my tenure at Y-95 was a happenstance encounter with my next mentor. Our station was part of a bachelor, bachelorette auction fund raiser for multiple sclerosis at an area hotel. At first when asked I declined. It felt weird putting myself out there like that and have women bid on you. Though after some coaxing, I agreed to do it.

As I entered the hotel for the event, I noticed several clusters of men standing around chatting in the ballroom. I introduced myself to several groups, but the conversations were pretty lame and boring. As I moved to another group, I noticed a guy on the other side of the ballroom doing the same. I watched him walk up to a group, stay for a few minutes and then move on. I had to go over to say hi and share my observations. I walked over to him and he introduced himself as Tony Ashe. He said he was from outside of Baltimore, Maryland and was founder of a company called Family Find. They advertised a year-at-a-glance calendar that his teams sold ad space around the border of the calendar to local businesses. His company name rang a bell. When I inquired, he told me he advertised on my radio station. We had a lot in common coming from Italian families and became instant friends. It was as if our chance meeting was supposed to happen. I truly felt we were kindred spirits, and I was being directed to events in my life once again, and I was along for the ride.

Tony would take me under his wing and share his many golden nuggets and lessons about sales and life in general. We'd spend hours talking business, sales, life, and of course, women. What a great combination. I was 29 years old and found his friendship and guidance invaluable, considering my immediate family was on the other side of the country. We became best of friends and remain so today.

HPC Apartment Guide

Destiny calls again. I signed up for a booth at the Arizona Multi-Housing Association's trade show when I was with Y95. The event showcased various multi-housing vendors who sold products and services to the apartment industry. I had my booth with photos from my live property remotes, enlarged photos of our station's cold- and hot-air balloons, along with a half dozen testimonials from my property management clients, all hanging from my booth. I even had my sales manager, Kevin Malone, so excited he came out to work the booth with me.

The response from clients who stopped by was overwhelming. Kevin mused, "I guess you do work for a living." Others came by and signed-up on the spot for a live remote as word of mouth spread. This put a smile on both our faces. A good sales philosophy, "The more you hustle, the more opportunity and commissions one can put in your pockets." Kevin called me the apartment expert. A famous quote came to mind:

> Good things come to those who wait, but only the things left by those who hustle.
> —Abraham Lincoln

While at the trade show, a gentleman from the Phoenix Apartment Guide came over from his booth and introduced himself as Gary Austin. He was a dynamic individual, full of enthusiasm with a commanding presence. As we spoke, we seemed to have a lot in common and I felt drawn to him. He asked me if I'd like to have breakfast some morning, and I accepted; never turn down an opportunity to see what life has in-store for you.

Our breakfast was at Macayo's Mexican Restaurant on Central Avenue in downtown Phoenix. He was sent by his company to turn the Phoenix market around because of prior mismanagement and lackluster sales. He was looking for people like me. I told him I'd think about it, but as I left I had a strange feeling come over me, maybe not so much a feeling as an intuition. I felt, like I had with Tony, this meeting with Gary was supposed to happen; it was part of my plan, God's plan. I knew he would take me to the next level of my learning and earning curve. About two weeks after that breakfast, in September of 1989, I left Y-95 and was hired as an account executive with HPC Apartment Guides. Another chapter in my life was about to be penned!

> There are three types of people when it comes to opportunity: those who see the window of opportunity and jump through it, those who see the window and hesitate and then those who unfortunately never see the window.
>
> —Andrew Botieri

At Y-95 I learned the basics of outside sales and overcoming the anxiety of cold calling with the limited training I received. The Apartment Guide would give me tools and opportunity to tap into talents I didn't realize I possessed. Though I've always considered myself an outgoing, optimistic guy, with Gary's tutelage my confidence grew at an incredible pace. Confidence is such a key ingredient in the success of anyone's life and their life's achievements. Confidence is also the key to sales. I was coming into my own, working hard on refining my professional abilities and my selling skills. I shadowed Gary on sales calls and presentations. While he presented I watched, learned and absorbed. Selling in real time you pick up so much more than from role playing or a training audio. In contrast, Gary showed how to deliver the presentation, and then he'd "curbside" coach you.

> True leaders share by example; bad leaders lead by position. It's that simple.
>
> —Andrew Botieri

This style built instant confidence. It was a stark difference from the radio station; where you practice more baptism by fire than anything else. This technique of shadowing I'd use in my training from here on out.

I also found this type of advertising sale much easier than radio. Now I had a tangible product (magazine) to show a prospect versus marketing slicks and a spec ad from the radio station. Though if you can sell radio advertising, you can sell anything. I had an incredible passion for what I was now doing; I loved it! I was reminded of my life's dream: to work at something I love and get paid for doing it!

I loved this job, just like JC Penney and Y-95. I realized I'd been very blessed up to this point with every job I pursued. I was also blessed to have met two incredible mentors in Phoenix.

> *When you love what you do for work, it ceases to be work.*
> —Andrew Botieri

What about you? Do you have a mentor? What lessons and guidance do you remember receiving? Are these lessons still part of your foundation? Or have you been a mentor to someone? Are you still doing it? How does it make you feel? Is there someone out there you know looking for a mentor, looking for guidance? Can that "life changer" be you?

Many books I've read over the years I've noticed great leaders like Jesus Christ, Abraham Lincoln, John F. Kennedy, General George Patton, and Ronald Regan have had the ability to inspire, motivate, and create a belief in those they serve. I've always looked for these traits in my leaders. Gary and Tony were those types of leaders, though Tony would take me to a higher level, based more on humility, integrity, and compassion. This style of leadership and coaching hit home for me, and I soon embraced it. Tony and I were roommates for about a year now, but I yearned to work with him. I knew he'd make me more successful. Don't get me wrong I loved what I was doing, but I was getting antsy. So one day, I asked Tony if I could come work for him. He looked at me with a wry smile, said he appreciated my interest. What he said next took the wind out of my sail. "You're not ready yet. When you are, I'll let you know." I stepped back on my heels and was a bit disappointed. These words would prove to be prophetic.

In the first six weeks with the Apartment Guide, I sold 26 pages and two front covers, which at the time I was told, was a company record and garnished me recognition at the home office and by my teammates. Things were going incredibly well, and my regional director, Barbara Lewis, began considering me for a promotion to publisher in one of her markets.

It was now January 1990, and I was so happy, kicking butt in my sales career and meeting new friends. I loved the Guide and believed 100 percent in the product, my team, and the company. Barbara Lewis reminded me there were some markets that would be opening up soon and would be considering me. Yes!

Delving into the Psychic

During this time period, I was delving into my spiritual side. The deserts of Arizona seem to take you there. An encounter with a woman named Gertie Miles would change my beliefs about the power of the spiritual world. I was introduced to Gertie, a Phoenix area psychic, by Tony, who had gone to her for readings. Gertie was an interesting lady. She was full of life and love for everyone she touched. I'd never been to a psychic before, but I'm always up for trying something new and tried to keep an open mind about meeting her. We met and before she started to "read me" she asked if I had something on me from a deceased relative, like a chain or piece of jewelry, to help her connect with the "other side." I handed her my black onyx ring which belonged to my grandfather. It was given to me by my father after Gramp passed away. We held hands and she said a prayer to the Lord for giving her these wonderful powers and gifts. As she held the ring, she gave me some insight into some of my family who had passed before me. She hit on a few things about my life and even gave me the first initial of the girl of my dreams. (After subsequent readings Gertie decided to stick to reading my business future and past family members and stay away from my personal love life as that seemed to be a hard target for her to hit. Tell me about it!)

What she said next blew me away. "You will leave the Apartment Guide very shortly, though you will stay in the publishing field."

"That couldn't be," I told her. "I love working for the Guide."

She smiled and kept on reading me, "You'll get into a publishing venture," and she began describing what the front cover of this publication would look like. I sat there with total skepticism now. She said she saw the colors red, yellow, and orange splashed across the top of a newspaper or magazine and mountains or a cityscape in the background. I was amazed. That was very detailed information. I still had no idea what she was describing, nothing came to mind.

Before finishing, she reiterated, "You will leave the Apartment Guide to work for a man from the East Coast by the name of Charles."

Charles...Charles? I didn't know anyone named Charles. All this made no sense to me. The reading was interesting, and I thanked her. At least I went from skeptic to partially believing in the spiritual realm and psychics. I walked out saying to myself, "I can't be leaving the Apartment Guide, I'm having too much fun and besides, I love what I am doing."

I put Gertie's session in the back of my mind and didn't think much more of it. Until about a month later when Tony informed me he was closing down his Family Find operation and moving back to Maryland. He accomplished what he needed to do and wanted to be close to his son. The news was bittersweet. On the one hand, my best friend and roommate was moving away, but on the other hand he was going home to his family. How could you not want that for someone, though it made me feel a little homesick for my family and friends.

He said, "I'll be coming back every now and then as I am considering a venture with my business associate John," whom I'd met before. I was sad to see my friend go. When you move that far away from home, the friends you make are important to help fill the void. Not only was I losing a best friend, I was also losing a wonderful mentor.

Blueprint Unfolds

So life moves on. Things at the Apartment Guide were still cranking and Barbara and Gary mentioned Seattle as a potential market for me. Then in April, I received a call from Tony who was traveling back to Scottsdale for a business meeting with John and asked if I'd join them for dinner. "Of course!"

We met for dinner at a great Italian restaurant in the Borgata shopping area in Scottsdale. After catching up, Tony proceeded to tell me about a venture he and John were starting. It would be taking Tony's Family Find concept but instead of it being a year-at-a-glance calendar format they wanted to put it into a monthly four-color newspaper that would have a community newspaper feel to it. The information in it would range from highlighting local students, promoting the arts, community articles of interest, someone's favorite recipe, games, and coloring contests for kids. And in the middle of the paper would be a month-at-a-glance calendar highlighting events going on in and around the city from sporting to cultural events. Within the newspaper would be display adverting space for local businesses that provided a service or product. The sales hook was each advertiser would be exclusive by business category, just like the Family Find program. The paper would be mailed directly into people's homes, not tossed on the front lawn like some newspapers. John owned a printing and mailing company and that was his part of the business deal along with financial backing.

It sounded like a great idea, but how did it involve me? Tony looked at me across the table and said "Hey Drew, remember when you wanted to come work for me and I said you weren't ready?

"Yes," I said and recounted how that, "Pissed me off a bit you didn't want me."

Tony smiled and said, "Drew, you're ready now! I want you and me to run the sales organization. I've watched you over the last few years and think you're ready to move up and be my general sales manager." I didn't know what to think. I was a little taken aback. I was extremely happy at the Apartment Guide and my career was moving forward at a great pace. Out of curiosity I asked what the newspaper was going to look like. He pulled out a mock-up of the paper in question and laid it on the table.

The heading at the top of the newspaper read *The Arizona Extra* and in the background set behind the heading was a mountain range and palm trees with the skyline of Phoenix. What caught my eye and attention was the sun setting over the mountains and cityscape throwing colors of red, orange, and yellow across the top of the page. My mind immediately flashed back to what Gertie had revealed to me during my reading, "You will work for a publication that has red, orange, and yellow splashed across its front page." I looked at the mock-up and said aloud, "Oh my God, Gertie was right." I told them of my reading with Gertie months ago. They both looked surprised.

"Gertie called this!" I shouted at the table. However, I told them I was happy at the Guide as I was in line for a promotion. Then I said, "The only thing that doesn't make sense is Gertie told me I'd work with a guy from the East Coast by the name of Charles."

At that moment Tony's head shot up from the table and said "Drew, my middle name is Charles." I felt dizzy, I felt like I was in an episode of the "Twilight Zone." This had to be destiny. Everything unfolding before my eyes was meant to happen. But I felt a little scared, a little nervous; it was all unfolding so quickly.

The three of us sat at the table dumbfounded by the accuracy of Gertie's predictions. I looked at Tony and said, "So you want me to be your general sales manager for this newspaper?"

"Yes," the answer came.

My next question was, "When do you want me to start?"

"This coming week," he said.

"What? I have to at least give the Apartment Guide two weeks' notice."

But they were adamant. For them to hit their early sales targets they needed me to be on board this week to help hire and train a new sales force. Though I should've pushed for the two weeks there were too many strong coincidences for this decision to be wrong. I know most decisions in life shouldn't be based on what a psychic says, but this was too strong a connection. And the main factor was what I felt inside. It felt right. My head was still spinning. I was at a cross roads in my life, and I wasn't 100 percent sure. I asked if I could give him an answer tomorrow on Sunday. I had a lot to think about.

I left the restaurant and got home around midnight. I needed to walk around. Things were moving too quickly, and I had a major life decision to make. I was living in Scottsdale at an apartment community that sat on an executive par-three golf course at Indian School and 78th Street. As I walked the cart paths surrounding the course, a full moon shined over my shoulders. My mind was racing, taking in everything Tony rolled out to me; what Gertie had said three months earlier, and still I wasn't sure what direction to go in. I prayed for guidance, direction, and strength. I asked God for a sign. For two hours I contemplated my future as I walked the golf course. I thought of all the moves I'd made to get where I am. I knew part of my success so far in life had come from my belief in God, belief in me, a positive mental attitude, and perseverance. Why was this decision so hard? I knew I loved working for the Guide. I was part of a great team and felt I'd be letting the team down. But on the other hand I knew I'd always wanted to work for Tony. I felt confident he'd make me more successful, and it felt as if it was supposed to be, that it was part of my blueprint in life.

As I walked, I looked up ahead on the walkway and saw my shadow expanding out ahead of me, growing larger and larger as the moon illuminated over my shoulders. At one point my shadow stretched out about 30 feet in front of me as if telling me it was time to grow. This was my sign. I called Tony the next morning and said, "I'm on board."

Sunday night I made a very uncomfortable call to Gary, my publisher and mentor at the Phoenix Apartment Guide. As you can imagine, he was not happy at all. But I knew I was making the right decision. Even today I know it was the right decision.

The Arizona Extra

I was 31 years old and general sales manager for the Arizona Extra. It was all new and exciting. I'd managed people back in my retail days at JC Penny, but this was different, this was now managing an outside sales team. I found this ability to inspire my team with energy and purpose, to groom and grow them for success. I've always said that outside salespeople are a different breed of animal, a little off center. Let's be honest. Outside salespeople have to thrive on rejection, how wacky is that? I was again reminded how important a positive, can-do attitude is to success. Without that PMA (positive mental attitude) one goes into battle each day with one hand tied behind the back and risks failure or mediocrity.

Our young team worked hard along with the rest of the management team. I began to understand the power of building and growing a sales team with compassionate coaching sprinkled with tough love when appropriate. I got a rush helping people succeed and watching them grow. I now knew what my purpose was at this time in my life.

Though we had a good thing going, our four-color newspaper lasted just under one year. I think our biggest miscalculation was opening the paper in the heat of late spring, early summer in Phoenix and not waiting until the cooler weather of the fall and winter season. Oh well, chalk it up to experience, and what a great experience it was. We were all disappointed. We had put our heart and soul into this venture, and we walked away with a sense of accomplishment knowing we were providing the areas of Tempe and Scottsdale a unique look at the community around them. And the feedback was great from the consumer. Who knows, maybe that newspaper may resurface again sometime?

So after we closed our doors, I was sitting at my dining room table three days later having a cup of coffee and contemplating what I was going to do next. With a growth in confidence and faith in God, I didn't seem too panicked about my future. I knew something would come along. I wasn't in a hurry and wasn't going to jump on any job. Like in the past, I wanted a job I'd love, that I could wrap my arms around and embrace with great enthusiasm, much like my last four jobs. As I was sipping my coffee the phone rang. (Insert *Twilight Zone* music here.) It was a call that once again changed the direction of my life.

On the other end was my former Regional Director from the Apartment Guide, Barbara Lewis. She said she had heard the Arizona Extra had shut down and was wondering what I was going to do. I thought jokingly, she had a spy somewhere around Phoenix. Barbara was an incredible boss, she was tough, she was fair, and she was compassionate, a great combination for a leader.

As we continued talking, Barbara said her district director, Ernest Oriente, needed help turning around their Southern California markets. I'd met Ernest at HPC's Annual Sales Meeting in 1990 when

Ernest coveted the famed Publisher of the Year trophy for the *Orange County Apartment Guide* and our Phoenix team won Sales Team of the Year. We were all so proud of our accomplishments.

Barbara mentioned the Inland Empire market in San Bernardino County, California for me. In a serious tone she indicated because of the abrupt way I'd left the Guide in Phoenix, I would have to meet with Ernest to mend the trust issue corporate felt I injured, and they had a point. But I hadn't left because I was unhappy or didn't love what I was doing; I left because it was my destiny. I told Barbara I'd be very interested in the opportunity and in meeting Ernest. But before we'd meet I told her I was going to take a two-month sabbatical and drive cross-country to spend time with my family back in Massachusetts.

Déjà Vu: Back to the Apartment Guide

After returning from visiting my family, I flew out to Southern California to meet with Ernest. We hit it off great since we sort of knew each other from the sales meeting. While traveling to both the Inland Empire and his Orange County market we had our heart-to-heart talk. I knew he was aware of my quick departure from the Phoenix market and told me the company wasn't sure if they could trust me again. I told him I could understand. I spoke with conviction and passion about the Apartment Guide, the product, the people, and how I could help him turnaround the Inland Empire market. He said, "I'm looking for commitment, integrity, and loyalty from you." He got all three and a lot more.

There was something about Ernest that grabbed my attention immediately. It was his intensity, his passion, and his love of life that infected me. My intuition, like before, was telling me this was going to be a move that would be perfect for me. My blue-print was unfolding once again before my eyes, and it was happening as though I was on the sideline cheering myself on. In October of 1990, I was hired as an account executive with HPC Apartment Guides in the Inland Empire. It seemed my guardian angel and good timing were on my side again. It would be in Southern California I'd meet my next mentor and friend, Ernest Oriente.

With my previous experience with the Apartment Guide, I hit the ground running with the help of my publisher, George Miscevich and a great support team. We faced many challenges but we were up for the challenge. We had two major competitors, *For Rent* magazine and the *Rental Guide* but our focus was on our national competitor, *For Rent*. We knew we needed to do more and work harder than they were willing to do. The tools we used in Phoenix would help turn Inland Empire around, or as we began calling it "Hub of the Universe."

After a couple of weeks in the market, I began conducting free leasing seminars for our clients and prospects, as I had done in Phoenix. Our mission was to provide them with concrete tools to make their jobs easier. These seminars covered the importance of attitude, successful telephone techniques, overcoming objections and closing the lease.

Since we were a free publication, we needed to validate our existence every 30-days, so we also began teaching and implementing tracking tools so our clients could see how much traffic and leases we and our competition were providing each property monthly. Though tracking of traffic had been around HPC for a few years, in Southern California we took it to a new level. Getting concrete results for our clients was what it was all about. If we could prove we worked, we could sell and renew more business regardless of even rate increases. The way I look at it, if you are able to increase the learning curve of the people you do business with each day, you both win!

All of this helped increase our exposure in the marketplace and provided us a competitive advantage. Our clients and prospects began to notice. I began working with Ernest to conduct free seminars in his other markets.

I have to share a story. I had been aggressively working my new territory. My territory and that of another account executive (AE) was divided by a street. I worked the west side, he the east side. I noticed for several months there was a property on his side of the street that continued to advertise in *For Rent* magazine even to the point of having a banner hanging out front that read, "As Seen In For Rent." Every time I'd see that banner it pissed me off. I finally got tired of seeing it, went across the street and asked the manager if our rep had ever contacted her about advertising? She said, "No." I even mentioned his name, and it didn't ring a bell. I shared how I could get her to advertising in both books without spending any more money. She was interested. So I got her to downsize her For Rent ad, add the *Apartment Guide* and saved her about 70 dollars a month. A big win for both of us.

During a sales meeting I put the ad up on the whiteboard. The AE whose territory I sold into jumped up and complained that was in his territory, so it was his sale and commission. I rebuked him by saying the manager never heard of him, which meant, he'd never even been to the property. George, our publisher, took the two of us into his office behind closed doors to try and find a solution. I was adamant; I worked the sale so it was mine. George read our territory rules, and it stated if you sell into someone else's territory, it is their sale and commission. I was pissed. I did all the work on an account that was all but forgotten. I felt like I got screwed. I asked George if that was his final answer.

He said, "AB, that's what the rules say."

I jumped up from my chair pointed at George from across his desk and said, "Don't ever pull the reins in on your strongest horse," and I walked out, grabbed my brief case and left. About halfway home after calming down, I called George and apologized for the way I acted. To this day; we get a laugh out of that outburst. I can be very competitive, don't you think?

However, we still needed to grow our Guide quicker, and we needed to get the attention of the decision makers. When your clients and prospects get to know you as a person and not as a salesperson, then you earn their trust and business. I went to Ernest with an idea. If we could bring decision makers to a location for two-hours, have lunch brought in, and bring in apartment industry speakers to share their expertise, we could start building relationships with decision makers as well as their on-site managers. Ernest loved the idea and the Inland Empire's Management Company Roundtable was born. This program, along with our incredibly dedicated team and a world-class servicing program were the ingredients to one of the best comeback stories in HPC history.

As we continued to build our Guide in the streets of San Bernardino County and take away market share from our competitors, something else was beginning to happen. As a team we were creating magic. Some may call it synergy. To me, it felt as if this was supposed to roll out this way, as if it were part of a larger plan for all of us. It seemed everything we touched turned to gold. It was as if at this moment, our lives were supposed to be at this place in time. We were all experiencing an incredible journey.

I quickly rose through the ranks as an account executive, to associate publisher, and publisher in the Inland Empire. In fact, the HPC publisher path was structured as a 12- to 18-month publisher in training process. On my professional goal sheet, I'd penned I wanted to earn the publisher's position in six months. The powers that be informed me that was a very aggressive goal. I agreed, but told them I was still going to hit it anyway.

My publisher, George, was promoted to our San Diego market where he continued the magic. George, who was still overseeing my market, called me one night while he and the others publishers were at a publishers retreat to tell me our Inland Empire market had just won Sales Team of the Year for 1991. I was so ecstatic; all our hard work had paid off. What was also cool was in 1990 as part of the Phoenix Team, we won the Sales Team of the Year. Not bad, back-to-back wins! In about six months I was promoted publisher of the Inland Empire and with the help of a great team we turned the market around with triple-digit sales gains.

Shortly thereafter, I received a paperback book from my regional director, Barbara, published in 1948 called, *The Magic Of Believing* by Claude Bristol. Throughout the book, the author talks about how each of us has the power within through our ability to believe in something to make it happen. In his book, Claude talks about how belief is the moving and motivating force that enables us to achieve our desired goals. This book placed me in a frame of mind of wanting and having success around me because I believed it. I had faith in myself, my God, and the people I surrounded myself with. After reading and rereading this book, my life professionally and personally took off. I ask you to look for this book and may it be a guiding light for you as it has been for me. Written inside my edition is a note from Barbara. I'm sure she wouldn't mind if I shared.

> Andrew,
>
> The Power of Believing can make all your dreams come true. There's no doubt you are a believer, a person who makes things happen for not only yourself but for those around you. Congratulations on your promotion. Barbara Lewis, 9-13-91

I was jazzed to be publisher and thought life was going great. Then one day Ernest and George called me to follow up on the market. They asked how things were going, and I said, "Great!"

They voiced concern because some of my team had told them I was managing them too aggressively. As Ernest put it jokingly, "AB you're a wild man!"

As they debrief me I realized they were right. I was expecting my team to run as fast as I was; to be as successful as I was. I was a bit of a taskmaster, which, I learned from Dad. I realized I wasn't grooming them for success but rather creating a barrier between me and my team, limiting their growth. This call was the aha moment that changed the way I managed my sales team. That day I stopped being a manager and became a coach and teacher, and that's how I would lead teams from then on. As we finished our call Ernest gave me some things to ponder, and ponder I did:

1. The difference between a manager and a coach is a manger says, "Do it or you're fired." A coach says, "Let me share with you how to do it better."

2. Practice grace under pressure. Never let your team see you get frustrated or angry.

3. A leader's main job is to groom and grow their people.

4. Not everyone runs at the same speed.

5. You're always on video with your team. What are you saying and what are they capturing?

The next day I'd sit with my team and apologize for the way I'd been handling them. It would be different from now on, that as a team we were going to win and win big, and we did. In 1992, I was awarded the coveted Rookie Publisher of the Year award. When my named was announced at our national meeting, I was shocked. I stood up as the whole company applauded and turned and hugged my good friend Robert Hammond and started to cry on his shoulder. I was overwhelmed. When I accepted the trophy I called my whole team up on stage with me to accept the award. It was only fitting.

Because of our success and accomplishments we were able to turn around the Inland Empire market. I was then asked to take over for Ernest as publisher of the LA/San Fernando Apartment Guide. I was extremely flattered but didn't have my heart into it. I was having a blast where I was, but protocol dictated I at least speak with my regional director.

So I drove up to our San Fernando Valley office to meet with her. I've always been a big fan of Barbara's. As she was discussing the opportunity and what it meant for me, I kept thinking about the long commute. It would be about a three-hour round-trip commute each day...ugh. I was comfortable in The Empire, as we called it, and was having too much fun with my team. As we were closing out our interview, she offered me the job. Now what? I didn't want it. I thanked her for her confidence in me, however, then explained how I loved where I was and didn't want to leave. So I respectfully said no. I remember the look on her face. She wasn't expecting that. I'd just purchased a condo in Upland and was having fun turning it into a home and didn't want to leave. I apologized, got up and left.

I hadn't driven five minutes from the office when my cell phone rang. It was Ernest. He said with shock in his voice, "Do you know you just said no to Barbara?"

"Yes," I said.

He said, "AB, not many people say no to Barbara."

I chuckled, "Oops, I guess I'm one." Ernest reminded me of what a great job I was doing and what a great opportunity this was for me, and I was the only guy he knew who could replace him as the publisher of the LA market. He also reminded me about the commitment I made to him and Barbara when they hired me back. So after some serious contemplating, I called Barbara back, and in February 1993, I took over the LA, San Fernando Valley Apartment Guide. I must say it was an incredible experience; however, a short-lived one brought on by an incredible and horrific tragedy.

They say in business and in life that adversity is an on-going event; it all depends on what weight you give each challenge. I guess it's all in how you deal with these events that separates successful from the not so successful people. My day of adversity arrived on the morning of January 17, 1994 at 4:31 a.m., the day the Northridge earthquake devastated the San Fernando Valley in Southern California.

After the dust settled from the earthquake, the authorities informed us our office had sustained major earthquake damage, and we wouldn't be able to move back for about six months. This happened during the production of our March 1994 guide. My team and I felt like orphans not being able to work out of our office, you know, where phones, computers, fax machines, and supplies were. We couldn't stop working or put our monthly issue on hold. So without our office for the next six months, I had to create a plan for our team to stay together in some fashion. It was crazy, and the stress level was off the charts.

However I found myself operating more effectively in my controlled chaos mind-set, which this definitely was. So we'd meet in a restaurant down the street from our damaged office to conduct sales meetings and laid out our week's strategies over breakfast on Monday mornings. We'd then meet back at the restaurant at the end of the day or the next morning. It was important to look them in the eye each day, as I knew this horrific event could take its toll on them and their psyche. I was feeling overwhelmed myself from all that had transpired over the past 48 to 60 hours.

After the initial earthquake, each day another three to five aftershocks rumbled and shook the ground sending fear through everyone. Was the next big one going to hit again? No one knew. It was a lot to deal with, but I didn't have time for that. I had to put it out of my mind and focus at the tasks at hand. Keeping the team together, selling, renewing, and keeping the production of the guide on schedule were my main concerns. And this was just our business, what about all the other businesses affected by the earthquake in the area?

Sadly we lost a few clients out of our book after the earthquake due to property damage. For one client, Northridge Meadows, we pulled their ad out at production, out of respect for the 17 people who died. The apartment building collapsed onto the underneath parking garage, crushing to death those who were sleeping on the first two floors of the building. It was devastating. I visited Northridge Meadows just two weeks earlier to get new photos approved for their ad.

Over the next few months a few more apartment communities dropped out due to the damage they sustained from the quake. Many came back months later after repairs were completed. It was a challenging time for everyone in the area. The senseless deaths, the total destruction of property, the chaos that surrounded the San Fernando Valley was so surreal. Though tragedy hit many people, the police, fire departments, rescue workers, local governments, and hundreds of volunteers sprang into action and made such a difference in helping people deal with the devastation.

Within the next 30 days we found a surrogate office in Burbank just down the street from Walt Disney's corporate office. Each day was downright crazy. We didn't have the luxury of any distractions, we had to keep focused, because if we didn't, I felt the emotions and devastation of the earthquake could hit my team and all could come tumbling down, including myself. Again, attitude and perseverance were the weapons we possessed to get through this ordeal!

> "Adversity is God's Way of Helping Build Ones Character."
>
> —Andrew Botieri

After I secured the new office and had the operation back up and running, I informed Ernest and my corporate office I wanted out of Southern California. I needed a break, a long break. I'd stabilized the market with the great effort of my team and the other Southern California markets who chipped in to help. I felt uneasy about earthquakes after this ordeal, mainly because you have no control over your destiny. I'd been through hurricanes, intense thunder and lightning storms, and New England's famous Blizzard of '78, all allowing some days, or at least hours, to prepare and react. An earthquake gives you no advanced notice. I don't like those rules. The whole earthquake event affected me and still does to this day. I was very proud of that LA/San Fernando team for getting through the whole crazy ordeal with only minor challenges. They went above and beyond to serve our clients and keeping their own sanity after the devastating aftermath. When adversity hits, you find out what you're truly made of, and you latch on to anything that might help pull you through your ordeal. For me it was faith in my God, faith in myself, not giving up, and the support of my team and corporate office. At the end of it all 57 people died in the Northridge earthquake on January 17, 1994. God Bless their souls.

While in Southern Cal I had many wonderful experiences and made many friends. Though, I also experienced the darker side of humanity. It was as if Armageddon was starting to erupt right underneath my feet. I was there during the Rodney King beating and the subsequent trial of the accused police officers who were eventually acquitted; which then brought about the devastating LA riots of 1992. I could smell the smoke at my house 40 miles away caused by the fires of the rioters. Both fires and emotions being ignited during that regretful time.

I'll never forget as I watched in horror the live pictures of Reginald Denny being pulled out of his truck cab and beaten to a pulp with bricks and rocks for no other reason than he was white. I was there for the whole OJ Simpson farce, the white Bronco ride (which interrupted my NBA playoff game), his murder trial and subsequent acquittal.

Another time, Julie and I were on the ready to evacuate the Woodland Hills area during the massive fires of Malibu in 1993. At night from our outside deck we could see the orange sky from the fires which were just below the tree-lined ridge coming up from the Malibu Canyon. These were the ones that made national news. I kept saying to myself what was going to happen next?

Two years later, the Northridge earthquake hit. I had enough; I was ready to get out of town. It was time for a new chapter; it was time to be on terra firma! Shortly after my request, I was promoted to district director for HPC and would be based out of Philadelphia. I was heading back east and a little closer to my family.

Looking back, the teams in Southern California were like no other sales teams or business experience I've ever been part of. They say life and events are all about timing, and I couldn't agree more. We were a group of high-energy people, with the same goals, from different walks of life, brought together by strong leadership, and when it was all said and done, we reinvented the way to sell and renew business in the multi-housing industry. I have no doubt that destiny put us all together in Southern California for a moment in time to see what would transpire. And in that moment, we created some incredible magic, and in doing so, became the driving force in those markets and eventually across the country.

Though it wasn't all about magic; what enabled the magic to be created, in my opinion, was implementing a proven system, the system that I helped develop, of sales and sales management techniques, which was an accumulation of the best of the best. But most important of all, we built accountability into the sales organization from top to bottom. No one could hide; everyone had to participate in the success of their market or be exposed. Today when consulting or coaching with clients, one of the first things I do is implement the system into their organization because it works. It has a proven track record, and the system can be replicated anywhere, with any company, with the right team.

In September of 1994, I was Philadelphia bound. I now had a chance to implement the system once again. One chapter in my book of life was ending, and a new chapter was about to be penned.

The City of Brotherly Love

I knew Philly was going to be a challenging market from the reports I received from my direct report Ray Tilson and COO Gary Austin, my former publisher in Phoenix. I knew I'd have to hit the ground running and put some long hours in to turn this market around. Failure was not an option.

Before I flew out to Philly, I spoke with the market manager to see when the salespeople got together for their Monday morning meeting. She hesitated and stated, "They usually waltz in around 9:00 or 9:30." I was taken back as her response gave me a good indication why the market was hemorrhaging revenue. It told me the team wasn't highly motivated and had no structure. It seemed as if they felt like members of a country club. I knew from past experiences I could turn them around and have fun while doing it. All they needed was a coach, some structure, and accountability.

I instructed her to let the sales team know we'd have a sales meeting that following Monday promptly at 8:00 a.m.; unless of course they had a note from their doctor. I could already hear their grumbling from Southern Cal. My question is: how can a team be successful if they get into the office at nine to nine-thirty in the morning, grab their coffee, chat with everyone, and next thing you know it's close to eleven, and most of their morning is gone? As the old saying goes, "The early bird gets the worm!"

Our President, Bob Metz, challenged me to re-create the success we'd experienced in Southern Cal. He directed me to take the system we developed and bring it to the East Coast. Many markets on the East Coast were doing their own thing, and he was looking for consistency and success. I was up for the challenge and felt very confident with the help of a strong energized sales team, we'd get the job done.

I'd now be running the day-to-day operation of the Philadelphia market and overseeing markets in New Jersey, Richmond, and Tidewater, Virginia. Not long after my move to Philly our company purchased two apartment magazines, one in Baltimore and the other in Washington, D.C. from Adler Publishing. Upon picking up these new markets, I was promoted to Regional Director and National Sales Trainer for HPC Apartment Guides and now added Baltimore, Boston, Connecticut, and Washington, D.C., to my portfolio and ceded Richmond and Tidewater to the late Ray Tilson.

Monday morning came and I arrived at the Philadelphia office at 7:00 a.m. to get set-up. Around 7:45 a.m. some of the sales and support team started filtering in and came into my office and introduced themselves. Most were sincere; a few were trying to position themselves. It never fails to happen that way. So at 7:55 a.m., I went to the conference room to await our sales meeting, and as I suspected, some salespeople tried to test the new guy; just like you test a substitute teacher.

At 8:00 a.m. most of the sales team were in the conference room, yet a couple showed up late for our first meeting. Today would be their only grace day. I looked around the conference table, looked everyone in the eye and used a line from Mel Brooks' movie *Blazing Saddles,* "There's a new sheriff in town." I told them I expected everyone to give 100 percent each and every day to help turn this market around. I was brought into this market because of the success and proven track record I'd earned in Phoenix and Southern California. I asked them to push themselves like never before, and if they followed the system, I'll be putting in place, they would be successful and put more commission in their pockets. All they needed to do was participate in that success.

"You may not like the new system; I do guarantee you will make more money than you're making now." Now I had their attention! They all straightened up in their chairs. "You can choose to follow my system and coaching style, or if not, you won't last very long." I then looked around the table, let go a chuckle and said, "Are we having fun yet?" They all had blank looks on their faces. I could imagine what they were thinking. What a great first impression that must've been. There was no structure, no discipline to succeed, the message needed to be sent.

We started engaging on what their challenges were: from problem accounts, production and personality issues. Ah! I felt at home again. We discussed action plans to fix immediate issues to take those off their plates. They were pumped; I could feel the excitement and energy race around the room. A small smile came across my face. I wondered, could this be Southern California all over again? Not so fast, slow down young man! My intuition told me with the right commitment from everyone, we could make a big statement in this market. One brave soul asked at the end of our meeting if we'd always have to meet at 8:00 a.m. Yes; I explained why getting in early and planning your week was so critical from many standpoints:

1. They weren't hitting their numbers.
2. Clients were dissatisfied with a lack of servicing.
3. The team had lost their competitive edge and needed to get back on track
4. The 8:00 a.m. Monday sales meeting was part of the system.
5. And I was the boss making the rules.

Before the meeting ended, I informed them moving forward if they were up to five minutes late getting to our meetings, they'd owe one dollar to our meeting kitty. If they were five to ten minutes late, they'd owe five dollars, and if they were over ten minutes late, I'd lock the conference door for the duration of the meeting. That only happened once in a while. Again the message needed to be sent. This practice started building accountability. Needless to say they had motivation to make it to our future meetings on time unless they were sick, had a meeting with a client or their death fell within the acceptable "death category" listed in *my* employee handbook. All fines would accumulate and at the end of each month, I'd buy pizza for the office.

It was all about having a plan. Any venture or goal you try and achieve in your business life or life in general you have to build a plan. After the first couple weeks, I assessed most of the team was in good shape, from sales to office support. Though there were a couple salespeople who challenged me right off the bat. They were now on my "radar." I had to make sure the sales team was ready to roll up their sleeves, work hard and follow my direction and a desire to succeed! I'd spend every chance I had sharing stories with them, examples of strategies used in other markets. I was excited because I knew, whether they did or not, they had the potential. They needed to believe in themselves, the product and services they were selling, and me.

So as the months passed, the team started gelling, and I could see the increase in confidence as they grew professionally. They started to understand what it would take to be successful. I continued arriving into the office around 7:00 a.m. because once my team arrived I devoted my time and energy to them. For any executive or manager, your main responsibility is to groom and grow your people. Once they arrived in the office, it was all about them. Leaders can't focus on themselves; they have to focus on the team. As my mentor Tony Ashe always said "We're in the people business, handle with care." I couldn't agree more.

The more the team implemented the system, the more they started to see and feel their progress; which included accountability modules, sales and customer service modules, and our one-of-a-kind ten-point service checklist. Every property and client had to be touched in some way every 30 days. Properties would get a monthly onsite visit to help the client solve their occupancy issues. It was a business meeting not just the usual social visit.

As more accountability took hold, I began witnessing what I experienced in the California markets. The sales team started coming into the office earlier and earlier. At first it was 7:45 a.m., then 7:30 a.m., and before you knew it they were trying to beat me into the office at 7:00 a.m. The best part about it, I wasn't doing anything overtly. I was silently sending a message: this is what it takes to be successful. Work long and solid hours to be prepared and increase your learning curve to stay one step ahead of the competition. In Southern California we played this game, where if a sales person beat his publisher into the office it's called, "swooping the publisher." I must admit a few times I got swooped.

They were beginning to believe in what was happening in the market and their contribution to it. They could feel the momentum shift. They began working harder and smarter than their competition; they were getting out in the field spending quality time with clients solving advertising needs. They were following the three legged sales stool: Prospecting, Presentations (sales and renewing), and Servicing. They could smell success and accomplishment; they were beginning to replicate the success strategies that months earlier I told them would happen. Magic was beginning to fill the air.

So what is this system I keep speaking of? That'll have to wait until another book.

Challenges

My first major challenge occurred with our two biggest clients who called to complain the Guide wasn't working, that they never saw their account rep, and they wanted to drop all of their advertising from our magazine. I spoke at length with both valued clients, Larry Korman of Korman Communities and Maria Jacobs of First Montgomery. They were unhappy with broken promises from the previous publisher and team. I explained why I was brought into this market and shared with them my Phoenix and Southern Cal story.

I asked for face-to-face meetings, and during that time, I asked them to give me 90 days to prove the Philadelphia Apartment Guide would work for them and improve their advertising results. I challenged them on making sure their onsite teams were properly tracking their traffic, which from prior shopping reports I'd taken showed they were not. I reasoned if their onsite teams were not properly tracking the advertising sources, how could they say my guide wasn't working? I told them if we failed to produce after 90 days, I'd let them out of the Guide, no questions asked. However, if I proved we could get the desired results for their communities, they would keep their existing ads in and place all of their remaining advertisable properties with us. They agreed. Because of the weak shopping reports from some of their communities, I asked to conduct a series of free leasing seminars for their teams to increase their closing skills and help them better track their advertising. They loved the idea! My team and I had a lot of work to do.

After the 90 days were up, I met with both Larry and Maria and shared with them the great results we were getting at their properties. I shared our service frequency reports, which showed properties were getting monthly visits, and the traffic and lease results they were receiving from us and our competition. It was all part of the system. They realized I was serious. They both commented I was true to my word and would be supportive in my mission to turn this market around. Eventually they put the rest of their properties in our book. This was just one example of what we were accomplishing in the market.

Over the next few years our clients and prospects saw the strides and accomplishments we were making, and they liked what they saw. We became their advertising and marketing partners, and as these relationships got stronger, the pages in our Guide continued to grow. When I first took over the Philadelphia market, the *Apartment Guide* was 354 pages, and when I handed the market over at the end of 1997, the Guide had grown to 640 pages. That's an 81 percent increase in revenue-generating pages. However the most satisfying part of my whole Philly experience was watching a team, who only a few years earlier felt defeated and had no direction or purpose, now believed in themselves individually as well as a team. They were now creating magic.

The Philadelphia market was another exciting turnaround for me. But to make it all happen I became consumed in my work once again. I put my heart and soul into this market, but I also realized I'd been putting a lot of hours in. I found myself, as I had in the past, working many weekends and always bringing work home with me. I admit I was a little obsessed about my work and justified it by telling myself if you love something and want to succeed, you have to put the time in.

Setting Goals

Like in the past, I'd come in every other Saturday during any given month. It was Andrew's time so I could get the stuff done I didn't have time for during the week, when it was my team's time. That still freed up enough weekends to have some fun, but instead of two days off, it was more like one-and-a-half-days off. But as I rolled into Sunday nights around 7:00 p.m., I'd go into a transformation that had been going on for a while since my radio days in Phoenix. My mind automatically shifted from weekend mode to work mode. It was almost like flipping a light switch.

I didn't realize it till an ex-girlfriend pointed it out to me. She said when we were at a party or out to dinner, around 7:00 p.m. on Sunday I'd get this look in my eyes as if I was in a faraway place. I was thinking about my week ahead, what needed to be accomplished and what tasks were at hand for the week and the month. If I was home around that time, I'd take out a legal pad and start planning the week. To me it was like a manager of a baseball or football team preparing for the big game. I was putting together my game plan. Wasn't this a big game? You bet it was. To me it was about winning, by exceeding expectations set for my market, growing my team, beating my competition and having fun, all at the same time.

My life was moving in fast-forward. I began achieving personal and professional goals at a fast and exciting clip. I knew from past experiences (Sales Team and Rookie Publisher of the Year awards) that to attain greatness you must possess the discipline to create a clear focus to guide you and your team to achieve goals and facilitate the success of your life's ambitions.

> Without a goal you have nothing in life to strive for.
>
> —John Hannah, Football Hall of Famer, New England Patriots

As I continued to accomplish one goal after another, I looked to see what the constant was in that success, and the constant became apparent. I was writing down my goals. I've read many different books and articles on goal setting, some ideas made sense and others didn't. Goal setting should be one of the easiest exercises you do. I wrote down my goals focusing on the daily, weekly, monthly, and yearly targets. I even knew where I wanted to be in the next five to ten years.

The key to goal setting is simply to write them down. They are your dreams. If you don't see them with your physical eye first by writing them down, you'll never realize them in your mind's eye (actually achieving your goals). Just like some people trying to lose weight: they may place a picture of a large unflattering animal on the refrigerator so they'll think twice about that ice cream. There's been study after study proving writing your goals down in a structured format will help you achieve those goals faster and effectively. Here's my rational for it.

Everyone at some point in their life has set some kind of goal. Some have accomplished their goals and others have not. Reasons for not achieving personal or professional goals may be laziness, no stick-to-itiveness, making your goals unrealistic, not having strong support, and not having a written plan or simply thinking goal setting doesn't work.

Using Your Subconscious

I've always been a believer in the power of our subconscious. They say Einstein used around 22 percent of his subconscious mind; a person who has telekinetic powers uses around 30 percent and the average person uses less than 10 percent of their subconscious mind. What does this say? It says we have a lot of room for improvement.

I like to keep things as simple as possible in understanding how goal setting works and how to make it work for you. So here it goes. Your subconscious mind is a very powerful and incredible tool that works 24/7; your conscious mind only works while you're awake.

Remember when your parents use to say to you, "I have to sleep on it," when you asked for something? There is some truth in that statement. When we go to bed at night with something that preoccupies our mind and we wake up the next morning with a resolution to that problem, what happened? How did we arrive at a solution while we were sleeping? Well it's your subconscious mind working on the problem while you're asleep. Let's face it, when you set goals it's very hard during the craziness of your day to stop and assess where you are in each goal setting stage. So if we prompt and reinforce our goals into our subconscious mind by reading those goals out loud every morning and before we go to bed at night, we set in motion the ability of our subconscious mind to take over and help us realize these goals. Our subconscious mind guides us during the day to act upon the steps we created in achieving our goals by acting upon what I call the "triggers" that direct us to our choices. Your subconscious mind will make the right choices for you so you can achieve your goals quicker.

Goal Setting Made Easy

You must try this to believe it. In a nut shell:

1. Write down your goals with a proposed date of accomplishment.

2. List the steps you'll require to achieve each goal.

3. Write your deadlines in pencil; be flexible.

4. Read them out loud twice a day for the first 45 to 60 days.

5. Keep focused and watch what happens.

Looking back on the success I've had with my teams, the common ingredient was goal setting. If you are a goal setter or you've been exposed to goal setting, you know it works! Being optimistic, having a positive attitude and setting goals can make such a difference in a person's life. It did

> *A goal is a dream with a deadline in writing.*
>
> —Unknown

in mine and others. And if you don't set goals, what are you waiting for?

My Philly team loved what we were accomplishing in exceeding our markets objectives and goals. I truly loved what I was doing, I always have. I've been very blessed over the years to love everything I've been a part of. Now looking back on it, maybe I began to enjoy my work a little bit too much, the high energy, the high expectations, the controlled chaos, and the thrill of victory. I always thought I'd have time for my personal life later on. How quickly life passes us by. I realized as each year passed into the next I was losing on average three to four vacation days, which was our company's policy; use it or lose it. For some reason I felt I

> *Life is there for the taking. Are you going to participate or be an innocent bystander?*
>
> —Andrew Botieri

couldn't be away from the office for long periods of time. I should have realized this was a red flag. I was obsessed with my work, some days it felt like an addiction. How come I never saw the red flags back in those days?

I always challenged my teams, if you don't love what you're doing for a job or a career, then look within and ask yourself if there is something you'd be better suited for? This is so important to how the rest of your life will unfold. You need to find something you can enjoy;

something you can latch onto and be passionate about. Why go through life surrounded by prison walls built by you and you alone?

CHAPTER 11

Fate Comes a Knockin' Again

As I stated earlier, "Life is all about timing." I am not sure if this was timing as much as it was a case of fate.

Back in 1996, while with HPC, I attended the Atlanta Apartment Association Trade show and had a chance meeting with a gentleman, who two years later would change the course of my life. He was Mike Mueller. What was presenting itself to me again showed how the choices we make in life play a role in and create and direct us to our destiny. From there it depends on our disciplines and sacrifices to reach that level or place we strive for.

Mike and I met at a party and hit it off immediately. Mike kept talking about finding and refining a better mousetrap when it came to computer technology and how to apply it to the property management industry. He was operating his apartment fax program in Phoenix which allowed people looking for an apartment to use their telephone to punch in a series of numbers on their phone pad based upon voice prompts. Based on your selections, your information would be faxed to the apartment communities with all your relevant information. But Mike looked at me and said with a mischievous grin, "I can make it even bigger."

Mike was on the ground floor of something revolutionary, only time would tell. We shook hands, parted and wished each other good luck and said we'd stay in touch. And one year later, in 1997, he did make it bigger. With the backing of Marcus & Millichap, Mike started AllApartments.

Back in Philadelphia, I'd left the Apartment Guide in November of 1997 after eight wonderful years. I loved working for HPC and learned so much about myself and what it took to be successful. I'll always look back on my time with HPC as some of the best years of my life. However, there was an upper management shift away from the business philosophy that originally helped build the company. The old philosophy, which was tried and tested, of building relationships, constructive coaching and having fun while striving to succeed. The new philosophy was all about driving revenue, regardless of how it impacted the clients or its employees. Clients felt abandoned. The environment had changed; it wasn't fun or rewarding any more. It was management by fear. One thing led to another, and it was time for me to move on. In fact, within about 14 months, the company lost many key people with over 200 years of experience through firings and forced resignations. These people had been the face of the Apartment Guide. It was an old fashion house cleaning for all the wrong reasons. What a brain drain! Many of the people back in those early HPC days are now in top leadership positions within the multi-housing industry.

In January of 1998, I created Total Peak Performance, a motivational sales, leadership and coaching company. I'd always loved training and inspiring people to be better at who they were and what they did. I seemed to have this ability to inspire others through my words and actions as I witnessed during my market turnarounds. I was now going to do it with my own company. I already had several Philadelphia, New Jersey, and Mid-Atlantic property management clients signed up.

That chance meeting with Mike Mueller in 1996 set into motion a series of events that would eventually leave me lying in a hospital emergency room four years later on the brink of death. How's that for destiny?

CHAPTER 12

The Beginning of the End

Grabbing the Golden Ring

No one can ever confirm why something happens or doesn't happen, that's always the unknown question. Some call it luck, others call it fate. Or "being in the right place at the right time." I'll let you be the judge of that.

I was attending the National Apartment Association's (NAA) annual trade show in Las Vegas in June 1998. My new company, Total Peak Performance was doing well as an early start-up. I was running at my own pace; definitely not the 60-plus hours a week I'd been putting in over the past ten years. In fact, I took solace many afternoons, weather permitting, to strap on my rollerblades and blade along Kelly Drive for my daily exercise and relaxation. I called it my "2:30 blade."

I attended this conference to network and promote my new company and catch up with old colleagues and business associates. It was great seeing everyone. As I walked around the trade show exhibit floor, as fate would have it, I bumped into Mike Mueller once again. We had some catching up to do.

I informed Mike I'd recently left the Apartment Guide in November of '97 and formed my new company. Mike's eyes lit up. He began sharing how his new company, AllApartments, had recently hired John Helm (a former McKenzie Consultant) as their CEO and just received a second round of venture capitalist funding. He said they were in the process of interviewing for a strong Vice President of Sales. In fact it was down to two candidates, though Mike confided in me, neither one had real property management experience, which he felt the position required. Mike's exact words to me were, "This job has your name written all over it." I was very flattered. I'd worked very hard over the years on my career and reputation. Lessons learned from my parents, grandparents and mentors.

I thanked Mike, but since I'd just started my own company, I wasn't looking for a change just yet. As Mike likes to tell the story, my response was, "Mike, I only work four days a week. I have Fridays off and everyday around two-thirty in the afternoon, I go rollerblading...blah, blah, blah."

Mike's response, "Big f'n deal!" Mike pressed on.

I told him, "I really appreciate the offer, however, I'm not interested."

Frankly, I was tired of moving around the country and tired of the grind of working 60-plus hour weeks. I felt I had to give my new company a chance. I guess I wanted to prove to myself, not anyone else, I could make this venture successful as I'd done with HPC.

Persistent Mike would not give up. He followed me around the trade show floor like a lost puppy dog, and with passion shared about the power of the Internet and the technology being developed and what was coming on the horizon. He had come a long way from his Apartment Fax concept. I didn't know that much about the Internet at the time, though at HPC we were starting to delve into the technology as a supplement to our print advertising.

Mike said I had the skill set he and John needed to make this venture successful. I still wasn't buying. Mike was still selling. He rolled out the salary and compensation package, which would be six figures and six figures worth of stock options. As he began to add up the whole compensation package, I started thinking more seriously about the offer. As Mike put it so eloquently, "You may never have to work again after we take the company public." As I added it up myself, it didn't take long to figure this could be the big ticket, that big opportunity everyone looks for in life. This could be the accumulation of all my years of hard work and the payoff of a lifetime. Grab the golden ring. It was beginning to sound more interesting.

I looked at Mike with my mischievous grin (Mike's not the only one) and said, "What's the next step." That once in a life time chance to make it big and find the pot o' gold at the end of my rainbow was at least worth investigating. From previous experiences I've had I'd always known things happen for a reason. There is a place and a time in one's life when the planets align, the universe comes together, and windows of opportunity open up for us. The question is: are we paying attention? I thought about my situation in Philadelphia. I'd found a new place to live, my company was moving along, and I had great friends. But I didn't have anything else holding me back.

As I say when it comes to opportunity, it's those three groups again: the first sees the "window of opportunity" and jumps thru; the second group sees the window of opportunity, however, their insecurities or fears makes them hesitate, and the third group, never sees the window at all. Let me ask you. Which person are you? What opportunities have you embraced or lost recently? If you embraced it, what was the result? If you didn't jump through the window, do you regret it? I told Mike, "Okay, I'll interview for the job. Now let's go get a beer!"

Starting with AllApartments

While at the trade show, a group of former HPC associates, now representing other vendors in the industry got together at the show. The same group I'd worked with back in the good old days when Marshall Haas owned the company. It was a "who's who" of the most talented group in the multi-housing industry. This group helped establish HPC as one of the most respected companies in the apartment industry. How fortunate to have had our lives intermingle and changed because of it. Can you say the same about your company and those you work with? If so, good for you, be thankful for that. If not, maybe it's time for a change. You deserve to go through life enjoying what you do and the people you work with. Our little get together was coined the "Haas Been Reunion!"

While sitting around talking, Barbara asked me what I had planned for the following day, Saturday. I was planning on seeing General "Stormin" Norman Schwarzkopf of the 1990 Desert Storm War, who was speaking at the closing event of the four-day trade show. She asked me to reconsider and escort her to a wedding in Los Angeles that same day. I was curious and asked, "Whose wedding?"

"Larry Flynt's."

"You mean the same Larry Flynt who publishes Hustler magazine?" I asked.

"The one and the same," she said.

Of course my next question was, "How do you know Larry Flynt?"

Barbara had been a high-stakes poker player for years, and she's a real spitfire. She plays in many big tournaments in Las Vegas and was, at one time, ranked amongst the top female poker players in the US. So eventually, a group of men including Larry Flynt, comedian Gabe Kaplan and others asked her to join their marathon poker sessions. In high-stakes poker you don't play for a few hours, you could play for 24 to 36 hours with only a few breaks in between. Maybe the guys thought having a woman in their midst increased their chances of winning. If they had any questions about her tenacity and boldness, they could've called anyone of Barbara's former teams and we could've told them.

Barbara mentioned there would likely be Hollywood celebrities at the wedding. So let me get this straight, General Schwarzkopf or Larry Flynt's wedding at his home in Hollywood Hills. It didn't take me long to make a decision. It was on to L.A.

The next day we flew into Burbank and I checked into the Beverly Hills Hilton. Barbara checked into the Peninsula Hotel. After a few hours, she pulled up in a chauffeured Jaguar and off to Larry Flynt's home. I had to remind myself not to get starstruck. As we approached his house, we saw armed bodyguards standing outside, which was somewhat intimidating.

If you aren't aware, during Larry Flynt's successful and controversial career, he'd been arrested on obscenity charges for selling *Hustler* magazines in Georgia, and after a court appearance, he and his lawyer, Gene Reeves, Jr., were shot after leaving the court house. They were critically wounded by an unknown assassin. Reeves was in a comma for 20 days, but recovered. Larry took two bullets in the stomach which damaged his spine. He'd never walk again. Larry would later go on to fight for his and our first amendment rights, our freedom of speech. He eventually took his case to the United States Supreme Court and won.

The Jag came to a stop, and one of his bodyguards opened our door and led us to the front of the house. On the porch was a heavyset man in a wheelchair, it was Larry Flynt and his soon-to-be wife, Barbara, not the Barbara I was with. From what I gathered, his bride-to-be had been his physical therapist, and I assume that's how they met. My Barbara gave Larry a big kiss. Larry smiled at me, said, "Hi," and then teased her about, "Her handsome young man."

I introduced myself and thanked them for making me part of their happy day. Larry told us to go inside where his daughter took us on a tour of the house. How cool. I was amazed at first how simple and quaint their home was. I figured, we're in Hollywood, so wouldn't someone who is worth tens, if not hundreds, of millions of dollars live in a big mansion? But the house had a nice warmth and charm to it and was full of incredible pieces of art, from priceless paintings to ancient Chinese vases.

After the tour, she guided us through the kitchen toward the backyard where the ceremony would take place. As we passed through the large kitchen, at the other end, I recognized Woody Harrelson, of *Cheers* fame. I looked at Barbara, "Shit, that's Woody Harrelson!"

Barbara said. "Oh didn't I tell you the cast of the movie *People vs. Larry Flynt* were going to be in attendance?" Wow, this wedding could be really interesting.

After a quick gawk at Woody, we went outside into the backyard and were greeted by Larry's brother, who led us to some drinks and hors d'oeuvres. As we approached the bar, my eyes widened and my jaw dropped. On one side was a large open cart with fresh ice and huge pieces of chilled shrimp and raw oysters; on the other side were bottles of Dom Pérignon, I mean dozens of bottles. I thought I was in heaven. Two of my favorite things: raw oysters and champagne. Very, very cool. As I stood there, I kicked into CSM (celebrity sighting mode).

After munching on these fine delicacies, we were led to our seats. They had set out white wooden folding chairs in his grass driveway and side lawn separated by a middle aisle. At the front of the makeshift wedding altar was the trestle where Larry and his bride would be married. The scene was very classy and romantic.

Shortly after sitting, a young blonde woman sat down next to Barbara to my left. Her long straggly hair was multi-colored. I remembered thinking; hey this is Hollywood, enough said! I leaned over and asked who she was; it was Courtney Love. In the movie, *People vs. Larry Flynt*, Courtney Love played Althea, Larry's wife at the time. Althea, according to the movie, had a bad drug habit, which resulted in an apparent overdose. After seeing water spilling out from underneath the bathroom door, Larry wheeled himself in and found her tragically drowned in their bath tub. Damn, what a tough thing to happen upon. I wish I'd seen the movie before I went to the wedding so I could've had a better understanding and appreciation of the ups and downs in Larry's life.

A few minutes later, Woody sat down right behind me with his wife. We nodded at each other. Wow, he seemed like an average guy. Then I thought, he is an average guy who happens to have been led to acting.

It was June and a bit warm as the wedding got started; it was a sweet ceremony. You could see the happiness in their eyes. The ceremony was quick, and after they were pronounced man and wife, we all applauded. As we were leaving our seats for the dinner tables, I turned as Woody was pulling off his bowtie. Being a big fan of Cheers and a few of his movies, I had to say something quick as I might not get another chance. I turned and said, "Boy you must feel a lot better with that tie off."

He smiled and replied, "Yeah, no kidding." Wow, Woody spoke to me...cool. Now I've met celebrities and rock stars from my days at the radio station in Phoenix, so I was used to seeing and conversing with them. So I don't get that starstruck, but I was excited to talk with him, being a fan. As Barbara and I left our seats I noticed other celebrities; actor Ed Norton, then Bill Maher from *Politically Incorrect* and former conservative, now turned liberal, talk show regular and political pundit, Arianna Huffington founder of the online *Huffington Post*.

We made our way to our assigned table and sat with some of the poker players Barbara played with. The meal was exquisite, as you can imagine, and was first class. Cornish game hen was the main attraction. After dinner, I noticed Woody and Bill Maher walk past our table and ascended a spiral iron staircase leading to an outside deck. Finishing a conversation at the table, I looked at Barbara and with a mischievous grin said, "I'm going to see what is going on upstairs."

As I made my way to the top of the spiral staircase, I noticed Woody, his wife, Bill Maher and two beautiful blonde women sitting and partying at a rectangle shaped table in the corner. I was in the right place. But in the same instant, it hit me, "Okay, you're up here, now what!?" Good question! So I took a deep breath and walked over to their table and stood next to Woody as they were debating social and political issues. I knew I was in the right place.

(This is the censored version) When there was a pause in conversation I leaned over, shook Woody's hand, and introduced myself. Bill Maher then stood up and we shook hands. Woody introduced his wife and Bill in turn introduced the two ladies at the table. As they continued their political discussion, Woody looked up and asked for my opinion. This was 1998 and they were discussing leadership in our country. I spoke with pride almost bloviating about Ronald Regan, his conservative approach to governing (less government), how he put the backbone back into our country after the dismal Presidency of Jimmy Carter (hostage crisis and 20 percent interest rates) and in doing so gave Americans hope and belief. When I finished, Woody commented, "Wow, you really know your shit don't you?" I chuckled. He pulled out a chair and asked me to sit. Of course, Maher and I were on opposite ends of the political spectrum, which lent itself to some spirited conversation.

After about an hour of talking and "partying", Arianna Huffington approached the table to say hi and Woody introduced us. I'd seen her on news talk shows, as a conservative Republican pundit. She tried, unsuccessfully to get her then husband, millionaire Michael Huffington, elected to the US House of Representatives from California. As we talked, she asked if I was married, and when she found out I was single, took me by the arm and escorted me around the party introducing me to as many single women as she could . She introduced me as her, "new handsome friend," in her Austrian accent. I was very flattered, a little embarrassed, though, it was fun.

After our walk, I bid adieu to Arianna and made my way back to the deck. Maher had gone down stairs so the rest of us sat around the table and continued chatting. I told them I was from Boston and how Cheers gave the people of Boston a local and national identity, but most of our discussions were on political and social issues; it was unadulterated conversation. It was people having conversation and debate about how everyday issues affect our lives.

As Bill came back to the table he bellowed out "Hey, who's this Andrew Botieri guy?"

My eyes shot up. "Hey, that's me, I said "What's up?" He said "your wife (Barbara) is down stairs looking for you." I laughed and said she was my ex-boss and good friend. At this point Woody made a whipping sound and motioned his arm as if snapping a whip. Insinuating I was "pussy whipped." I laughed and reiterated she was just a friend. They teased me for a while and had a good laugh at my expense.

I said, "I'll be right back," and went down stairs to see what Barbara wanted. After finding her I told her of my encounter with Woody and Bill and convinced her to come up stairs to meet them. I introduced her to the group and we sat around the table enjoying everyone's company.

It was getting late, and the wedding party began breaking up. Woody came over, shook hands said, "I'm glad we met. You're really cool Andrew, it beats talking with these Hollywood types all the time."

I can imagine! Woody huddled up everyone to take some pictures, so we all jumped in and out of photos: Woody, me, Barbara, Larry Flynt, and his new wife, Bill Maher, an exotic dancer, and Arianna Huffington. It was a memorable and very fun night. I couldn't wait to tell everyone back home about this crazy night. When I look at these photos today, a warm smile comes to my face, and I remember a great lesson. No matter who people are and where they go in life, we all put our pants on leg at a time.

Landing the New Job

After returning to Philadelphia from Vegas and the Larry Flynt adventure, it was time to focus and consider a new chapter of my life: the new opportunity with AllApartments.com. I flew to Scottsdale to meet with Mueller, the management team, and the CEO, John Helm. The meeting and interview with John went great.

The next day, I met with the AllApartments management team, which was a little awkward as some members of the team knew in the backs of their mind they would have to relegate some control of their departments to me as the vice president. Though they were interviewing me to see if I'd fit in, I was interviewing them to see if they would fit in moving forward. It became clear after these interviews and a few sidebars I had with sales and customer service people, that these groups weren't focused and weren't working as a cohesive unit. I made a note to spend more time emphasizing personal accountability. For us to succeed and beat the competition, we all had to be rowing in the same direction. After I was hired, some of these department managers challenged me from day one on varied issues. It was like a couple mosquitoes buzzing around my head. Having turned around five markets, I knew what needed to be done. I couldn't wait to get started.

After these interviews, I flew to San Francisco and met two of the Board of Directors for AllApartments, who were major principals in the new start-up. I felt a little intimidated at first as these two gentlemen commanded great respect within their circles. Bill Millichap of Marcus & Millichap, one of the largest real estate investment companies. Bill was a great guy who came up from the ranks to become a co-founder of Marcus & Millichap. The second gentleman was William Randolph Hearst III of Kliener, Perkins, Caufield & Byers, which at the time was the number one Internet venture capitalist group in the US. They were involved in taking Netscape, AOL, Intel, Google, and Amazon.com all public, just to name of few. These were the big boys, and I was finally going to get my chance to play in the big leagues. All my childhood I wanted to get to the big leagues, that was my baseball dream, and then I thought, hey though I was playing on a different field, wearing a different uniform, the game was the same; hone your craft, develop your team, beat your competitors, and have fun while doing it. Maybe that dream was about to come true.

When it comes to competing in sports or in life, gaining an advantage is so important in the success of any endeavor. I decided to take a different approach in these interviews with Bill and Will (as they liked to be called) than I had in any other interviews from the past. I needed an edge, something to set me apart from the other candidates who were vying for this same position.

Over the years, I've accumulated many letters of recommendations, promotion letters, kudo correspondence from higher-ups, articles written about me, and testimonials from clients. I placed them into a three-ring leather portfolio book, which I called my brag book. After I sat down with each one at their offices and a little chit-chat, I told them, "I could sit here all day and tell you how good I am, but I thought it would be appropriate to have my 'brag book' speak for me."

I handed them the book and sat back and said, "Here's what others say about me!"

It was a bold move, but as they leafed through the book, they'd look up and say: "What a great idea." "Very impressive." A smile cracked at the corner on my mouth, it worked!

After about a 60-minute interview and asking many questions, both Bill and Will commented if they had the final say they'd hire me right on the spot. Wow, a proud moment. I felt so much relief and confidence especially after the anxiety I had going into these interviews.

Within a few weeks, I was officially announced as vice president of sales and operations for AllApartments. What a whirlwind of events. It had only been 45 days ago when I reconnected with Mueller at the NAA Conference in June and now in August of 1998, I was putting my new company Total Peak Performance on the backburner, leaving my beloved Philadelphia, and heading back to Scottsdale for a second time. Before moving out to Scottsdale, I flew back home to Hanson once again to say good-bye to family and friends before heading back to the Southwest. Let the games begin!

Starting with AllApartments

Every time I've made a move (this would be number 15) whether it was geographically for business or a career change, I've always looked for a sign to reinforce my decision. Sometimes the sign appeared before my decision, and other times it came after. I feel these signs enabled me to connect the dots that I was on the right path. This move back to Arizona wasn't going to be any different. It didn't take long for that sign to appear.

As part of my compensation package, AllApartments would cover my housing costs for a period of time till I bought or rented a place. Before I came out, I called a few corporate housing companies to see what was available. Knowing the location of our office and having lived in Scottsdale before, I wanted to be near Old Town. After speaking to one of the companies, they gave me an address of an available furnished corporate apartment. The address seemed to ring a bell, but I wasn't quite sure. When I arrived in Phoenix and drove to the address they had furnished me, I realized this was my sign. The condominium community I was going to live at was the same apartment community, Harbor Pointe, that I lived at back in 1988 when I worked for the Apartment Guide and the Arizona Extra. The same community Tony and I were roommates at. How's that for a sign! I had a good feeling about this new venture! Remember when Tony and John asked me to come on board with the Arizona Extra and I walked the golf course looking for a sign? This was the same place.

It was mid-August; my first day at AllApartments had arrived. I was very excited and a little nervous at the same time. The first thing I did was meet the entire office, every department. My message was similar to the one I gave in Philly a few years ago: "People expect a lot from us, it's very competitive out there, and it's not going to be easy."

There was a lot of work to do in a very little amount of time. I explained to them, "Come to work because you want to, not because you have to. If you don't you won't last long with a poor attitude. I am here to help you be successful."

I rolled out my vision to the entire office and what was expected of everyone including myself. In most cases I was asking them to change the way they had been conducting business. We needed to make some major changes. From past experience, I knew I'd get some push back; I always did. Most people resist change. I had some of those change resisters in attendance during this meeting. When you know you'll get push back, all you can do is share your enthusiasm, your convictions and intensity delivered with belief and confidence and hope they seize on that energy.

> When we think and act pro-actively, we spend less time putting out fires.
>
> —Andrew Botieri

After I concluded the office meeting, I asked the salespeople to stay behind. This was the group I needed to connect with; they would be driving the success of this company. Prior to this meeting, I'd met separately with several salespeople to get a feel of where things were in their view; some discussions were open door and others were closed. It wasn't much different than what I found in Philadelphia. What became clear was:

1. There were no effective sales tools to sell and renew with.
2. There were no defined sales territories, just lots of confusion.
3. I inherited seven sales people, yet only three were allowed to sell.
4. The sales manager didn't know how to sell his product.
5. This was going to be quite an undertaking.

I believe it was Dale Carnegie who said, "How do you eat an elephant?" The answer, "One bite at a time." I had my work cut out for me to get this team competitive and successful. Mike had put the team together; my job, as I looked at it, was to help them take the football into the end zone. I began laying out my priorities and addressing them one by one. Though in my case, I decided to tackle three and four things at a time. The multi-tasker! The two interchangeable expressions I've always used when the pressure was on are: "balls to the wall" or "let's rock n' roll." It's hard to explain, but I've always enjoyed the controlled chaos aspect of business. It makes it a challenge and challenges motivate me! I like to be in there fixing things and making them more efficient and successful.

A light moment occurred as I began rolling out new sales processes and procedures. One of the salespeople, Tricia, respectfully kept interrupting me with comments like, "Well you don't understand," or "That's not how we do things."

After the second time I turned to her and said in a very direct manner, "No you don't understand, this *is* the way it will be done." The whole room got quiet. You could hear a pin drop. I then began to chuckle and others joined in. It was a funny and priceless moment, but the message was sent. "This is not going to be a country club atmosphere," as my old boss George Miscevich would say. Coming from corporate America, the culture here was a bit lax for me. I wasn't used to the dot-com culture. When I finished the meeting and left, Tricia turned to the person next to her and said laughing while pointing at her head, "Didn't he see this tiara on my head?" She later told me the story; from that day forward I call her Princess. A couple weeks later, I bought a fake tiara and presented it to her. Humor is such a great instrument to use when dealing with issues that call for a lighthearted approach. I'd put humor to the test in about nine months.

The first couple of weeks were spent getting a feel for the operation, the sales team and who was responsible for what, all 50-plus of them. I needed to find out who knew their jobs and who were play acting. I also needed to identify my self-starters and who needed guidance. This is the quickest way to assess a team's capabilities to appropriately divide my time to each team member's needs. I'd get my self-starters on their way and hunker down with those who needed help, whether it was sales training or other aspects of their responsibilities.

However, my biggest focus was the sales team. As my good friend and mentor Tony always said, "We're in the sales business. No sales. No business." You can't say it any clearer than that. The quicker I could get their learning curves ramped up, the quicker we could start selling and renewing business. In the beginning I conducted some form of a training workshop almost every day. It would run the gambit, whether it was learning their presentation, effectively working a sales territory, selling against the competition or overcoming objections, there was always something going on. I dove in and immersed myself into my work. There was so much to do in so little time. Sound familiar? In a start-up organization or for that matter any other business, you either sell your product or service effectively or you don't. If you don't have the proper tools to sell and renew with then why open your doors? The hard working crew knew what they were selling at AllApartments; they just didn't know how to sell it.

It was an exciting time because we were creating a new vehicle for people to shop online for an apartment. This was cutting edge Internet advertising. Over 40 percent of our population rents their home or apartment. That's a large number to attract. From the beginning we knew we had a winner, we were on the cutting edge of technology with visions of success and wealth. But with that looming challenge I was going to have to work even harder.

Though within the first week, I realized there was no formal sales structure or accountability. I guess that's why they hired me! At one point I walked into Mueller's office, grinning, and asked why he never let on how much retooling the sales department needed. He chuckled and said I might not have taken the job. It was another challenge along life's journey. I better get busy.

I had my hands full from the beginning. I sat down with my sales manager, who I inherited. From the outset I knew he was over his head, nobody on the sales staff listened to him, and he couldn't even sell our product during a role play. Want to see what someone knows or doesn't know about their sales presentation, role play with them. Needless to say, he didn't last long.

I had so many people scampering for a piece of me there'd be a waiting line outside my door. Someone joked they needed a deli ticket number dispenser. There was always an array of questions to be answered, egos to be massaged, hands to be held, and upset customers to console. So Monday through Friday I was at the beckoning call of my sales and office support teams. Not any different than before. I loved every minute of it. However, after a few weeks it didn't take me long to realize the work pace within an Internet company seemed ten times faster than of a normal company.

Those who wanted to succeed worked hard and those who didn't have their heart into it didn't last long. Darwin's Theory of Evolution, survival of the fittest! Within the first 45 days, four salespeople and a sales manager were let go, by 90 days I had my core team and was hiring more talent. Now I could move forward with purpose and not be dragged down by office politics and egos.

I was determined to get the sales team up and running as quickly as possible, the quicker we grew revenues, the faster we could execute our business plan. Then the more attractive our company would be to potential investors, increasing our chances of taking AllApartments public. My thinking was the quicker this all happened, the quicker we could cash out of our stock options, make significant money, and then pick our next endeavor. It seemed simple enough. For good or bad, visions of stock options kept dancing in my head.

For the first 150 days I was working six days a week, with an occasional Sunday thrown in for good measure. Between the office and my home I was putting in a combined 65 to 70 hours a week. I totally immersed myself in my work; okay maybe a bit obsessed. Controlled chaos rules! But I was in my element, having fun developing the sales tools and sales systems for the team with the help of the great marketing department. I loved the thrill of the sale and going up against my competitors. To me it was like playing competitive baseball or hockey. Since my days as an athlete in high school and college I knew the importance of showing up ready to play each game to the fullest, with passion and perseverance. In this case, this was the game of life. I have to admit, I hate to lose. But on the occasions I did, I wouldn't wallow in self-pity. You shake it off; reflect on what you did wrong and understand how to do it better the next time.

Victories are short lived. As they say in sales, it's not what you did last month, it's what are you going to do for me this month. So to stay ahead of our competition, it was critical for this team to have whatever ammo they needed to succeed. My job was to provide them with the weapons.

> We should learn more from our mistakes than from our victories.
> —Andrew Botieri

Once these sales issues were in the pipeline of being handled, I could focus on the next looming challenge: the proper distribution of the sales territories. Before I came on board, Mike had instructed his top three salespeople to place their name beside the accounts they had been working. Seems easy enough? Well there was a loophole. They put their names on pretty much every property management account across the country, even ones they weren't actively working.

The urgency was the other salespeople, including new hires, who only had scraps to prospect. My first reaction was comical. But I realized this was a pressing issue. Salespeople are hired to sell, not to make collection or copy change calls from clients like they were doing. I sat behind closed doors for many days and weekends analyzing how to properly divide out the territories, so I could begin hiring hungry salespeople, so they'd have a "hit list" to sell from. The three, Tricia, Julie, and Ann Marie had strong relationships with many of their clients so I needed to free up more time for them to up-sell within those companies. The ladies found the process a bit painful at first, but it all worked out in the end. I now had all the appropriate sales territories broken out as equitably as possible and quickly grew my sales team from 7 people to 15 in 6 months, which was my goal. Once this albatross was off my shoulders, we could rock n' roll!

As the team continued to grow, belief and trust in each other was beginning to form. As they began to grow and bond something magical was happening that could surpass what occurred in Philadelphia. Remember in Philly and Southern Cal as the teams grew in confidence and saw what it took to be successful they began putting in that extra time and effort. The Scottsdale team was catching on quick. Like before, I found myself coming into the office pretty much every Saturday to pump out a few hours of corporate reports/requests, sales and marketing pieces, "to-do" lists for my direct reports and spending "alone time" to plan our sales strategies.

You never get alone time in an office full of high energy people. Since receiving their sales territories, they were eager to learn and sell, so some began coming in on Saturdays. I'd hear the office door shut and then hear "is anybody here?" A smile would come to my face. This is an important sales character trait: assertiveness. I was looking for commitment. I didn't expect salaried people to come in on weekends, but management and salespeople, yes, as we don't work a typical 9 to 5 job Monday through Friday. It demonstrated their true commitment to the cause.

Rob and Ann Marie started coming in on Saturday to get a jump on their upcoming week, and of course, to schmooze me and get undivided attention, which was getting harder during the work week. We'd sit around and discuss sales and marketing strategies, pending proposals, challenging clients, and needed enhancements to our website to create a better experience for our end users. So 20 minutes would lead to 45 minutes to a few hours. Where did the time go? You know how that goes? Don't get me wrong, I didn't mind, it's why I was there, to help them be more successful. Don't forget. It's all about your people! Once others caught on the boss came in on Saturday, I'd hear the door shut more often. A leader must be compassionate, must listen to his people, find out what they need and then act. And another tip, never let them know you work weekends!

So with "Andrew time" being whittled away on Saturdays, I began defaulting to Sundays as a day to "stop by" the office to get some things done. The office was five minutes from my apartment. However, one hour turned into three, three turned into four, and so on. The joke in my family was if they wanted to get a hold of me on the weekends, they'd have a better chance calling my office first. Looking back on it now, it should have been a red flag and not a badge of honor. But I wasn't thinking like that; I was hired to do a job, not only revamping the sales department but getting operations (office and service support) working in conjunction with the sales team. If you want to operate a true sales organization, everything you do has to be to support the sales team's ability to sell and renew business. Too many companies forget about that part!

Even though I was working at a hectic pace, I was back in wonderful Scottsdale after an eight-year hiatus. Though it felt a little strange coming back to the Southwest where I first experienced personal, professional and spiritual growth back in 1987. It was wonderful reengaging with old friends and of course my Cousin Paula and her family.

It may sound like all I did was work and never take my head above water. I did enjoy myself, but admittedly most of my waking time was focused on AllApartments and building a successful sales team. I spent free time after work with my team getting to know them better at happy hours trying to mesh their personalities together creating a bond. If you can get a group to know each other outside the office a stronger bond takes hold and they'll step up to help each other succeed. The old work hard, play hard adage. We began to bond, not just as a group of co-workers but like a family, sincerely interested in everyone's welfare. One of my regional sales managers Rob and I became good friends. Rob was my go-to guy and he always seemed to enjoy playing devil's advocate with me enabling me to see problems and challenges from different perspectives. Rob didn't win many of our debates, but he did win a few.

As we gained traction I elevated several salespeople to team leaders and with their help continued to groom the sales team. Those that caught on were finding success and those who didn't got weeded out for poor performance. That's the world of sales. Andy Grove's (founder of Intel) philosophy "you retain the top 10 percent of your people and you turn over the bottom 10 percent of your people." It's a necessary part in building a super star sales team; you can't have your emotions involved in hiring and firing decisions.

I was about six months into my new endeavor with AllApartments and our business was growing quickly from all sides. We had an outstanding executive team headed by CEO John Helm, a strong board of directors and an awesome Technology Group, who were developing incredible software programs for website functionality and helping to create a better mouse trap to take the company to the next level. I began traveling around the country more often for client meetings, sales blitzes and industry trade shows or flying to San Francisco on a weekly basis for executive or board meetings. It felt as if things were non-stop. I'd fly into a city late at night, get to the hotel, have room service delivered around 10:00 or 11:00 p.m.; then to bed and wake-up early the next morning for client or prospect meetings. I'd skip my workout at the hotel gym to get an extra hour of sleep.

Back home I also noticed, with my self-imposed work schedule, I was missing more workouts which should've been used to help burn off the excess stress that we were all dealing with. I began eating less healthy than I was accustomed to. Too much fast food and eating at late hours of the night, sometimes even missing lunch. In the past, I found ways to reduce my stress but now I didn't seem to find time to work out, to relax or even sit and play my guitar. Though I didn't feel stressed out, I felt I was operating in that controlled chaos.

We began assembling a strong group of diverse talent. Some were veterans of the apartment industry and others were novices, possessing raw talent waiting to be unleashed onto the multi-family housing world. We needed people who were ready to meet the challenges of growing a new company, who didn't mind working long hours and not complaining about it. Of course we hired those with strong, positive attitudes.

> When it comes to Attitude, you either hire for it, or fire for not having it.
> —Andrew Botieri

I continued working 60 to 70 hours a week, though frankly, I loved every minute of it as strange as that may seem. I enjoyed building and turning around sales organizations, watching people grow and succeed, making those companies profitable and have fun while doing it. There was a lot of pressure with our start-up; in fact, any sales organization has pressure, pressure to make sales. That had been my experience with Y95, Arizona Extra, and HPC, and this was no different. I loved the pressure. Bring it on!

Things were coming together; we were having nice sales gains, but not big enough, not fast enough. Heard that before? Our biggest challenge was the infancy of the Internet in the eyes of many clients and prospects. They weren't sure the benefits Internet advertising delivered. We needed to convert more property management companies over to the Internet as a way to cost effectively market their apartment communities around the country, around the world! We needed to educate our customer base. Knowledge is power.

I asked the marketing department to develop a series of sales blitzes around the country targeting our most opportune markets to grab larger market share. We would invite groups of prospects and current advertisers of AllApartments to a local hotel in their area, provide a continental breakfast and conduct a three-hour presentation on the history of the Internet: how and why the average consumer used the Internet, how easy it was to advertise their properties online. We shared important Internet facts and statistics, though a few clients and prospects still thought Internet advertising was a fad and wouldn't last.

These blitzes helped turn that tide. It was a great educational tool not only for the clients, but for me and the team. Let's face it, the more educated your customers are, the sounder decisions they can make in investing in your product or service. After a three-hour presentation my sales team would set appointments with prospects at the seminar and stay behind for two to four days running appointments. Sometimes, if time permitted, I would stay an extra day and run appointments with them. I would fly into a major city like Atlanta, San Diego, Orange County, or Houston and do my thing.

These blitzes worked great and it was a chance for me to meet many new clients. Though the traveling was fun and I enjoyed hanging with my team, the traveling was starting to take its wear and tear on me, but I wasn't paying attention.

Everyone was working hard as a team with a common goal in mind, "Let's make this thing happen!" You either work as a team or you don't and within a company it's apparent very quickly. Let's face it; you spend more time together at work with your work family than you do at home with your own family. Everyone seemed committed and willing to work hard to help this company succeed. There was magic in the air. I thought of Claude Bristol's book *The Magic of Believing;* it was happening again. I could see it coming together. I sat back in my chair and grinned.

Everything was moving along as we had planned and hoped. I was at a level I'd never played before; in a game with players who were bigger than life and this kid from Hanson was along for the ride. Then came one night in February 1999, which would set into motion a series of events leaving me facing the biggest threat to my life.

Stress, Success, and First Symptoms

I had just returned from Atlanta after another successful sales blitz. I did my usual to unwind from a stressful and intense trip like this so I sat down to play guitar. It is such a source of inspiration and relaxation and it helps to relieve stress. I played a couple favorites. It felt good to unwind. After a while, I put the guitar down and walked to the kitchen for a bite to eat. Within seconds sharp pains began shooting up and down the fingertips on my left hand. I shook my hand trying to shrug off the sensation. My whole body felt sore and tired from the long plane ride. After I ate, I made my way to bed. At about 2:00 a.m., I awoke and realized both hands were numb with that pins and needles feeling shooting through them. *Don't you just hate that feeling?* I figured I must've slept on my hands so after a few moments the prickly feeling went away. I fell back to sleep, not even thinking twice about what had happened.

The next morning brought no thought of the sensations. I knew I'd been working crazy, nonstop hours in anticipation of making this new start-up successful and on a bit of the greedy side taking the company public with its anticipated IPO. We felt no different than any other start-up dot-com company who'd gone public before us like, AOL, Netscape, and Yahoo. It was an intoxicating carrot dangling off the end of my nose. For those who are unaware, an IPO (initial public offering) allows a company to sell shares of its stock to the general public to help raise needed capital to help that company grow.

Looking back on it now, I realize I might've become a little obsessed with striving to get the sales team cruising in over-drive so quickly. The executive team, board of directors, and I had high expectations for everyone involved. We all seemed to be operating in a gear called intensity and with that intensity came more stress.

The stress started leading to some sleepless nights. I'd wake in the middle of the night with my mind racing with business stuff. I'd lie awake for hours as a barrage of business and personnel things began running in and out of my head. I even tried dumping all my thoughts on a pad of paper just to get my head clear before bed, but even that didn't seem to work. When I couldn't sleep, I'd turn the light on and read a book or magazine until I dozed off. Some nights even that didn't help. I also realized I was waking up more frequently with the numbness and pins and needles in my hands. It seemed like clockwork around 2:00 a.m. I'd awake to the pain and numbness. I got frustrated lying there, not being able to get back to sleep. On a few mornings I'd get up and make it into the office around 5:00 a.m. I wonder if I took that old English idiom, "The early bird catches the worm," a bit too seriously. I also noticed my fingers tips were becoming very sensitive to touch. I still dismissed it as being over tired and over worked.

There was a lot of excitement in the air at AllApartments. We were in the midst of using a research company to find a more definitive brand name and identity for AllApartments. So March we continued our momentum, but we needed to grow faster as discussions were taking place to take our company public, and we needed to show our investors a strong and consistent sales growth and sales model. We needed to make a big statement throughout the industry; we meant business and were serious players looking to dominate the niche of online apartment search referral. We needed to make a big hire. Funny how good minds think alike. In our hiring net, Mike and I kept discussing, low-keyed, the possibility of hiring one of the most respected people in the multi-housing industry, Marcia Bollinger. Marcia was currently a vice president of my former employer HPC Apartment Guides. It was like my radio days at Y-95; you need to make a big splash.

I had worked with Marcia for many years at the *old* HPC before it went through all of its changes that dethroned it as one of the best in the industry. In fact, at HPC we ran the two largest regions generating well over $40 million in annual revenues. Mike and I met with Marcia several times and finally negotiated to bring her on board. It was a big coup de grâce. In March 10, 1999, Marcia Bollinger came on board as my director of sales for SpringStreet.

Six days earlier, on March 4, we had our launch party to announce the name change from AllApartments to SpringStreet. The thinking was SpringStreet would allow us to market more than just apartments to the public. We could do home rentals, roommate searches and provide our users a greater experience to return to our website. It's all about the eyeballs! There were a few of us, including Mike and me, who preferred we stay AllApartments. Our name said what we did. SpringStreet just didn't seem to do the same. But the majority won out. Our goal was to either take SpringStreet public through an IPO or be attractive to a larger company that might want to buy or merge with us. Regardless, the pace at SpringStreet was about to be placed into overdrive. Things would get crazier than they had ever been. As an overachiever, I needed to kick it into sixth gear and continue to operate in controlled chaos.

With Marcia on board, we also kicked into an aggressive hiring pace. Fortunately, most of the talent we were looking at were people from our old company, HPC, and our print competitor, For Rent. This enabled us to hire superstars with proven track records. I know this infuriated both companies. We were offering less money, we were much smaller, and we didn't have the finances to be world-class, yet! However, we did have one enticing advantage, the same main reason I came on board, we offered stock options which the magazine competitors couldn't match. We were even threatened with possible legal action for pilfering one company's salespeople, but that never came to fruition. The way I looked at it, if their employees were happy, they wouldn't have left to work for us.

When the majority of the hiring was done, we had brought on about 20 superstars. I joked I could envision my face on a dart board at both HPC and For Rent's corporate office for their execs to throw at. Oh well, all's fair in love and war!

You could feel we now had the right team. You could see it by the "pep in their step and the glide in their stride." With our new team ramped up, the intensity increased. We were training nonstop, flying into markets to run in the field with our salespeople. We were continuing to develop and pump out more sales tools and setting up meetings with big decision makers from property management companies all over the country. The pace was daunting.

Symptoms Spread

Within a few months, not only were my fingers and hands still experiencing the sensation of numbness and pins and needles, but now something strange was going on with my feet. I'd wake up each morning and as I placed my feet onto the carpet to stand, it felt as though someone took a baseball bat and whacked the bottoms of my feet in the middle of the night. My feet felt swollen and stiff, just like my fingers and hands had become. Though they felt swollen there was no swelling. For the first 15 to 20 minutes each morning I'd have to limp around my apartment until the blood got flowing in my feet. After a few minutes the pain subsided a bit, though the soreness and aching lasted throughout the day. Even at the office, if I stood on my feet for more than an hour at a time, my feet started throbbing along with shooting pains. The only way to alleviate the pain was to sit down. As the vice president of sales and operations, I was either conducting sales trainings, or traveling around the country. Sitting wasn't an option. There were many painful days.

Over the next few months, I continued to shrug off the pain in both my hands and feet. My executive assistant, Stacy, started giving me a hard time about not going to see a doctor about my worsening condition. I couldn't seem to pull myself away from my mission to see a doctor. I was busy, we were busy and I was thinking to myself that it can't be that bad. Maybe it's a guy thing, but I felt as though it wasn't serious, probably just a result of being overly tired from the crazy hours I was working and traveling. My response was always, "I'll go when I get back from my next business trip."

After the third or fourth time I used that excuse, Stacy called a local doctor and set up an appointment for me. She wouldn't give in, and when she got like that, you didn't win. If I procrastinated, she'd sit on the top of my desk and not move until I left for the appointment. She took good care of me. In fact this wasn't the first time Stacy had to intervene to get me a doctor. After I had my head-on collision in December of '98 in Scottsdale, she called a chiropractor, made the appointment and then made me go. She'd get so mad if I broke any doctor's appointment. She'd scold me and not talk to me all day. People joked and asked if we were husband and wife. We bickered back and forth, like Oscar and Felix in the *Odd Couple*. I was definitely Oscar!

So off to the doctor I went, and after some pokes and prods and asking questions about where it hurt, he then asked how old I was and I told him I'd recently turned 40. He paused, and then deduced I probably had some type of arthritis, maybe even the beginnings of rheumatoid arthritis. I shook my head and told him I couldn't have rheumatoid arthritis because it's not just in my knuckles, it seemed to be everywhere throughout my hands and feet. He looked me over once again and said unless further tests revealed anything else; he thought it was just a case of me, "Getting older."

Maybe he was right. At the time, my 95-year-old grandmother and my 72-year-old dad both had rheumatoid arthritis in their fingers. He told me when people get to be around 40 or a little older, arthritis can begin to set into their joints. It still didn't seem to ring true to me but I wasn't quite sure what I had. I thought, he should know, he's the doctor. It seems when doctors don't quite know what's wrong they defer to the, "You're getting older," conclusion.

Hmmm…in hindsight, a lifesaving tip for you, next time a doctor gives you this advice as his unscientific diagnosis, please run and get a second opinion. As my good friend Angel says, "No wonder they call it a practice!"

As the months went by, my travel schedule became even more intense. Almost every week I was flying to San Francisco for some type of meeting. I traveled to Washington, D.C., for a multi-housing industry conference, then onto to Austin, Texas, for that states' annual apartment industry trade show, then to San Diego for another sales blitz, and many other places in between. Physically, I noticed the pain and stiffness I'd feel in my hands from carrying my briefcase or luggage. But I pushed it to the back of my mind. It seemed I was always packing a suitcase and flying off somewhere. Sometimes I'd wake up in a hotel room in the morning, not quite sure what city I was in. When I remembered, I'd chuckle to myself. If only I'd known at the time, at this current pace I was running it was far from funny.

Doctors and an Elusive Verdict

After I had my first appointment with the doctor, who told me, "Well you're getting up there in age, and you must be having early symptoms of arthritis," I requested to see a rheumatoid arthritis specialist. I was given some routine blood work, and though some results showed some irregularities, there was nothing conclusive to say what might be causing the pain, stiffness, and numbness. In June of '99, I was tested for carpal-tunnel because of the pain in my hands. But the final results showed nothing concrete to pinpoint a cause. So I kept moving forward, working long hours, getting a lot accomplished, and taking on more at a faster velocity. As the months went on, the doctors continue with their arthritis conclusions, though I still had my doubts.

During the summer of 1999, prior to the merger with HomeStore, our Board of Directors and CEO had been adamant about me relocating to San Francisco to be closer to the action and work more intimately with the other vice presidents and board members. So in July, I gave in and moved to San Francisco. Early on during my interview process, I was asked about moving to San Francisco at some point. I wasn't too keen on the idea, having gone through the Northridge earthquake in Southern California in 1994. California was the last place I wanted to live.

The second reason, I resisted the move was I'd be leaving my sales and support teams behind in Scottsdale. How can a VP of Sales be hundreds of miles away from the pulse of their sales team and out of the loop living in the next state? It never made any sense to me. But when your direct boss who controls your destiny asks you to do something, you do it. My only consolation was Marcia would be in Scottsdale as my director of sales.

This would be move number 16 since leaving my parents' house in 1982. I became a whiz at packing and acclimating to new areas, whether it was Scottsdale, Southern Cal., Philly, and now San Francisco. Whatever it takes! So I took the long drive from Scottsdale heading to San Francisco. When I got to Frisco I moved into a very, very, very small studio corporate apartment at Union Square in downtown San Francisco. It was so small there wasn't even a door for the bedroom, but it was clean and in a great location.

Ironically, about 30 days after I moved, the board of directors of SpringStreet worked out a deal to marry us with another company, Realtor.com and HomeStore.com was born. After the deal went through, my board and CEO John Helm were now out of the picture. and I had new bosses and a new board with Homestore. This marriage would make HomeStore the largest, most comprehensive real estate site on the Internet at the time. Once the deal was completed we were on track to take HomeStore through an IPO sometime in August of 1999. How exciting!

The day had finally arrived. On August 10, we had our IPO Party in San Francisco, and on August 12 we had another IPO party to celebrate with our team in Scottsdale. It was official! All the accumulation of everyone's long hard hours of dedication and commitment manifested itself into success for all. We also knew it was far from over. We now had to run even faster because as a public company, we were now beholden to our new stockholders (the public), and as a public company, we had to report earnings and financials to the Security Exchange Commission (SEC). From the beginning my game plan and exit strategy was to work about two years with this venture, and if we achieved a successful IPO, I'd cash out of my stock options and move on to other opportunities. So I plowed ahead.

Along with the craziness of the merger, I was now dealing with other health issues that started to exacerbate throughout my body. There were changes going on with my skin. The skin around my fingers began tightening to the point I had trouble even making a basic fist, and the pins and needles and numbness were more prevalent. I also noticed the skin on my forearms and inner thighs began to tighten, which created a weird sensation that felt like my skin was crawling. It was very uncomfortable.

> *Short term sacrifice for long term reward!*
>
> —Andrew Botieri

These events were all happening at the same time. It seemed bittersweet because on the one hand, the accumulation of all my hard work and efforts over the past two decades positioned me for a once in a lifetime opportunity. On the other hand, the stress and pressure was not letting up, and my body didn't feel like it was getting any better. But I kept focused and kept trying to push to the back of my mind the inevitable; something was going on with my body. Something was happening inside of me, and my doctors still had no idea what it was.

As the fall of 1999 approached, the skin on my fingers began to tighten even more. My fingers on my outstretched hands were starting to turn in with a pronounced curvature to them. As I looked at my hands, I started taking this whole medical thing a lot more seriously. My fingers felt stiff, and the joint pain seemed to increase more frequently. Over the next few weeks my fingers began curling under, toward the palm of my hands. I lost the ability to play my guitar. I couldn't get my fingers to form a basic chord. That was devastating. I put the guitar down, and a rush of fear and anxiety jolted through my body. For the first time I felt scared, I was dejected. To make matters worse, my family was on the other side of the country, and at this time I decided not to share the depressing news with them. Music had been such a large part of my life. I enjoyed playing guitar and now that joy was being taken away from me.

As the weeks went by, I noticed even buttoning a shirt or tying a shoelace became a difficult chore. Okay, something was going on with my body other than the doctor's diagnosis of arthritis. What was going on, and when would it get better...or worse? I began to pray for an answer.

After I moved to San Francisco one of the first things was to find a primary doctor and a rheumatoid arthritis specialist. Maybe these guys would know what the hell was going on with my body. My primary doctor was located between my house in Oakland Hills and my office in downtown San Francisco. As I walked into his office, I couldn't believe my eyes. The guy looked and acted like Christopher Lloyd's character Doc, the mad scientist in the *Back To the Future* movies. He even had the same hairdo. It was really weird, almost uncomfortable. Welcome to California, where even the average person looks like a celebrity. After that initial meeting, I could never look him in the face or take him seriously because all I could think of was Doc. He began to tell me, "Man has pain throughout his body because we do activities, like walking upright, lifting heavy objects that counteract the way our bodies were structured to work when we were apes and chimps."

Hmmm...Okay, Doc, anytime now you can refer me to an arthritic specialist, quickly, so I can move on. So I received my referral and called for an appointment.

I kept thinking all of this made no sense whatsoever. I'd always been a picture of good health. I ate well, exercised often, and kept my spiritual side active. But now I was working 60-plus hours a week, finding no time to exercise and burn off stress. As for Church, I wasn't even finding time to attend services. I was just praying to help take this company public, work hard, keep the stock price high, and cash out. It seemed never ending. I was getting caught up in the moment and never realized it could be costing me my life. I was focusing on the money and not enjoying the honey of life.

By October all the major joints in my body were aching and stiff; I had no idea what was going on or what was happening to me. I had trouble standing up straight after squatting for short periods of time. My hands were so tight now I couldn't even pinch any excess skin between my fingers or my hands. Even my temples would swell up every time I chewed any textured foods. They'd swell up about the size of half a golf ball. My elbows hurt, and anytime I slightly bumped them into a wall or chair, the pain would shoot down my arms. and it hurt like hell. At the same time, my hips, knees, shoulders all began to feel stiff and achy. You name it, it hurt. Was this just the arthritis becoming more pronounced and aggressive? Or was something else going on? I kept putting it to the back of my mind, I was busy. Maybe it's that macho thing that men look at themselves as invincible. Hey guys and gals, we're not invincible, we do bleed, we do cry, and we do have fears. My biggest fear was not knowing.

With the referral slip in hand I received from Doc, I went to see an arthritic specialist in the Bay Area. I was nervous to say the least with all the changes going on with my body. What would this guy say? Would he tell me what I'd already been hearing or would he find something different? I could only pray for resolve to this unsettling medical condition.

I arrived at his office, signed in as a new patient, filled out my paperwork and waited. A few minutes seemed like half an hour. Moments later the doctor came out into the waiting area and greeted me. As we shook hands he kept hold of my right hand turning it from side to side and then reached for my other hand. What happened next blew me away.

After a moment or two he looked at me and said, "You have scleroderma."

I looked at him and said, "I have sclero-what? What the hell is scleroderma?"

"I'll need to run more tests, but you have all the symptoms."

He took me into his examining room poked and prodded for a while, did some other tests and then proceeded to tell me about scleroderma. All I remember from that meeting was hearing him say, "It has no cause and no cure." It sent my head spinning.

After he gave me his prognosis he laid out a plan for me but kept emphasizing there wasn't much they could do. In most cases you have to let it run its course unless it becomes life threatening, and then they'd have to go from there. He told me that 80 percent of people who get scleroderma are female and the mortality rate is 50 percent. "You got to be kidding me!" I said.

"No," was his response, in a serious tone.

I had to find something funny to say to brush of this devastation, so I said, "Sure. I had to go out and get a chicks disease." All this time I thought it was arthritis, and now I find out I have a disease that has no cure and can kill me. It felt like someone punched me in the stomach. I grabbed the arm of a nearby chair to keep from falling as I felt faint and nauseated. This was serious.

I shot other questions at him like, "What's the mortality rate for men?" He said it was too new of a disease to have many men's statistics. He gave me a few more instructions: what to look for, making sure I notice any other significant changes and had me schedule a follow-up appointment, and I left. I drove back to my apartment in a complete daze.

When I got home, I either sat or paced back and forth in my apartment. What was I going to do? How was I going to deal with this? How would this affect my work, my livelihood? I knew I needed to call my family, but it was late back on the East Coast, so I'd have to wait till tomorrow. But how was I going to tell my family I had a disease that might kill me?

That night I jumped on the computer and tried searching for information on scleroderma, and what I found was pretty scary. It talked about being entombed in your own skin as it began to harden, not having the ability to move your mouth or jaw and the claw effect from the fingers curling under your hand as the skin tightens, as your fingertips fuse to your palms. I felt a jolt of panic run through my body. I had to take control. I had to choose an attitude, a positive attitude, and that's created from positive thinking. And when you're faced with adversity, a positive attitude is a must ingredient.

So now what? I knew I had to be strong: mentally, physically, and spiritually. If I didn't, what advantages would I hand over to this disease? I knew from past experiences that positive attitude is a force in helping change the direction of life for the better. I also knew I'd never faced anything as powerful and destructive as scleroderma. I began reading as much as I could find about the disease. I figured if it had the ability to kill me, I'd better know as much about it as possible. The next day, I placed a call to my family back home to give them the news. There was a lot of stunned silence. In their defense, I'm not sure they knew what to say or what to do, considering the far distance between us. I had referenced a couple of books for them to read. Unfortunately, the books were not that encouraging, and my family began to worry even more. I reassured them I was feeling good, and I'd stay strong to beat this disease.

> *Spirit of heart facilitates action.*
> —Andrew Botieri

From October of 1999 to May 2000 it was business as usual with a few minor business and medical changes. The disease was spreading to different areas of my skin, but so far, according to my doctors, I was doing okay. Their biggest concern was making sure the disease didn't go internally and affect my major organs like my kidneys or lungs.

On the business front, like most companies experiencing a merger, HomeStore brought in their own management team to run things; so I moved over to national sales along with Marcia B and Mike. I asked to be relocated back to Scottsdale in January 2000 to be closer to my team and friends. I even bought a home. For the past 23 months I was overseeing a sales and operations group of around 100 people every day and now I was responsible for me and 25 national accounts. Wow, what a change. It was great to be back with the AllApartments team.

Around this same time, I'd rekindled a relationship with a former girlfriend, but unfortunately after a few months, things weren't going so well. It was a smorgasbord of emotions, both highs and lows, and it was tearing me apart. I've had my heart crushed a few times as I'm sure we all have, and I know I've broken a few as well. It's the way things go. There's a reason everything happens. Between the stress of work, dealing with my medical condition, and now a break-up, I was feeling the stress even more.

My body hurt, my spirit was dampened, but I kept moving forward. Upon returning to Scottsdale, I noticed other changes in my body. The skin on my hands became even tighter, and it became even more difficult to do simple tasks like opening jars or bottles, and most frustrating, I still was unable to play my guitar. The pain and stiffness in my knees, elbows, shoulders, and hips became more prevalent. I couldn't move or take a step without something hurting. Before I left California, my doctor gave me a referral to a couple of doctors in Scottsdale who specialized in scleroderma so they would now keep an eye on me. However, like the doctors in CA, they said we can only let time take its course for now. They kept an eye on my blood pressure and other vitals because any changes might indicate if there was major organ involvement (as major organs fail your blood pressure increases). So I sucked it up, prayed for a cure, and tapped into my two weapons: positive thinking and perseverance. That's all I could do. There were no known cures on the horizon, so I plugged along at work. All the while in the back of my mind was the disease.

I also wasn't talking much about the soured relationship after it came to an end with anyone, I kept it in. I kept my disease quiet for the most part from my co-workers because I didn't want anyone fussing over me or using it as an excuse. Those who knew about my disease were very helpful and compassionate. As I rolled into February, it had been one year since I experienced the beginning symptoms of pins and needles. Wow, a whole year had passed. My doctors now had me on three different medicines to control pain and my blood pressure.

The only positive note: about 30 days after I returned to Scottsdale, with just me to worry about for a change, I noticed the skin on my forearms began to loosen up and my temples stopped swelling. I reflected on why this was occurring, and to me, it seemed simple, I was less stressed from a work perspective. I no longer had lines of sales and office support people outside my door; part of me missed that. I was no longer dealing with sales quota issues; it was just me and my handful of accounts. I told my doctors about these findings, but without medical evidence, they couldn't say for sure it was stress related or not. They didn't have to know. I knew. I knew my body, and it seemed to be responding. But the rest of my body still ached. What I noticed now over the last few months was the extreme fatigue I was experiencing. I couldn't make it through the day without feeling totally spent. Some mornings I'd wake up and couldn't muster the strength to get out of bed. Yes, I was still working hard; just because I had a disease didn't mean I could stop working. I still had to pay bills, and I was still "rocking n' rolling." I called my doctor and he explained it was the scleroderma affecting my body, and I would just have to ride it out. For how long, was my question, he didn't know.

As June came around, we were gearing up for National Apartment Association's annual trade show and conference in New Orleans. It was June 21, 2000; a fuse was lit.

CHAPTER 13

The Powerful of Attitude

The following is an article I penned in 1992, "Attitude is the *Fuel* to Accomplishment" by Andrew Botieri.

As a sales trainer and coach, I've had hundreds of people over the years ask me "How do you always keep yourself so motivated?" It's a question at first, I'd never really thought of. All I know is over the years I'd wake up every morning ready to take on the world and all the opportunities it had to offer. My sales staffs used to roll their eyes when on every Monday morning, I would be all "pumped up" as they came walking lethargically through the door ready for our sales meeting. To me, Monday has always been the best day of the week. As I like to say, "the velocity of your Monday dictates the velocity of your week." If you have a slow Monday, you have a slow and unproductive week. It's all up to you!

I guess what it comes down to is having the "right" ATTITUDE about your life and your professional path. Let's face it; life is not a dress rehearsal. This is the only chance you have to go around and do what you were put on this earth to do. Remember that five percent is understanding; 95 percent is application. Do you know what your "purpose and reason" for being is? Everyone has one. Some find it early, some find it later and unfortunately, some never find it at all. I realized years ago my purpose and reason for being was to be a "coach" and "teacher" to those I work with and those in my life. This has been my driving force…for my entire life.

So, how can you keep the right attitude? "Attitude can't be manufactured. It's almost a spiritual thing. It comes from within. It is a love of **LIFE, SELF** and your **BELIEF SYSTEMS**. These three ingredients are the essence of ATTITUDE." Let's look at these important ingredients:

Love of Life. You have two choices every morning when you wake up... either make it a great day or make it a lousy day. Which do you prefer? What is keeping you from making the obvious choice? There is so much to get out of life that some people take for granted what they have and how they spend their free time. After my recent "brush with death," I now fully understand how precious each day is and what a reward it is to be alive. Why is it some people spend more time thinking about how to spend their money which is replaceable, but less energy on planning their "time" which is irreplaceable? Think about that! You create your own destiny. You owe it to yourself and your family to stop and smell the roses.

Love of Self. One can never succeed in life unless they are comfortable with themselves. Who are you and what do you stand for? What are your convictions and what are you passionate about? Without an answer to these questions you have no foundation to build upon. This should be an ongoing self-analysis where eventually you are able to identify your shortcomings and set written goals to achieve them.

Belief Systems. Life is a spiritual journey as well. We need humility in our lives and this comes from our belief and faith in a higher power, a higher being. It is this faith that allows us to persevere when the going gets tough and we're not sure which direction to go. The power of prayer and belief can get us through our daily challenges in business and in our personal lives. On a personal level and during my recent illness, I firmly believe the prayer of family and friends is one of the main reasons why I am still here today.

Total Peak Performance Tip. Here are three action steps to help you get started. The first thing you do is to write down the three most relaxing things you would like to do. Make it easy on yourself. Schedule it in your day planner and just go do it! No excuses! Point number two, take out a piece of paper and draw a line down the middle with a straight line across the top. Hopefully it looks like a "T." Now make a list of the things you like about yourself and the things you don't like about yourself. Each week take one item from the "don't like" column and work on it until you can move it into the "like" column. Last but not least, take a moment of "quiet time" and ponder what is important in your life and what your priorities are. Remember priorities will change, so be flexible and have fun!

Positive attitude and positive thinking play such an important role in each of our lives, whether we realize it or not. Our ability to change our attitude into an action-orientated mind-set when you face adversity or a challenge is key. God gave each and every one a truly wonderful and unique gift: free will. This allows us to reason and weigh the pros and cons of a situation during our decision making. This is what sets us apart from all other animals on this planet. With that said, each and every day we make choices that shape and mold our destiny, via our free will. The biggest choice we make every day upon rising from bed is which attitude we're going to choose.

> *Some people wake up and choose to create a mediocre or shitty day and take others down with them; while others chose to make it a great day, on purpose.*
>
> Thanks Patrick!

Attitude first begins as a conscious choice, and as you continue to be consistent with those positive choices, it then becomes an unconscious effort. You don't even have to do anything to summon it. It's just there. Like the example I used earlier on goal setting, you can eventually condition your subconscious mind to summon your positive attitude without much effort. On tough days, it does take extra effort to summon it. So how do some people always stay upbeat? That's a great question, but there is a better question.

> Attitude, it can't be manufactured; it's almost a spiritual thing. It's a love of self, life, and your God. These three ingredients are the essence of Attitude.
> —Andrew Botieri

Who Motivates the Motivator?

Do you realize the power you have within you? Realize how important your attitude is not just in your daily life, but the life of those around you. Negativism, pessimism, and plain old bitching or whining is like a cancer, and like cancer, it can spread throughout organizations, friendships and families with devastating effects. Positive thinking and optimism on the other hand are contagious; it's infectious and can spread like an out of control wildfire, if you're fortunate enough to catch it! You wear your attitude for everyone to see, whether it's positive or negative; just like deciding on what clothes you're going to wear that day.

If you're able to maintain your level of positive mental attitude through adversity and challenges, then you open up your opportunities to achieve more in your lifetime than you would've otherwise. Throughout your life, there comes a time when you will need to reach down deep and find that spirit within, that little extra bit of motivation to help you through life's many challenges. Your ability to harness the power within is such an important life skill.

Dealing with Dialysis

During the first few months after coming out of my coma, my life was full of uncertainty. The doctors weren't sure if the scleroderma would return or not. I could be fine or the disease might become active again and do more damage, even kill me. They didn't know. That left such a hollow feeling inside. As you can imagine with that hanging over my head some days were tougher than others; like not having enough energy to even get out of bed. And then there were the three-and-a-half hours of dialysis, three days a week. I had days where I felt depressed. Dialysis was the most harrowing experience by far. Dr. Kris hoped in my case to kick-start my kidneys with dialysis. But there were "no guarantees." At least there was some hope, where there is hope, there is faith, and where there is faith there are miracles.

My first experience with dialysis outside of St. Joseph's Hospital was extremely emotional and uncomfortable. First, it's the most humbling experience I've ever encountered in my life. Imagine being dependent on a machine to survive as you sit and watch your blood drain out one tube, enter the machine that cleans your blood, and then your clean blood is returned into you from another tube. This leaves one extremely fatigued. Second, after being told I may never come off of dialysis, I'd be anxious during each treatment. But the toughest part is the dialysis unit itself; it is a very depressing place. I kept thinking everything I'd worked hard for all my life seemed to be slipping away slowly as I confronted this deadly disease and its aftermath. But this whole ordeal reinforced in me I had to take on every day, every moment, every disappointment, and even small successes with the best possible attitude I could muster. I'd call on my two weapons to help with this ordeal: positive attitude and perseverance.

Mom drove me to the Scottsdale Dialysis unit for my first treatment. I got out of the car, walked through the door and was met by a nurse. I didn't let my mother come in the first time. It would be too hard on her. I was led into the unit and was taken aback by the number of patients sitting around a large square room in their chairs receiving treatment. The machines were all humming in chorus. There were over 20 chairs and each one was occupied. Most were senior citizens; others in their 30s, 40s and 50s and as I walked by some patients to my chair, you could feel their pain and anguish, it was so surreal. You could feel their despair!

After I was placed in my chair, the nurse began connecting the lines to the catheter port hanging from my chest. I looked around the room more closely and saw patients who had amputated legs due to diabetes which can exacerbate kidney failure. The nurses informed me over the first couple weeks most of the patients were receiving dialysis three to four days a week and had been for years. So who could blame them for the way they felt? As I sat in my chair, I felt panicked. I started wondering if I'd end up like they were. I started buying into my negative self-talk. You know that little voice? Could I be destined for an amputation because of my situation? My first thought was if that's what it's going to be like, I'd rather die now and get it over with. A nurse mentioned a few patients had been receiving dialysis for over 15 years. At this moment it felt like a spear being thrust into my chest. I felt like a thousand pounds fell upon me; my heart and spirit dampened. Nausea set it, and I felt faint.

For what was to be many three-hour sessions my time was divided between watching a little eight-inch TV attached to a retractable arm coming off my chair. Or reading, sleeping, fainting, or staring out into space wondering what the hell was going on. Each session created physical and emotional trauma. At the end of my sessions Mom picked me up and drove me home.

As I lay in bed that first night after my first dialysis, I made a couple of promises to myself. One was not to allow anyone to drop me off inside the dialysis unit because I didn't want them to have that picture in their minds of how depressing the atmosphere was. Second, maybe the lesson here was not about me. Maybe it was about the other patients who were worse off than me at this point. I made a commitment to try and make their lives a little better, a little brighter. It may not turn their lives around, but maybe make them feel a little better as they were hooked up to their machines.

Even if I wasn't in the best of moods heading to dialysis, I'd put a smile on my face and say, "Hi," to the patients and nurses on my way to my chair. I got to know many of them by name. I'd stop and ask how they were doing. I began to tease and joke with them. I then started teasing the nurses to help relieve their stress from dealing with all of this.

One nurse told me, "You're very popular."

I inquired. She said after a couple weeks, the patients kept asking her, "Is Andrew coming in today?" When I heard this, my eyes filled with tears. That was my sign. I now made it my mission to cheer everyone up. Was this what God had intended this lesson to be about?

It seemed for the first few weeks a couple doctors at the D unit reminded me there were no guarantees of the kidneys kicking in. They pointed out the length of dialysis time (in years) of some patients. How could they be so defeatist? Maybe they were being realists, but how can someone who is an optimist be a realist? I knew they didn't want me to get my hopes up too high. They expressed a concern of possible depression if I didn't come off.

A bad day at dialysis: looking back I'm glad I didn't have many bad episodes during treatments like the other lifer patients had. Some constantly moaned and groaned in their chairs for hours. Others, especially a few of the amputee patients, moaned how they wanted their life to end; they were tired and didn't want to go on anymore. Even as I mustered up a positive attitude before treatments, I'd still find myself asking, "How long would it take before I started saying this?"

My bad or tough days came about once every other week. The most painful occurred when the nurses drew out your blood (to clean it) and water (urine and other toxic liquids) from your body. Their challenge was to regulate the proper amount of water to take out of your body. Sometimes they'd take out too much water, and your body went into severe cramping. My toes, feet, hands, and fingers would constrict and cramp. It was so painful and discomforting. I'd have to call a nurse over to pull my extremities back into place or massage them to reduce the cramping. The pain got rather intense. Sometimes there was nothing they could do about the cramping, and it hurt like hell as tears came to my eyes.

To give you an idea of how much water they drew out after each treatment, my average weight loss from water weight was about six to seven pounds. I began calling it my dialysis diet.

The worst part during dialysis was the fainting. Again, the nurses tried to regulate how much blood was being drawn out. Every patient reacts differently depending on what they ate before they arrived or how well they slept the night before. There were so many different variables. The dialysis chairs looked like a reclining chair, though the chair back was designed so it could quickly be pushed down when you were in the process of fainting. The nurses threw the chair back so your head was almost touching the floor and your feet were up in the air to allow blood to rush back to your head. Sometimes the nurses made it in time to revive you, and other times you passed out for a few seconds or minutes. I hated that feeling of slipping into faint mode.

Sometimes I had both the cramping and fainting during the same session. Boy did that suck!! It also sucked the energy out of my body, where I'd spend the rest of the day recuperating back home. Most times I came home from dialysis and went straight to bed and slept for three to four hours. But to its credit, the dialysis machine is an incredible invention and a life saver. My hats off to every nurse who works or has worked in a dialysis unit. You truly are heroes!

Post Event Reflections

By now I'd been out of the hospital for almost two months. Between the hospital and home I had ample time to think about what happened and what these events were supposed to mean. What was the purpose of all this? Was it part of my master plan, my blueprint? One night I started thinking about my purpose and reason. Not that I hadn't before in the past because I've always felt a need to put a concrete hand on why we are all here and if it's part of God's master plan. I do believe our journey through life is to identify what our purpose and reason is and then take action to fulfill or enhance it.

I believe people fall into three categories: those who find their purpose early on in life, others who find it later in life, and unfortunately, some who never find it at all. It's there, however. I think the ones who never find their purpose and reason didn't make consistent and good choices in their life and wandered off their trail. How sad! What is your purpose and reason? Have you really thought about it? Sit down with a piece of paper, a journal, or the rest of this page, ponder and write your thoughts down. It's a great exercise.

CHAPTER 14

Coming Back Home to My Roots

My medical situation wasn't changing anytime soon. My doctors in Arizona said it would be a long haul. Some said it could take about 9 to 12 months before I'd be back on my feet, but only if I came off dialysis shortly. Others told me if my kidneys didn't kick-start, the ordeal could take much longer. I guess I thought I could bounce back from anything in a reasonable fashion of my own choosing. I guess I was wrong.

My situation in Scottsdale was changing. My family needed to get back to their lives in Massachusetts, so it was at this point I decided to follow through on the promise I made to myself and Mom that day in the hospital. It was time to pack up my life in Scottsdale and go home where I grew up. The timing was right; both my body and a broken heart needed healing. What a better place to heal than back home. It was time to focus and put myself on a path to recovery physically, mentally and spiritually.

Saying Good-bye to Scottsdale

After returning to Scottsdale, I was busy between dialysis, putting my house on the market, and packing up my life once again. Ironically many of my possessions were still in boxes as I never finished unpacking from my January 2000 move prior to getting sick in June. As I wandered around my house packing, I realized I never had the chance to turn my house into a home. By now my co-workers and friends knew I wasn't coming back to work. Over the next few weeks many friends dropped in to say goodbye. I felt sad. I felt a little lost.

This was supposed to be a new beginning for me in Scottsdale; alas I've also realized that change is constant.

A very touching moment occurred attending a SpringStreet office get-together with my old team at a nearby hotel. The same team I hired, trained, and loved. The same team that was handed a big challenge, and through creativity, perseverance, and long hours, we did it! We helped Mike Mueller realize his incredible vision. I was very proud of that group. During the party, a small group of close co-workers took me to an outside patio. I wasn't sure what was going on. We stood in a circle. They began sharing their thoughts about how I had inspired them, how I touched their lives, and how important I'd been to them. I was completely blown away. I started to tear up. What a sap I am. I guess we never know the affect we have on someone until moments like this.

My team knew I was a collector of the famous contemporary artist, Thomas Kinkade. When I was transferred to our San Francisco office, they presented me a Kinkade painting called "Chinatown" depicting a scene in San Francisco's Chinatown. As they finished up their emotional words, they presented me with another Kinkade painting; this one depicting a lighthouse and cottage on the edge of a rock-laden embankment above the ocean. Strong waves crashing up and over the rocks below. The beam from the lighthouse shines against morning's first light as the lights from inside the cottage casts a reflection on the rocks below. The painting is called "Beacon of Hope." How appropriate.

As they handed me the painting, I looked down at the beautiful painting, read the title, and began to cry. I couldn't stop. Love comes in many forms. They were my beacon of hope. After we caught our composure, they wanted me to say something. Wow, this was going to be tough. I wasn't ready for this. I tried to muster what self-composure I had, and through a crackling voice and flowing tears, I told them how much I appreciated and loved them and thanked them for this wonderful gift. Through continued tears I said, "I will never forget you or this moment."

We all stood in the circle hugging and crying in one big love fest! Today, I proudly hang both paintings in my house as a reminder of how in my hour of need, they were there for me. How blessed I truly am.

When my sister Karen flew out to spend some time with me, it wasn't all site-seeing and fun; she had to endure a second procedure to replace the shunt catheter in my chest. For a couple weeks the tubes on my shunt were being forced to close as my body rejected the lines in my chest. In some cases, if your body recognizes a foreign object it will try to destroy it. That's what was happening, so it had to be replaced. What was cool was the inventor of the Schon catheter, Dr. Donald Schon, replaced the shunt and catheter. He was a great guy and effortlessly performed the replacement. Again I asked not to be put under sedation.

Karen drove me to dialysis and hung at my house until my time was up. After about five days and a great visit, she flew home. I was sad to see her go. She had been the glue back home holding everything together while I lay in the hospital teetering on death. I said my goodbyes, but told her I'd see her soon. After she left I had to count on friends to bring me to and from dialysis, and if I couldn't, I'd drive myself. I wasn't supposed to, as I could get fainting spells after treatments. I can be stubborn at times, but I knew it wasn't smart. This was another reason in my decision to move home. I knew I'd always have a ride.

One of the last things I had to do before I left was go for my last kidney check-up at Dr. Kris's office. The same office I collapsed in to begin this strange ordeal. I shuffled in and registered at the front desk. The nurses, who were there that fateful day, were shocked to see me standing in front of them. One nurse commented how much better I looked than I did a few months back. We all chuckled. My appointment was with Dr. Laurel, who, ironically, I had my original appointment with on the morning of Thursday, June 29.

A nurse led me into an observation room to wait. I heard someone grab my chart off the hook outside the door and heard the person say, "Is this the guy who collapsed in our office a few months ago?"

"Yes," the nurse said.

I'll never forget his words, "Wow, he's alive?"

When he came in he looked at me and said "do you realize that you shouldn't be alive?" He continued, "Most people wouldn't have survived."

I smirked and said, "Yes I'm told that a lot lately."

I was given a good bill of health to move across the country and back home. He made sure to forward all my records to my new nephrologist in Massachusetts. He also confirmed my new treatment schedule at the Weymouth dialysis unit. After leaving the examining room, I sought out Dr. Kris and found him in his office. I thanked him again for saving my life, and said I'd never forget him. He sheepishly took my compliment. With a warm handshake we parted.

Another chapter in my book of life was coming to an end and a new chapter not yet penned. On October 5, 2000, the movers came to my house in Scottsdale, packed up my "life," and at 3:25 p.m. on October 7, my buddy Greg drove me to the Phoenix airport for my flight home…on a one-way ticket. "Lord Jesus, may Your bright light be my protective shield." The sun was about to set on another chapter of my life.

CHAPTER 15

The Power of Miracles, Part 2

As I was writing the article "My Celebration of Life," I reflected and pondered this whole new experience and what it meant. What lessons were within? Did it mean my life as I've known it was over? Would I have to live on dialysis or was this just the beginning of the disease and its disabling affect? Why did God give me a second chance? I'm still not sure, though in my heart-of-hearts, I know there is a reason. I feel there were three key factors in my miraculous recovery from my brush with death.

First, of course, were God and His son, Jesus. I strongly believe Jesus came down and placed his healing hands on me, pulling me from the grips of death. Some of the doctors that day in the ER thought I wouldn't make it. They were ready to give up. I don't think they realized who I had fighting in my corner. Even today, while attending Church, the first thing I do is look up at the cross, at Jesus, and thank Him for my life. The two of us have a very special bond now and forever.

Second, thousands of people were praying for me all over the country. Maybe it's my faith or my belief, but I believe in the power of prayer, the power of our Lord. Prayer works. I am a living testament to that. I am not a religious fanatic; I learned from firsthand experience. When troubling times are upon you, prayer and faith are the intangibles to help you through your crisis. Give it a try. Give it to God.

And third, I never let up on my strong positive attitude and my strong will to persevere and survive. I obviously wasn't ready to check out yet. I have no doubt in my mind that Divine Intervention played a crucial role in surviving this life threatening crisis.

Nancy's Story

A few months after my life-threatening event, a friend of mine, Nancy, told me of a chilling incidence she experienced involving my illness and a small wooden box. Here is Nancy's story in her own words she gave me shortly after I came back to Massachusetts in 2000.

It was around 4:00 a.m. on a Monday; I was tossing and turning as we (myself and Andrew's family and friends) had all been doing for days after hearing about Andrew's sudden medical crisis. As I lay in bed, I kept hearing my name, but thought I was dreaming. Confused and restless, I got out of bed. I heard a familiar voice coming from the hallway. Thinking I was losing my mind for hearing voices in the dark, I sat at the top of the stair to clear my head. Then I heard the voice more clearly. I looked around and saw no one. Curious and scared I sat very still, listening. The voice came again in a low, comforting whisper as if to keep me calm. The voice said, "Tell him to put it in the box with the Angel on it."

The voice repeated this phrase three times. The second time, the voice became familiar, a female voice that I recognized but couldn't get it to register. I sat for a moment and stood up intending to go back to bed. At the time I wasn't even wondering what the voice had said, because it made no sense to me whatsoever. I was thinking about the voice.

I then looked down the staircase and noticed my kitten, Sedona, standing at the bottom of the stairs staring up at me. I went down, sat on the last step and put her on my lap. Then in a startling louder voice she said, "He must put it in the box, look at it, cherish it, but never wear it!"

I nervously looked around again and saw no one. Now I was beginning to become frightened. Sedona jumped off my lap and went into the living room where she sat and whined and whined. Confused and sleep deprived, I went and picked her up. I then noticed an object next to her. I thought she might've knocked over a picture frame off the bookshelf. I picked the object up, not really focusing on what I held in my hand. I stood for a minute and felt a warm rush of calm and comfort which overcame me. I now knew that voice! It was my Nana's. She had recently passed away, and when I called out my Nana's name, my kitty stopped whining.

Next, I walked into the kitchen and turned on the light. I felt like I was coming out of a sleep. I now realized that I had the object in my hand. I looked down and couldn't believe what I saw, a small wooden box about four inches by four inches and two-and-a-half inches deep. I looked closer and there it was, an Angel on the top of the box, a cherub's face. I suddenly recognized it as being like the one I had long ago, but I hadn't seen it in many years. Amazed and stunned, I sat down looking at the picture of the Angel. I held the box while thinking of my Nana's voice. I opened it and the box was empty. I closed the box and went over in my head again what the voice was saying. I was sure now that I wasn't dreaming.

Then, I remembered what I was thinking about earlier before I heard my name being called from the darkness of my bedroom. I was recalling a visit to a spiritual advisor over a year ago. I've been to see spiritual advisors in the past and had always seemed to get fairly accurate information about my job or my love life. I had been making mental notes to remind Karen (Andrew's sister) of something the psychic told me.

The psychic asked me, "Who is Karen? Tell her to tell him not to wear black onyx. It's the stone of death. Tell her not to wear it either."

I wasn't sure what the psychic meant by this and that's probably why I never mentioned it to Karen earlier.

During Andrew's crisis, Karen and I were on the telephone constantly. Seeing I was in the medical field, I ended up being the translator of medical information from the hospital where Andrew was in Phoenix to his family here in Massachusetts. I was on the phone with his cousin Paula, herself a heart specialist nurse of cardiac care. She would relay information about Andrew, and I then put it into words the family could understand. In the beginning the prognosis was not encouraging. His family was so distraught and full of anxiety it was the least I could for them. We all felt so helpless being over 2000 miles away, not knowing and not being able to be with him to let him know we all loved him and wanted to give him our support and comfort.

As I lay in bed, I recalled I'd spoken to Karen earlier that day about what the psychic had said about her and the black onyx stone. What Karen said next stunned me, even to this day. Andrew had a ring left to him by his late Italian grandfather. It was a simple, yet beautiful black onyx ring. That was it! The ring! It was Andrew's ring that was meant to go into the wooden box with the Cherub on it! I felt a cold chill go through my body. I was filled with relief to finally understand what the psychic meant when she warned me, "Tell her to tell him not to wear black onyx. It's the stone of death."

I was feeling very eerie and spooked. But now I had another dilemma; how did this box mysteriously appear in my living room? I could hardly sleep for the rest of the night after what I had experienced. The next morning I immediately called my mother and asked her if she remembered the box with the cherub on it.

She said, "Yes, I saw it yesterday when I was dusting the bookshelf by the fireplace, why?" I asked her to go and get it. She came back to the phone and said, "Well it was here yesterday."

I recounted my bizarre story to my mother, and then I told her I was holding the box in my hand. Everyone was so concerned about Andrew during the first few days of his illness because no one knew if he was going to make it through the night. After I mentioned to my mom that I was holding the Cherub box, she said, "Good, that makes me a lot feel better. Because if he is to put his ring into the blessed wooden box, then we must know that he'll need to get better, so he can place the ring in the box himself."

Every time I read this I get chills accompanied by tears. It would be months later that Nancy made some additional comments about the night she had a spiritual reading. In addition to the psychic asking, "Who's Karen?" and the whole black onyx ring thing, the psychic also said to Nancy, "There's a Sagittarian who's going to get a wake-up call next year."

At the time, in 1999, it made no sense to Nancy. That was until she found out my birthday is December 19, a Sagittarian. Kind of freaky, huh?

Kicking Dialysis

As you know for months I continued telling the doctors, "I'll be off dialysis in six months."

I was becoming a pain in the ass I bet. At one encounter, a doctor pointed his finger at me saying in a frustrated voice, "You don't know what you're dealing with."

I looked him right back in the eye, lying in my dialysis chair, pointed my finger at him and said, "No you don't know who you're dealing with; I'm off this in six months."

Five-and-a-half months after my first dialysis treatment, I was sitting in my chair and the doctor was running my blood numbers and levels as he always did. Chuckling he said, "I don't believe you."

I said, "About what?"

He looked at me and said, "Today is your last day on dialysis!"

By the Grace of God, your prayers, and a positive attitude: in fewer than six months, I was done. My kidneys kicked back in. I was off dialysis! My prayers were answered. Some would call it a miracle.

"What!" I yelled. I had to call Mom. I dialed my cell and she picked up. But all that came out were tears.

She urgently said, "What's wrong?"

I said through my tears, "Everything is good. I'm coming off dialysis!" I couldn't believe it. God answered my prayers, the prayers of family and friends, and your prayers. I can't thank all of you enough. My family and I celebrated by popping a bottle of champagne and of course drinking it!

As the months went by my skin began to soften, became more supple. I could pinch skin again where before it was too tight. My fingers began to straighten out and the stiffness started to diminish. After four months of coming off dialysis, I began playing guitar again. It was a true miracle! Thank you God. I am now playing guitar and singing regularly at local establishments in the Plymouth area.

And after six months, once the catheter was taken out of my chest, I could take my first shower. No more sponge baths for me.

Guardian Angels Revealed

It wouldn't be until 2005, when I'd sit with a local medium, Maureen Hancock, who's received national attention and television exposure, where she revealed to me my guardian angels. For those who are not familiar with the term, a medium is someone who has the ability to channel the spirits and souls of those on the "other side" through themselves. In other words, they can talk with the dead. You may be familiar with John Edward of "Crossing Over" fame who is also an incredible medium. I can understand some of you may be skeptical, I used to be skeptical as well, but Maureen turned me into a believer. She knows she gets her ability to talk with the dead from God. As a little girl growing up, she'd hear voices around her and her family thought she was crazy. Years later she would see the gift she was given. Prior to this, she was a stand-up comedian in Boston.

I accompanied my two nieces, my Aunt Laura, and Cousin Nancy, to a private reading with Maureen. My aunt had lost her husband, Uncle Ralph, a few months earlier. I want to share what Maureen got through me. Keep in mind she didn't know me or anything about me. In the past when I've visited a psychic, I don't divulge much information so I can test them; to see if they truly are in tune with their powers. It doesn't take long to find out.

Maureen approached me and placed her hand on my knee and instantly pulled back with a small smile and said, "Do you realize you have two very strong Guides around you?" I felt at least one, but two, that might explain some things. She continued, "Most people have only one Guide, I haven't seen many people with two."

One was an older Guide, the other a young man. She said the older Guide, was a proud Native American Warrior, but what she confirmed next is something I've felt since a young child. She told me the young man with her, of teenage years, was speaking to her by showing her images. This is how she can interpret what those from the other side are trying to communicate. She said they communicate at such a fast pace she can rarely understand what they are saying, so they use images. If you've seen John Edward and "Crossing Over," you know how symbols play an important part in his ability to interpret what these spirits or souls of the deceased are trying to say to him.

She told me this young man was taking her outside, walking her through some woods, down to the edge of a pond and to the water's edge. She looked up at me and said, "Did he drown?"

I knew this had to be Andrew, my name sake. But I wanted more confirmation. She then said, "Who wanted to be a priest?"

Now I knew it was Andrew. As a teenager, he was very involved in his Catholic Church and was an altar boy who'd been considering entering the seminary. My eyes started to fill with tears.

But there was more. She looked at me making the, "Yer out!" signal, like a home plate umpire does. She leaned in and asked me if I'd recently come close to dying, something sudden. The room went silent. I shook my head in the affirmative, but didn't offer any more information. Mediums who are good will "see" the information and reveal it to you. Maureen is good. She related that they, my relatives from the other side, were telling her that on that fateful day when all the doctors working on me thought I wouldn't last the day, I began to crossover to the other side. I was dying. I was lying in a coma and had no idea what was happening. Maureen told me my relatives (Andrew, Uncle Louis, and Gramp to name a few) instructed me to turn back. To live. They said it wasn't my time to go, there was more for me to accomplish. Without missing a beat Maureen mentioned it may have something to do with making cassette tapes and public speaking. At the time she had no idea what I did for a living. She said they were making fun of me because I kept talking about writing a book, but never got around to it. Well I got around to it. Interesting yeah?

I sat there frozen, dumbfounded, in a daze. This is what I'd been hoping to find out. How close did I come to dying that day? The doctors said I shouldn't have survived, it was that close, but I needed to hear this as painful as it may be. I began to cry. My relatives who had gone before me, were there that day in the hospital keeping an eye on me. They sent me back, but for what purpose? That's the journey I now find myself on.

Maureen says when our relatives or close friends die and crossover, they never leave us, and they're always there for us. Maureen jokingly says our relatives don't visit during the three S's (shit, shower, and sex). She emphasizes they do hear us, and they are around us. Remember, if you have a grandparent, parent, sibling, or friend who has died and crossed over they can hear you, and they want you to communicate with them. This is the power of love. Since Maureen shared this with me, I speak to my relatives every chance I can. She has helped me deal with the feelings and emotions I felt after my crisis and helped put some missing pieces together in my puzzle.

Your Master Plan

You see there is a master plan for all of us, and I feel a large portion of that plan has been predetermined for us. God being the Architect. Does that mean we have no say in this predetermined life of ours? I say we do have a lot of say in our destiny and in the direction it travels. You choose your destiny every day. You also choose your attitude every day. How? By consciously making better decisions to increase the joy and successes in your life, or the reverse is you'll make bad, ill-informed choices that steer you down the road to mediocrity and unhappiness. It truly is up to you! So what are you going to do to increase your sound decisions and opportunities available in your life today?

The reason I keep bringing up choices is because that's what life is all about: choices.

> Destiny is not a matter of chance; destiny is a matter of choice.
> —William Jennings Bryan

As mentioned earlier, I've felt I had a purpose, a reason for being. It's part of that master plan that's out there somewhere, and it included me! That's how my public speaking career got started. Over the years I had this ability to inspire others, to motivate them to reach great heights, to share my knowledge and nurture and grow them. So many people come up to me months after an engagement, or maybe a former sales person who worked for me, and they'll say how I changed their life! That is my purpose and reason for being!

I can say, over the years I've touched many people, and they've touched me as well. Though sometimes, you wonder how much you've meant to the people you know or encounter. Is what you're doing making a difference? That's the big unknown. Is what you're doing changing the way people think about their own lives? One of the most rewarding things about what I do now as an inspirational speaker is the feedback I receive about the impact I've had on someone's life. One such incident occurred when an attendee of a just-completed seminar walked up and introduced herself to me. She mentioned she had seen me speak two years earlier and how what I said changed her life. Here's her story:

> I've seen you speak before and you told us about how we had the power within us to make better choices in our life, and we need to take responsibility for our actions and by doing so we can create positive events to occur in our lives. Well I listened and thought about what you had to say. I was in a bad marriage, I knew for a while what I had to do, but I didn't have the nerve. I went home after your seminar, asked my husband for a divorce, and now, my son and I have been living on our own for over a year. We have a wonderful new life that has opened many possibilities. What you said Andrew changed my life for the better, thank you so much."

I'll never forget that encounter as long as I live. Me, the big baby, my eyes began to water up, and I got a little short of breath. It was incredibly overwhelming. Words can't describe that feeling. See your life is *all* about the choices you make each and every day.

You need to reach and strive toward your own personal dreams and goals and challenge yourself to take something from this book. Think about your life and what changes you can make to enable you to live longer and enjoy life the way it should be lived. Make better choices. I didn't, and I almost paid the ultimate price. What about you?

I grew up knowing there was so much more out there in our endless universe and that somehow we are all connected in some way if not at least sharing a common bond. Every single person reading this book has the ability, has the potential, to overcome almost any obstacle in life by applying positive mental attitude to the situation or challenge, to be persistent, never giving up, and putting those thoughts into action. But you have to choose to do it! And this is where your discipline becomes into play.

Discipline is the art of identifying our bad habits and making positive changes and having the stick-to-itiveness to keep at it long enough to turn a bad habit into a good and productive habit.

CHAPTER 16

Why This Book?

After that day on June 29, 2000, my life and how I would live it changed forever. Even the doctors weren't sure of my outcome. They told me I would also experience emotional mood swings as I struggled with the feelings and emotions of my crisis. Of what it was like to teeter on the edge of death and then contemplating the prospects of dialysis maybe for the rest of my life. I had a lot of choices to contemplate from the onset of my crisis. I knew from here on out my choices truly would affect my health and my life, from a renal diet to weekly dialysis to weekly doctor visits. Is this what I had to look to forward to? I knew it came down to my daily mind-set. The same in your life. Could I continue to handle the medical and mental challenges from here on forward? Could I overcome it? What would I choose?

So what finally prompted me to write this book? A few months after my ordeal, a friend and business associate, Jeff Smedley, was the editor of an industry magazine called *The Apartment Professional*. Jeff kept in contact to check up on my health. During one such phone call, he mentioned he was looking for a different kind of article than the typical leasing or marketing articles he ran in his magazine. This was not the first time he'd asked me to pen an article. In fact, I'd written several articles for Jeff and other apartment industry magazines over the years; however, no article was going to be as hard as this one. This time, the article would be about something very deep and personal to me, my struggle and triumph over an autoimmune disease called scleroderma.

"My Celebration of Life," by Andrew Botieri

The following article, with a few slight changes based on updates from my doctors, ran in the January/February 2001 issue of *The Apartment Professional*.

We can all remember a time, a day, and an event that not only changed our lives, but re-shaped our thinking about life completely. My event was June 29, 2000. It was the day that my physical life on this earth almost came to an end. Because of a misdiagnosis from a doctor, I went into complete renal kidney failure, hypertensive crisis, I had hemorrhaging in the brain and I went into a coma for 28 hours due to an autoimmune disease I contracted called Scleroderma. The disease has no cure and can be fatal. I feel emphatically that the disease, in my case, was brought about because of stress. I was working over 70 plus hours a week. I also feel that stress is the "trigger" for so many other diseases and illnesses that affect us today.

When I was brought into the emergency room in Phoenix my blood pressure was 270 over 170 and the doctors who were urgently working on me told my friends that they needed to call my parents and a priest. My parents flew out from back east not knowing if I would be alive when they got to the hospital. It was that close! I believe now that I am here for these three reasons: The Grace of God, Prayers from Family and Friends and because of my Positive Attitude on life.

The reason for this particular article is not to get your pity. Pity doesn't get you anywhere in life. What I'm hoping to get is your ATTENTION. This is an article on prioritizing our lives and how attitude plays a major role in what we become…an article that after reading, I hope you really do make a change in your life. A life where family, friends and you are the priority…not work or complacency. I spent 14 days in the hospital recuperating, six of those days were spent in the Intensive Care Unit as they tried to stabilize my blood pressure and rid my body of the toxins caused by my kidney's complete shutdown.

As I lay in my hospital bed thinking about all my accomplishments and what my life was about, I realized even with all my successes and fortunes, I almost went to my grave never having an opportunity to really enjoy life as it should be lived. Why? Because most of my focus in life was work, work, work. Never taking needed vacations, never relaxing, always on the go. Sound familiar? When I awoke from my coma and realized that I had been through a "brush with death" experience, my mind really started to wander and wonder. I thought of my family, my nieces and nephews who would have never really known who their uncle was and for me never seeing them alive again. I actually visualized what their lives would be like without me in it. It was very scary!

Every day since my crisis my life has been full of challenges and frustrations. Like being hooked up to a dialysis machine three days a week, three and a half hours a day. But the one thing that helped me through it was my strong positive attitude about life. I had been on dialysis for five months after my crisis and then another miracle happened...I was taken off of dialysis by the Grace of God. I prayed everyday as I still do today, thanking God for sparing my life. I think of all the people all over the country that were praying for me. It was and still is very overwhelming.

Though I will never be fully out of the woods, I am so thankful to be alive and I find myself enjoying even the smallest of pleasures in life. Please take a close look at your lives...Are you living or just existing? Reevaluate and reprioritize what you are doing in your life. God has given me a second chance to fulfill my "purpose and reason" for being...not everyone is given a second chance. So live your life to its fullest today and follow your dreams because every day is precious.

As I was writing this particular article I wanted to generate some immediate benefit to the reader. I had to get the readers to think about the important issues in their lives. I wanted people to feel something after they finished reading this article. The proverbial wake-up-and-smell-the-coffee story or almost in my case wake-up-and-smell-the-coffin story.

A few days after the article was printed, phone calls and emails came pouring in from all over the country from people sharing their concerns and best wishes for my recovery. They expressed how the article, "My Celebration of Life," had truly affected their lives. Some recounted stories about themselves or a family member who had an illness or disease and how that whole experience changed their lives forever. I also heard stories from people who knew others who needed to make changes in their lives but wouldn't make or didn't take it seriously and ended in a sudden illness or death. Others shared how the article made them think about putting some immediate changes into place, so they could consciously move their lives forward in a more positive direction. Many others said they were working way too much and forgetting about the things that were most important to them, like their families, children, friends, and the balance they were trying to achieve. I am sure that sounds familiar with many of you reading this book.

Others made copies of my article and handed them out at work, to friends and family members who were border-line workaholics. These are the people who tend to focus totally on their business stuff and forget about taking time out of their hectic life to stop and smell the roses. I was this workaholic. I almost died striving for the golden ring without taking care of myself along the way. Today I consider myself a recovering workaholic and still try to find a good balance. In my humble opinion, I believe this is the way life is supposed to be lived. But I can only bring the horse to water, I can't make it drink. You must take action in your own life. You must decide what balance you want and strive to achieve that place. How? First by writing a game plan on how to balance your life, then list what's most important both personally and professionally and lastly put it into action. Make it happen. This is just another form of goal setting. Have at it!

I shared my article with family and friends, many who didn't really know what I'd experienced or gone through. As they read the article, I could see from their body language the look of disbelief, horror, and the tears that came to many eyes. Not only was it affecting people in the apartment industry, the article was now beginning to change the lives of those most important to me, my family and friends. Instantly, my mom, my new marketing manager (inside joke), made dozens and dozens of copies and began handing them out to all her friends at the local grocery store. Leave it to a mom to always be your biggest fan. Though she still doesn't talk much about what happened that fateful day, I know it hit her like a ton of bricks. In her wildest dreams, I know she never envisioned her oldest son, or in fact any of her children, dying from a deadly, unknown disease. As the old adage goes, parents should not outlive their children. Like my dad, she comes from that generation where they don't show a lot of outward emotion or talk about things. But on the inside I know it was tearing them both up. She has honored me by placing my article in a beautiful gold-trimmed frame she displays in her home for all to read and be touched by.

Something else happened as a result of the article. Several people told me either they or their pastor or priest began reading my article to their congregations. I was stunned! I was on dozens and dozens of prayer lists all over the country during and after my release from the hospital. Words cannot describe the love and humility I felt. I found out later, I was still on some prayer lists a year after my incident. Why? Why me? What had I done to deserve this? Had I touched that many lives over the years? I was overwhelmed.

Even my Aunt Laura got into the act. She told me, "The congregation sat in still silence as my minister read your article. There wasn't a dry eye in the place."

Even Father Mark at my mother's parish anxiously read my article to the entire congregation. Not a sound could be heard. After he finished, tears flowed from the pews. Now every time I see Father Mark, he says "Jesus Loves You." You know what Father? You're right.

These events were some of the first inklings that maybe I survived this ordeal to fulfill something important, something I am supposed to accomplish, some type of unfinished business. I feel in my heart and soul that God definitely gave me a second chance. Maybe there is a higher reason why I survived enabling me to share my story with others. Maybe to help tell others to make some minor or major changes in their lives before they get their wake-up call. Not everyone gets a second chance.

I've sat and wondered for hours why I survived and others don't. Events like this bring those thoughts out. My first nephrologist here in Massachusetts, Dr. Birjinder Singh, a well-respected and an incredible, compassionate human being who gave his all to his patients was killed in a car accident on Christmas morning of 2000, while driving to a hospital to make his rounds. And before I had a chance to finish this book my scleroderma specialist, the renowned Dr. Korn would die of cancer. Why? Why is it that some get a second chance and others don't? I know it's so easy to say, "That's just the way it is," but it still doesn't make sense.

I realized that life isn't fair, and you better get the most out of your time on this earth because you *never* know. You never know when the end is the end. I guess it has to do if our purpose and reason for being is realized, and we've accomplished what we are supposed to. And then it's time for us to move on to the next life. I guess this falls under the mysteries and miracles of God. All I know is I am so thankful God and his son, Jesus, saw within their infinite wisdom and power to spare me. I now continue on a journey to find out why and to follow His path and purpose for me.

As I finish this book, my health is good. I've come to grips knowing I'll always have this disease, but so far the doctors feel it will stay dormant. I am now only taking one 20 mg of blood pressure medication a day and a Prilosec for my acid reflux. Life is wonderful after a frightful journey with this deadly disease called scleroderma.

AFTERWORD

So, What Have I Learned?

Though this is the last chapter of this book, it's by no means the end or the end of the "living" chapters in my book of life. It's the beginning of a new journey and I hope, after reading this book, a new journey and new consciousness for you, your family and your friends.

I feel I've reached a different place in my life, a place that's still very hard to explain or sometimes hard to understand. Even as time drifts forward from that fateful day, it's still hard to realize and comprehend how close I came to dying. Without having a chance to say goodbye to family and friends. In my mind, I still go back to that uncomfortable and strange emotional feeling of waking up out of a coma and hearing what my body had gone through.

After any life changing event, the subtle things in life begin to look different, and you begin to see, smell, taste, feel, and hear everything in a different way. Things are a little more detailed bringing more pleasurable experiences. I think it's because the event itself makes you slow down, makes the whole pace of your life slow down and it allows you to appreciate everything around you. But it has to be a conscious decision, because you can easily fall back into the grind of life. It's not always easy to keep on track.

I know I'm in the right place, whether it's the sound of birds chirping, the baby squirrels chasing each other through the trees in my backyard, or standing in an afternoon spring shower getting soaked and enjoying it. You don't worry about the little stuff anymore; all you are doing is actively enjoying life and living for the moment. When is the last time you've done something like that for yourself? If you haven't, open up your calendar or make a note on your to-do-list and do something outside the box. Learn to step out of your comfort zone and be a participant in your life, not a bystander. As Nike says, "Just Do It!"

Since my crisis I've had a lot of time to reflect and ponder on my Celebration of Life. I mostly think back to all the people who've affected my life and how I am the better for it. I thought about all the hours I put into my career, the commitment and sacrifice to help make those companies more successful. I also realized that it all didn't really matter in the end. What matters most is that we try to make the world a little brighter, a little better and hopefully look back to see how we've made a difference in the lives of others and hopefully changed those lives for the better. That's what my mission is. In all the companies I have worked for over the years and all the teams I've help build and nurture, I feel I've had a positive effect.

I believe there were little hints from the good Lord for me to slow down that I didn't pay attention to. I believe my medical crisis was supposed to happen. It was part of my Divine plan. It demonstrated to me again when going through adversity you must tap into your inner power of mind-over-matter, the ability to tap into your positive mental attitude (PMA). Life is about paying attention to the lessons and being pro-active versus reactive with your life's choices. We all have these moments where we must learn lessons. So stop making excuses and create a plan and new direction for your life and execute your plan. The key is to not only learn, but change and shed your bad habits. By engaging your PMA you can change the course and direction of your life, a course you chart. If by reading these words you can see to it to make changes for the better in your life, then maybe that's what it's all about? Could this be my purpose and reason for being and surviving? To help you change? I think so. No, I know so!

Since going through this life-altering event, I've found a sense of wanting to give back. I guess when something is almost taken away from you that you cherish; you feel a desire to give back. I think this feeling stems from the fact, at least in my case, having been given a second chance at life, you must show your gratitude and love by giving back and helping to encourage others who may be less fortunate than you are. I feel a special joy and fulfillment when helping others, whether it's as a reading tutor for first graders, helping deliver for the organization Meals on Wheels, speaking to schools or sitting on a non-profit board or offering pro bono consulting to struggling business owners. This feeling of making a difference in the lives of others is very rewarding and having the right balance in life allows these opportunities.

I've had many people ask me how my ordeal has changed me or what lessons did I learn? In some ways I haven't changed. I still seem to be the same person I've always been, loving life and being optimistic. Yet in other ways I have changed quite a bit. I've slowed my life down, somewhere between third or fourth gear on a six-speed stick shift. Here are some other things I've learned:

- Diseases, tragedies, and other heartaches in life do not discriminate regardless of your race, religion, or how much money you make.
- Life is truly precious and in a blink of an eye, it can all be taken away from you. End of story!
- When we say we'll try harder to stay true to our beliefs and convictions, we sometimes fall short. That's okay; we're not perfect or indestructible. God made us that way.
- I know we could do a better job with anything we desire by giving it one more degree of effort.
- The power of giving back without asking anything in return is the true reward.
- Sunsets can consist of over eight different color blends.
- Small things or small issues really don't matter that much.
- There is someone watching over me.
- I truly believe in guardian angels
- Our loved ones who have died and have gone before us are around us every day. They can hear you and want you to talk to them.
- We don't tell one another we love each other enough.

- Some people have gone back to same-ole, same-ole after 9-11. Our civilization as we knew it has changed forever. Wake-up!
- God has a plan for all of us; we just need to ask Him to reveal it to us.
- Miracles do happen.
- I'll always be indebted to so many people who were there for me when I needed them the most and those who prayed for me when I was in the hospital. Thank you! thank you!

After the responses I'd received from my article and from continued hounding, okay, encouragement from family and friends, I felt this story needed to be told. That this book, like my life, has a purpose and reason. I hope you enjoyed this story, and that in some way it has touched you and demonstrated how important balance is in your ever seemingly out of control life. To realize how important family and friends are to us and that life is to be lived today, not tomorrow, because tomorrow may never come.

> *Life is not a dress rehearsal.*
> —Rose Tremain

I would like to leave you with this thought. When you're sitting on your proverbial porch, in your proverbial rocking chair, do you want to look back on your life and say, "I wish I had..."?

> *There are no luggage racks on a hearse.*
> —Clotaire Rapaille

All of us should examine what's important in our life.

God Bless and Celebrate Your Life!

Bibliography and Resources

Coyle, Walter. "A Brief History of Scleroderma" http://www.scleroderma.org/medical/other_articles/Coyle_2001_4.shtm (accessed April, 3, 2012)

Mayes, Maureen D., M.D., M.P.H and Khanh T. Ho, M.D. *Understanding and Managing Scleroderma,* Byfield, MA: Scleroderma Foundation, 2009. http://www.scleroderma.org/pdf/NewlyDiagnosed/2009/U&M.pdf (accessed April 3, 2012)

Steen, Virginia D., "Scleroderma renal crisis." *Rheumatic Disease Clinics of North America* Vol. 29 (2003): 315–333.

Helpful Websites

National Scleroderma Foundation (http://www.scleroderma.org)

Fresenius Medical Care (http://www.ultracare-dialysis.com/HealthyLifestyles.aspx)

International Scleroderma Network (http://Sclero.org)

National Kidney Foundation (http://www.kidney.org)

To get your *FREE* ebook from Total Peak Performance, email Andrew@AndrewBotieri.com with "Ebook" in the subject line.

Who the Heck Is Andrew Botieri?

Andrew Botieri has over 60,000 hours of hands-on experience helping small, medium, and large companies reach their potential through his coaching and world-class sales, customer service, and leadership training programs. As an award winning sales professional, Andrew's endeavors include founder of Total Peak Performance®, a motivational sales and leadership training company; national sales trainer and turnaround specialist for HPC Publications, a national advertising company; vice president of sales and operations for AllApartments/SpringStreet, a real estate start-up dotcom company, now Move.com.; radio advertising sales for radio station KOY/Y-95 in Phoenix; and senior merchandiser manager for JC Penney, where his departments broke many company sales records. Andrew is currently the publisher of the *New England Apartment Finder* magazine.

Aside from being a published author, Andrew is a national motivational speaker, and leadership trainer with dynamic programs mixed with humor and real-life stories. In his spare time, he volunteers for nonprofits and performs at local establishments as a songwriter and acoustic guitar player. He lives in "America's Hometown," Plymouth, Massachusetts. Check out www.andrewbotieri.com and subscribe to his free newsletter "Success Strategies," or if you'd like Andrew to speak at your company's upcoming meeting or event, email him at andrew@andrewbotieri.com. Also visit his website to order his top twenty nationally published business articles.

"*I am passionate about helping people be more successful not just in business but in life. I'd love the opportunity to inspire your teams to their Total Peak Performance!*" Andrew Botieri

Made in the USA
Middletown, DE
10 August 2016